Advance Praise for
Michael Smerconish's *Morning Drive*

"Michael Smerconish is a feeling, thinking American. He has an open heart and an open mind. Read *Morning Drive* and you hear someone trying to put it together for himself. He believes in borders and roots for the police, but never forgets the precious individual freedoms they are there to guarantee. It's good that Michael Smerconish airs in morning drive-time. Because when it comes to defining the America debate in the early twenty-first century, this guy's right where the tire hits the road."

—Chris Matthews, host of *Hardball with Chris Matthews* and
The Chris Matthews Show

"I have known Michael Smerconish for two decades. In that time he has distinguished himself by being an independent thinker in an industry that tends to define the terms of debate. For this reason, and many others, *Morning Drive* is a must for Washington insiders and citizens across the country who are interested in preserving not just a healthy two-party system—but also their ability to get access to balanced, impartial news. Michael takes an unvarnished look at ways in which radio and cable television hosts can organize the news for dramatic or controversial effect. Further, he boldly goes where few Republicans have been willing. He prescribes a course of modernization for the national party that makes logical sense and is politically prudent."

—United States Senator Arlen Specter,
Commonwealth of Pennsylvania

"The nation is lucky to have Michael Smerconish as a political commentator. He says what he believes; he doesn't part on ideology or a partisan political agenda, and he sure as heck isn't predictable. It's that same independence and unpredictability that make *Morning Drive* a great read. A fascinating look into Michael's experience in government and politics, this book provides meaningful insight into colorful characters and is an extraordinary memoir of how this young neophyte blossomed into a nationally syndicated commentator."

—Governor Edward G. Rendell, Commonwealth of Pennsylvania

"Every so often there's political commentary that urges, shapes, and critiques political change seamlessly, fairly, and convincingly. Even rarer, there are commentators who hold all politicians accountable for what they say and write, and apply the same standard to themselves. Michael Smerconish personifies this kind of commentary, and *Morning Drive* provides terrific insight into who Michael is, how he came to be, and how independent thinking is essential to achieving smart political results."

—Harold Ford, Jr., former United States Congressman,
Chair of Democratic Leadership Council

MORNING DRIVE

Things I Wish I Knew Before I Started Talking

MICHAEL A. SMERCONISH

The Lyons Press
Guilford, Connecticut
An imprint of The Globe Pequot Press

The Lyons Press is an imprint of The Globe Pequot Press.

Text design: Sheryl P. Kober
Layout: Joanna Beyer

Library of Congress Cataloging-in-Publication Data is available on file.

ISBN 978-1-59921-517-4

Printed in the United States of America

10 9 8 7 6 5 4 3 2 1

Contents

Preface

Paragraph No. 4 of my contract for this book with The Globe Pequot Press, under the heading of "Manuscript Delivery and Deadlines," says:

> *The Publisher shall prepare an Index for each of the Works through its own resources. The cost of construction of the Index shall be charged to the Author's royalty account up to $750.*

No thanks. I'd rather have the $750. Additionally, I don't want an Index because I know what an Index begets. It invites the "Washington Read." Do you know what that is? A fellow Philly guy, *Hardball*'s Chris Matthews, came up with the term after having sent copies of his 1988 book *Hardball: How Politics Is Played Told by One Who Knows the Game* to some reporters and politicians. He got some pretty frank responses, including one from George H. W. Bush, who was vice president at the time (and in the middle of a presidential campaign). Bush said he'd be happy to read the full book, but only because he'd already used the Index to look up any mention of himself and was satisfied that he'd "emerged unscathed." As Matthews wrote in the *Washington Post,* "Here, in our busy, ambitious city, many people ravage books like Wild West hunters once attacked the buffalo. Unlike the Plains Indians who harvested the entire animal—meat, horns, skin, hooves—for their needs, we buy a book simply to cut out its tongue—that one tasty tidbit that justifies the read."[1]

So I say no way to the Index. I'm not about to let the Washington intelligentsia stand in the Barnes & Noble on M Street in Georgetown scanning a list of subjects and names in a hasty bid to determine whether to buy my book. Plus, I need the $750.

But I am feeling benevolent, so here is what I *will* do. You want names? I got your names right here. They're not in alphabetical order, and I'm not going to tell you where they appear or why they are mentioned. But each of these folks is the subject of some discussion in the pages to come. So thumb if you'd like.

Or better yet, just buy the book.

Pat Croce, Pat Tillman, Ayman al-Zawahiri, Pervez Musharraf, Ronald Reagan, Bob Dole, George H. W. Bush, George W. Bush, Osama bin Laden, Rudy Giuliani, Arnold Schwarzenegger, Michael Bloomberg, Bill Frist, Ann Coulter, James Dobson, Nancy Pelosi, Terri Schiavo, Barry Goldwater, Sid Mark, Rush Limbaugh, Larry Kane, Don Imus, Dr. Laura Schlessinger, Arthel Neville, Mel Karmazin, Frank Rizzo, Arlen Specter, Ed Rendell, Mumia Abu Jamal, Danny and Maureen Faulkner, Chris Matthews, Barack Obama, Joe Biden, Chris Dodd, John McCain, Khalid Sheikh Mohammed, Harry Reid, Russ Feingold, Marcus Luttrell, Jim McGreevey, Pat Buchanan, John Kerry, John Edwards, James Carville, Michael Dukakis, Karl Rove, Al Gore, John Roberts, Colin Powell, Saddam Hussein, Hans Blix, Bob Kerrey, Michael Scheuer, Patrick Murphy, Lou Barletta, Barbara Walters, Richard Lamm, Bill O'Reilly, Larry King, Bill Maher, Tom Marr, Tucker Carlson, John Lehman, Roger Ailes, Glenn Beck, Matt Lauer, Tom Ridge, Bob Graham, Sean Hannity, David Gregory, Lanny Davis, Joe Scarborough, the Reverend Jeremiah Wright, Michelle Obama, Larry David, Peggy Noonan, D. L. Hughley, Bill Clinton, Catherine Crier, Neal Boortz, Michael Savage, John Gibson, Bill Bradley, Mel Gibson, Michael Richards, Tim Hardaway, Geraldine Ferraro, Samantha Power, Howard Wolfson, Bill Cunningham, Bob Casey, Harris Wofford, Michael Nutter, and Larry Ceisler.

Introduction

War Games

In October of 2006, I found myself deep inside a United States Central Command (CENTCOM) military hangar in Doha, Qatar. CENTCOM refers to a geographical designation used by the U.S. military that encompasses the Middle East, East Africa, and Central Asia. It's an area that includes Afghanistan, Iraq, Pakistan, and twenty-four other nations and is home to 651 million people. To say our interests in the CENTCOM region are vital would be an understatement. Our nation's crack-pipe dependence on foreign oil extends directly to the sands beneath these countries; 65 percent of the world's known oil supply is here.[1]

There I stood in this massive military nerve center, watching war in real time. Two wars, actually: Iraq and Afghanistan.

I stood about fifty feet from two different combinations of giant television screens. Facing a wall of video to my left, on a radar-like screen I watched movements of our military's air position in the skies over Iraq. Another screen transmitted images of the ground that were being relayed by unmanned predator drones. On one jumbo television screen on the left, they were showing live coverage from Fox News at home. Then I looked to my right. Over there were more screens with similar images, only they were monitoring the war in Afghanistan. In the midst of the Afghanistan transmissions was another television feed from home: CNN. When one of the military brass serving as an escort asked me what I thought of the images, I told him that they had Fox News and CNN on the wrong sides, ideologically speaking. Lucky for me, he laughed.

The maps of Iraq and Afghanistan showed a beehive of activity: lots of aircraft, and plenty of movement. I noted that the U.S. military activity in Afghanistan was heavily concentrated on its border with Pakistan. But there, at that line, all the action stopped. In fact, emblazoned on the map hanging for all to see in the cavernous CENTCOM facility was a warning that said activity in Pakistan was prohibited unless certain protocols were followed. I thought that was significant given that Pakistan, in particular its North Waziristan region, was presumed to be the hiding place of Osama bin Laden. We had no military presence in Pakistan, at least on the map in front of me, nor could we establish one without first notifying the Pakistanis.

I wanted to believe that unseen were the movements of some Pat Tillman–type American heroes, combing the rugged terrain of Pakistan's tribal region, wearing burkas, paying off the locals, cutting deals, using sophisticated spy gear, and doing whatever was necessary to find and kill bin Laden and his lieutenant, Ayman al-Zawahiri. Now, I was beginning to think otherwise. Even before taking this trip at the invitation of the Pentagon, I was slowly coming to believe that five years removed from the events of 9/11, we were no longer aggressively hunting the two men most responsible for the worst attack on America in my lifetime. It galled me to think we'd outsourced that responsibility to Pakistani president Pervez Musharraf, who had himself recently reached an accord with the tribal leaders from the area where bin Laden was believed to be hiding, promising not to fuck with them if they did likewise. Again, I couldn't be sure.

I have never believed I have a right to know all aspects of how we are waging the war on terror. But my comfort level with my government does require a degree of confidence that everything possible is being done to avenge the deaths of three thousand innocent Americans. By now, in 2006, I no longer had that confidence in the Bush administration. This was quite a departure for me, given that I twice supported this president's election and had even served as the master of ceremonies at his final Pennsylvania campaign rally in 2004. I also regarded it as a poor reflection of the political party to which the president belonged—the party I had joined when I registered to vote some twenty-six years prior.

I signed on with the Republican Party in the spring of 1980 soon after turning eighteen. Although I have voted for plenty of Democrats, I had always supported the Republican candidate in the presidential races. In each instance, part of my vote was predicated upon the view that I was supporting the most hawkish of the candidates running. I came of age politically thinking that military strength was a priority and that the GOP was the party of record on all matters of national defense.

George W. Bush was the man who had visited Ground Zero just days after the 9/11 attack and, standing in the rubble, borrowed the bullhorn of a firefighter named Bob Beckwith to say to rescue workers, "I can hear you, the world can hear you, and the people who knocked down these buildings are going to hear all of us very soon."[2] They roared their approval, and at home in my Barcalounger I did likewise. Then in an address to a joint session of Congress, the president further declared, "Either you are with us, or you are with the terrorists. From this day forward, any nation that continues to harbor or support terrorism will be regarded by the United States as a hostile regime."[3] It's that last part that I thought of while standing in CENTCOM watching two wars being waged on screens akin to a Saturday matinee. Wasn't Pakistan now harboring the most hostile of terrorists?

I came home with a growing sense of unease about whether we had been diverted in our quest to kill those responsible for the attacks on 9/11. Two weeks after my return home came the 2006 midterm elections, in which the Republicans lost control of the U.S. Senate and the U.S. House of Representatives, a development that touched off soul-searching within the GOP. Many voiced theories about what the party needed to do in order to regain its hold in Washington. I had my own views. With my concern over the non-hunt for bin Laden fresh in my mind, and my growing discontent with the GOP on other, primarily social, issues, I decided to put pen to paper and published a column in the *Philadelphia Daily News* that outlined where I thought the Republican Party needed to move. I would later refer to this "platform" as my Suburban Manifesto. I wrote, "I'm doing a personal political sanity check in the aftermath of Tuesday's vote to determine if I'm registered in the party that best reflects my views."[4]

I said I saw a battle looming for the direction of the party of Lincoln, and I wondered whether it would become a party epitomized by individuals with names like Giuliani, Schwarzenegger, and Bloomberg, or instead Frist, Coulter, and Dobson (I hoped the former). In questioning whether the GOP was still for me, I then offered my views on fifteen topical issues. No. 1 on my list was a reflection of what I had seen—or not seen—overseas. I'll share the full list shortly; here is an abbreviated version of what I wrote:

- *Immigration:* Our borders are porous. Only when they are closed should we decide what to do with the millions already here illegally.

- *Gays:* Homosexuals don't threaten my marriage. As we seek to find some accommodation for same-sex couples, we need to end that false argument.

- *Preventing terror:* We need to implement all of the recommendations of the 9/11 Commission.

- *Bin Laden:* I want a commitment of manpower directed toward finding and killing Osama bin Laden and Ayman al-Zawahiri.

- *Iraq:* We need an end game, and don't call it "cut and run."

- *Campaign finance:* Stop trying to regulate donations. Someone will always find a loophole.

- *Embryonic stem cell research:* Pardon my callous nature, but that which exists in a petri dish is undeserving of the full rights that are afforded to a viable fetus.

- *Abortion:* I want a party with room for pro-life and pro-choice views. Plan B should be available over the counter to anyone at least eighteen years old. I also don't want politicians determining my end-of-life plan.

- *Global warming:* Beats the hell out of me. But given the apparent stakes if the concerns are valid, err on the side of caution.

- *Profiling:* Let's look for terrorists who look like terrorists. In virtually every instance, they have race, gender, ethnicity, religion, and appearance in common.

- *Torture:* Once we identify the bad guys, we have to get the information from them on impending attacks by any means necessary, and that includes torture.

- *Term limits:* We need citizen politicians, not professionals. Two Senate terms and six in the House will ensure we get grounded folks who are capable of earning a living when not serving us.

- *Entitlements:* Social Security, Medicare, and other programs make up more than half our federal spending. We can't afford to continue the status quo. Yo, AARP: The retirement age has to be raised to seventy.

- *Death taxes:* We work hard trying to lead a comfortable life and leave a nest egg for our children. It's un-American that when we check out, Uncle Sam will stand there with his hand out to tax our earnings for the second time. The estate tax must go.

- *Guns:* A symptom, not a cause. Single-parent households pose more of a threat to safety than firearms. Let's address that issue.

So in which party do I belong? (And would any of them want me?) After publishing those views in the *Philadelphia Daily News*, I read the full list on the radio and also posted it on my Web site www .mastalk.com, where I invited people to weigh in and register areas of agreement and disagreement. In one weekend, 3,449 people did just that—a seemingly healthy sample compared to the conventional political poll, which questions several hundred or maybe a thousand people and makes national prognostications. My expectation is that the respondents were a combination of readers of my newspaper column and listeners of my radio program, and probably more of the latter. That means they are largely, but certainly not exclusively, white, suburban, Republican, and ideologically in the center, or to the right. These demographics are an important consideration because if they're accurate, the results are even more telling for the GOP as it looks to the future.

So what did the tally of votes on the fifteen points of my manifesto reveal? For starters, that people who responded agreed, on average, with about ten out of my fifteen positions. Specifically, there was significant agreement on the need for an Iraq exit strategy, even a timetable, and on the subject of hunting down and killing bin Laden—even if he's in Pakistan. A total of 80 percent of people agreed with my view that we need to screen everyone at airports and borders, but some more than others (yes, I refer to the dreaded "p" word, profiling). And there was a similar level of agreement on enacting all of the 9/11 Commission recommendations. There was also overwhelming support for my desire to: close the borders until we figure out what to do with the illegal immigrants who are already here; abolish the estate tax; and impose term limits. Each of these views was shared by 70 percent or more of the respondents. Already, I could see why the GOP got drubbed in the midterm elections. These positions should have been the core of the GOP platform, but they weren't.

The reaction to my positions on social issues was even more revealing—again, assuming that many of the respondents came from the moderate or conservative world of talk radio. Where I embraced embryonic stem cell research, half of the respondents agreed. The same result greeted my arguing for a party that has room for both pro-life and pro-choice folks, makes Plan B available over the counter, and rejects federal intervention in end-of-life cases like that of Terri Schiavo. Even where I said marriage between a man and woman is not threatened by same-sex unions, half agreed.

Is this confirmation that when the GOP leadership is decidedly pro-life, against Plan B dissemination, and for federal intervention à la Schiavo, or opposes gay rights on the grounds that it has an effect on heterosexual marriage, it is turning off 50 percent of its suburban base? I wondered.

There was another reason to believe that my issues exchange was not just me and 3,449 friends pontificating in our pajamas, but rather, that we were airing views that speak for many suburban nooks that have become the battleground of national and statewide elections. The Metropolitan Institute at Virginia Tech shed an important light on the Democrats' congressional coup in 2006, reporting that the Democratic Party garnered almost 60 percent of the vote for congressional seats in the inner suburbs of the country's fifty largest metro areas. That number had been 53 percent in 2002, the previous mid-term election. And, they won almost 55 percent of the vote in the next ring of suburbs—up from 50 percent in 2002.[5] In other words, these academic folks documented how gains made by the Democrats in neighborhoods such as mine had national political ramifications. I wondered whether my views were typical of those people who had been reliably Republican and were now less so. Perhaps when read together, the data from the Metropolitan Institute at Virginia Tech and my Suburban Manifesto suggest that there are many of us who want a party that's tough on the bad guys, not too preachy, doesn't piss away money, and is no longer willing to allow fringe elements to take over its platform. Might we even hold the keys to future national elections?

I learned something else from publishing my Suburban Manifesto. I realized that listeners and viewers who are often barked at on talk radio and cable TV shows, the same people who are supposedly enter-tained with the red-state-versus-blue-state equivalent of "Jane, you ignorant slut," actually have a thirst for intelligent discussion about issues. Of course there was the occasional rabid writer, but most of the people who wrote to me in droves about my proposed platform were anxious to engage me on matters of substance. Those are the people I try to entertain in my professional work, regardless of whether they ultimately agree or disagree with my personal views. My radio style is not to be doctrinaire, and my approach has never been one to wel-come only guests who agree with me or to ridicule those who don't. As my television work has increased over the last two years, I have tried to keep this in mind—specifically, that while the pointed sound bite might give the TV producers a chubby, it is not necessarily what people at home want to hear. It is possible to be both entertaining and informative, but sadly, that lesson has not been received in the offices of those who book and plan many of the well-known gabfests that dominate cable TV.

There's one more thing that has now gained significance. About a month after the midterm losses sustained by the Republicans, I hosted none other than Senator John McCain at a gathering of five hundred of my radio listeners. It was part of the informal book club I run, which enables me to bring high-profile authors to Philadelphia to discuss their literary works. This day, December 2, 2006, was a year and a half before McCain would traverse an unlikely road to the Republican nomination for president. I recently went back and listened to the tape, and one exchange caught my ear. First, I said:

> *It's my view, Senator, that the Republican Party is at a crossroads as we look toward '08, and we need to make a decision if we are going to be a party of ideologues or of pragmatists. I consider myself to be a part of the latter category. The question for Senator John McCain is whether or not a non-ideologue can win the Republican nomination.*

Senator McCain answered like this:

> *In 1976, we lost the presidency; we lost both houses of Congress. The Democrats had overwhelming majorities. We had just lost a war. There [were] assassinations, there [were] riots, there [were] demonstrations. We had a broken military because we just lost a war in Vietnam, and many people in America, particularly on the liberal side, believed that America's best days were behind us, and the Democrats thought they were permanently in power and that we would have to move far to the left in America. There was one guy—that I first heard about when I was in prison—who was a guy that was the governor of California, who had a very different view of America's future. He believed America's best days were ahead of us. He believed that America was going to win the Cold War that this mutually assured destruction and the Berlin Wall could not stand. And he gave us hope and vision for the future.*
>
> *Now was Ronald Reagan a rigid ideologue? No. I think that if you look at his record when he was governor of California, he even raised taxes. But he had a vision. He had a vision grounded in good fundamental conservative principles and an optimistic vision of the future and an unshakeable faith in America and its citizens and the unique role we played in history*

*and will continue to play in history. So I believe that the message
we have out of this defeat, my friends—and we were defeated—
is . . . we came to power in 1994 to change government and
government changed us. We lost our way on spending. We have
got to stop this unnecessary and wasteful spending that we have
engaged in, and we have got to give Americans a much clearer
view of our vision of the future of the country. We can do this. We
will do this. I still believe America is a right-of-center nation, a
more conservative nation than my Democrat friends are, and I
think if we learn the lessons, we will prevail and once again gain
the majority.*[6]

I appreciated Senator McCain's reply even though I believed it to
be unresponsive to my question. Where he sees America as a right-of-
center nation, I would argue that we are more centrist. But even if he
is correct, I think his party—my party—is being guided by forces that
wish for it to be a *far* right-of-center nation. He invoked the name of
Barry Goldwater, an individual whom I thought of as John McCain's
2008 bid for the White House unfolded. I think in many instances
McCain veered too far to placate forces on the far right with whom
Barry Goldwater would never have been comfortable. Remember,
Goldwater was the forefather of a movement that caught fire when
he said he wanted government off our backs, out of our pocketbooks,
and away from our bedrooms.[7] I think that is largely what I have been
advocating, and what I wish to explain in further detail here.

Well, congratulations. You've made it through the Cliffs Notes
version. Now allow me the opportunity to make the full case for my
Suburban Manifesto against the backdrop of my own political coming
of age and the presidential race of 2008. When my publisher, Scott
Watrous, first raised the prospect of my writing a political outlook, I
readily agreed, with one caveat. I said that I looked forward to delivering what he wanted, but only if it could be wrapped in a talk radio
memoir and behind-the-scenes look at the modern world of political
punditry. I don't think I can offer an outlook without first walking
you through where I started, and how I have been influenced along
the way, largely by the forces that now control the way in which many

Americans get their political news. I am a product of that talk radio and cable TV environment, and as I think about my career in politics and punditry, I realize there are so many things I wish I knew before I started talking.

Michael A. Smerconish
January 2009
Philadelphia

Chapter 1

The Champagne Bar

My path to political punditry began in my hometown of Doylestown, Pennsylvania, in the suburbs of Philadelphia. It once ran through a whorehouse in Brussels, Belgium, but I am already getting ahead of myself.

In the spring of 1980, I was a senior at Central Bucks High School West, best known for its perennial football champions. That year, my dad ran for the state legislature, and I, newly registered to vote, caught the political bug. My mom was then well on her way to being an incredibly successful real estate agent. My father was a guidance counselor for the public school system and had never before been politically active. The entire spring of my senior year was consumed with my father's one and only run for office. I was involved in absolutely every aspect of his campaign and I loved it. From voter registration and gathering petition signatures, to handing out leaflets at supermarkets—you name it, I did it. I went to meetings with him, watched his public speaking, and attended screenings for endorsements. We did it all together. All my dad had to say was that I was his son and a senior in high school, and everyone was happy to have me sit in on any kind of meeting. It was a great learning experience.

We ran hard but came up short. Dad was beaten in the primary by Jim Greenwood, who would go on to win the general election—dumping a several-term incumbent—then to the state senate and, eventually, the U.S. Congress. I was terribly upset at the loss, but developed a strong interest in politics as a result.

One of the very cool things about my first election season was meeting both Ronald Reagan and George H. W. Bush within days of one another. Both were still in the race at the time of Pennsylvania's primary. That summer, in the midst of the Republican National Convention, they would join forces. But in the spring of 1980, before Pennsylvanians voted, I met each during campaign appearances. Bush

1

came to the Shrine of Czestochowa in Doylestown, which is a huge replica of a famous chapel in Poland. He spoke and I got to shake his hand as he exited. I was very impressed with him. His slogan at the time was "a president we won't have to train," highlighting his extensive résumé, which by then already included his status as war hero, member of Congress, U.N. ambassador, envoy to China, and head of the C.I.A. I went home and told my parents that my first presidential ballot would be cast for him. And it would have been—but for my meeting Ronald Reagan a week later.

Charlie Gerow was a new friend then working for the Reagan campaign as a regional coordinator. He tipped me off to a Reagan tour of Philadelphia's Italian Market and I skipped school to be there. Together with a neighborhood friend, Mike Stachel Jr., I rode the train into Center City. After pulling into the old Reading Terminal shed, we headed down to 9th Street, where the merchants display their produce, meats, and fish in the street. A visit to the Italian Market was then a must for anyone running for president. There really were Italians in the Italian Market, though today they seem few and far between, having been displaced by Asians. Anyway, Gerow had told me that Reagan would walk a few blocks on 9th Street from Washington Street to Christian Street. Along the way, he said, Reagan would stop in Esposito's Meat Market, a big butcher shop. In fact, he said Governor Reagan would walk in the door at 2:50 p.m. and if we wanted to meet him, that was where we should stand.

The scene on 9th Street was bedlam. Ronald Reagan got out of a town car and worked the crowd, starting at Giordano's Market, a few blocks from where we were located inside at Esposito's. "Are you sure he's coming in here?" asked my buddy. I started to have my doubts. There was no one inside of Esposito's except the two of us and the butchers. Then I spied a large catering plate with a huge length of sausage spelling out "Reagan." I figured we must be in the right place. Sure enough, minutes later, in walked Ronald Reagan and a phalanx of Secret Service, and nobody else except the two kids from Bucks County who skipped school. Pay dirt.

I had a pocket Instamatic with me. Those cameras were all the rage at the time. We asked Ronald Reagan if we could each be photographed with him and took turns passing the camera. "Hold on fellows, I need to blow my nose," I remember him saying. I was elated to have met Reagan one week after meeting Bush. A few days later, I was crushed. I had not wanted to carry the flash attachment on the train and, as a result, the quality of the photographs was terrible. I didn't know it then but I would soon get another chance.

Late that summer, Charlie Gerow called again. Ronald Reagan, now the Republican Party candidate for president, was coming back to Philadelphia, this time for a fundraiser with Arlen Specter, who was running for the U.S. Senate. The date was August 18, 1980—the price $250 per person! Gerow told me that if I played my cards right, I might be able to crash the fundraiser at the historic Bellevue Stratford Hotel. There were no guarantees. I put on my only sport coat and headed back into the city. I simply walked up to the reception host table and filled in my name on a blank name tag, and walked in the door. Nobody thought to stop the youngest person in the room. (Ah, the good old pre-9/11 days!) That day, I not only met the future president again but also soon-to-be Senator Specter and his son Shanin, who was then a University of Pennsylvania law student and would soon become one of my closest friends. One more thing: This time I had not only my pocket Instamatic but also my flash attachment. I handed the camera to a stranger when Reagan worked the rope line and the guy snapped one shot. This time the photograph turned out clear, and it remains something I treasure.

That fall, I arrived on campus at Lehigh University as an incoming freshman, all full of piss and vinegar for the Reagan-Bush ticket and mistakenly thinking everyone else was too. Soon after my arrival on campus, I determined that the College Republicans were moribund, so I decided to form a rival club that I called Lehigh University Youth for Reagan-Bush. My efforts with the club were mildly successful, best measured by the registration of new Republicans. I remember that I was thrilled when my government professor, Dr. Frank Colon, agreed to give me one college credit for my efforts; that was my first credit earned toward my eventual double major in government and journalism.

Initially, it was rough sledding to enlist supporters in college for Reagan-Bush, so I decided that as means of recruitment, I would throw a party, a keg party, for all supporters on campus of Ronald Reagan and

George Bush. Little did I know that the very night I had selected for the affair would coincide with Game 2 of the World Series between the Philadelphia Phillies and the Kansas City Royals. Lehigh draws largely from Pennsylvania and New Jersey, home to lots of Fightin' Phils fans. Magic was in the air that night for the Phils, who rallied in the eighth inning and won the game 6–4, thereby going up 2–0 in the series. Needless to say, my beer blast was a bust. Hardly anyone showed up despite the combination of Republican politics and beer. I was embarrassed in front of the guest speaker, my now good friend Charlie Gerow, who had flown in to speak to the masses I was supposed to have assembled. I took the beer bar to my dorm, where the guys were celebrating the Phils' victory.

I was then living with 150 other freshman guys in the dorm known as Taylor Hall. It was a great place to live, but it was a dump. It has since been renovated and is now a showpiece. In fact, when the Philadelphia Eagles hold summer camp at Lehigh every August, I think some are now housed in Taylor. That would never have been the case back then. Life at Taylor was a very rudimentary existence and two things were in short supply—bathrooms and telephones. This was before cell phones, and no one had a computer. There was one telephone for an entire floor, and the guys were brutal in taking messages. If your girlfriend called and some prankster answered, he might tell her that you were on the can, or worse, in your room with another woman with a DO NOT DISTURB sign on the door! ("Hey, are you really sure you want me to disturb him?") If your parents were on the line, no matter the time of day, they'd say you were sleeping off a hangover from the night before. ("He really needs to rest.") That's why it had to be divine intervention that a call out of the blue from a locally based Pennsylvania state representative named George Kanuck actually got to me.

It was a few days after my beer bust. Someone yelled down the hall and told me I had a call. When I picked it up, the voice said, "Is this Michael Smerkonavitch?" badly pronouncing my name, something to which I was accustomed. I said yes, and he then asked, "Are you the one who has a club called Lehigh University Youth for Reagan-Bush?" I thought of the kegger and sheepishly said I was. I suspected it was a prank call until he introduced himself and said he was calling on behalf of Dan Sullivan, the head of advance for Ambassador Bush (that's how

George H. W. Bush was referred to back then). He explained that "advance work" was the term given to planning the logistics of a visit by a major candidate and that George H. W. Bush was coming to the area to tour the Bethlehem Steel plant. More importantly, he said that he desperately needed student volunteers to pull off the visit. Specifically, he needed motorcade drivers, press escorts, luggage handlers, and lots more. He needed my club! (If only I had one.)

I hung up the telephone and ran down the hall recruiting my neighbors—Republicans, Democrats, Independents, and Communists—whoever wanted to play a role in the upcoming visit of George Bush. Several friends from Taylor, namely Al Manwaring, Bob Fioretti, and Phil Hoffman, were all thrilled to do so, and what unfolded was an unbelievable experience for them and me. Part of my job was to procure a twenty-foot U-Haul, two four-door American-made sedans, a station wagon with a luggage rack, an eight-passenger van, three baggage men, and, finally, two attractive coeds who would tour the Bethlehem Steel plant as press aides with Ambassador Bush. My hometown girlfriend and that of my brother met the last requirement.

Ambassador Bush spent October 21 and 22 in Allentown and Bethlehem, Pennsylvania. When the future vice president, president, and father of a president arrived, I was able to accompany him during his visit to the Lehigh Valley. It was quite a high for a young political junkie.

Because of my small role in the campaign, I was invited to the Reagan-Bush inauguration and was given two tickets to the swearing-in ceremony. They said, "standing room only." I took my father. In a move that would symbolize both the political changes and love for the American people that Reagan would bring to the office, the president-elect changed the location of the ceremony from the east portico of the Capitol to the west side, so that he could be sworn in facing California and allow thousands of spectators to fill the National Mall to watch the historic moment. What I did not realize until we arrived, however, was that our tickets enabled us to stand somewhere closer to the Washington Monument—nearly a mile away! Still, we loved being there.

I went back to my studies; meanwhile Dan Sullivan was named the director of advance for the vice president. A year later, I was in Washington visiting my member of Congress and walked over to the

Capitol Hill Club, just to look at the facade. I knew it to be a place where Republican fat cats would dine and plot strategy. A few men were exiting, and I caught the eye of one of them. He looked at me and I returned the stare. It was Dan Sullivan. He invited me to become an advance man for the vice president, and I ended up interning in the VP's office and doing advance work across the country and even around the globe. As an advance man, I assisted in planning the logistics of a vice-presidential visit and seeking out volunteers in different communities who might be willing to help with the trip.

My first trips were the less-desirable locales, like Butler, Pennsylvania, where Vice President Bush was the guest of honor at a fundraiser for Eugene Atkinson, a Democratic member of Congress who had turned Republican. I arrived a week before Bush did and worked with other advance personnel and the Secret Service in planning the logistics of his visit. I had the time of my life. From there, my advance destinations got better. After Butler, it was Rome, New York; then El Paso, Texas; and then San Diego, California—all while still a university student. The domestic trips were soon followed by Brussels, Belgium, and Oslo, Norway. Although I was just a college geek, in each place the locals treated me like a member of the White House staff. My role afforded me the opportunity to see things while still a college student that many people would not see in a lifetime.

The vice president's trip to Belgium, February 2–4, 1983, stands out. The purpose was for Bush to meet with allies at NATO Headquarters and sell them on a proposed deployment of the Pershing and Cruise Missiles. But what I remember most is literally stumbling into a Brussels whorehouse—er, champagne bar.

The lead advance guy on the trip was Ronald Eberhardt. If he reads this story, he will be hearing what I have to tell you for the first time. Ron was an intense but talented fellow and a compulsive planner, a compliment that comes from one with many anal-retentive traits of his own. We worked long hours prior to the vice president's arrival, and I felt a little stir-crazy because I would go from the hotel to the U.S. Embassy and then back to the hotel late at night. Each night when we would return, I would see a very formal doorman in front of an unmarked building across the street from our hotel. Finally, I asked our hotel doorman what was across the street. He told me it was a casino. Great news for me—we often played cards in my fraternity, Zeta Psi. I was immediately interested in a couple of hands of blackjack and asked him if it was open to the public. The doorman at my hotel said I should just tell the doorman across the street that I was a hotel guest, and I'd "be fine." So I changed my clothes, grabbed a few travelers checks, and went to play cards.

The doorman at the casino welcomed me, opened the door, and directed me to the second floor, which did indeed house a small casino with maybe a half-dozen blackjack tables. I took a seat and started to play next to an Asian guy. I had a drink when a cocktail waitress offered some booze. Not bad. I caught a good shoe, meaning lots of face cards that increased my odds, and I was enjoying the entire experience. Here I was, a college student, a frat guy, traveling with the vice president's staff in Europe and playing some blackjack while sipping a White Russian. A White Russian. That cracks me up now just to think about it. I think I had no knowledge of liquor beyond beer, hence my strange order.

Anyway, I was soon making conversation with the dealer, and after replaying in my mind the speedy way in which I was shown the staircase to the casino, I asked the dealer what was downstairs. "A champagne bar," was his reply. That sounded pretty nice. Before too long I was up $200. Why not a glass of champagne to finish a nice evening, I thought? Wait until the frat guys hear I polished off some Cold Duck or whatever, to boot. I cashed in my chips and headed for the stairs. The same doorman now pulled back another curtain to reveal the "champagne bar." Once inside, it took a few seconds for my eyes to adjust to the dark. When I could see, I saw that I was the lone male in a room of about twenty women. Their clothing, or lack of it, left no doubt as to their employment. Oh, the guys at Zeta Psi were never going to believe this! Wait a minute. Was prostitution even legal in Brussels? (Yes, was the answer.) Panic quickly set in. I saw my work with the vice president pass before my eyes, so I asked somebody if there was a rear exit. There was and I took it. The last thing I recall about that night is jogging down an alley behind the casino/whorehouse, feeling like I was in a James Bond movie and hoping I didn't get lost heading back to my hotel.

For a time, I was simultaneously maintaining my responsibilities in college, doing advance work for Vice President Bush, and increasing my political involvement at home in Bucks County, Pennsylvania. In our suburban community I was named the political equivalent of a city Ward Leader. Many a night I would drive one hour from campus to Bucks County to attend committeeperson meetings for the Republican Party, and then return to school. This involvement led to my being elected county-wide as an alternate delegate to the 1984 Republican National Convention. That summer's convention was held in Dallas, and I was one of the youngest elected representatives at the national gathering.

After Lehigh, it was off to the University of Pennsylvania for law school, where my political involvement only increased. In my first year, I attended class and was a serious student. But in my second year of law school at Penn, I got diverted. The very seat that Dad had sought in the state legislature became open, and I decided to run for it myself, hoping to avenge my father's loss. Despite my opening a full-time campaign office, raising more than $50,000, and running a pretty polished campaign, I lost by 419 votes. Though the campaign was unsuccessful, I'm still proud of my run for state legislature at the age of twenty-four.

When my own race ended, there was no way I could focus on just law school, so in my third and final year I played a significant role in two campaigns: Arlen Specter's reelection to the U.S. Senate and the mayoral campaign of Frank L. Rizzo. In the fall of my third year at Penn Law, Senator Specter asked me to manage the city of Philadelphia portion of his campaign, and I said yes. His son Shanin and I were now close friends, and Shanin had been supportive of my run for the legislature. He told his father I had run a well-organized effort and that led his dad, Senator Specter, to invite me to join his campaign.

That 1986 Specter race is worthy of some mention. This was Arlen Specter's first reelection campaign for the U.S. Senate and he was running against congressman Bob Edgar. Having lost his fair share of elections, Specter was determined to run hard. He had done a fine job raising money during his first term and was far better focused and financed than his opponent. That money enabled Specter to supplement the activities of the Republican Party where it had no presence—the minority wards of the city of Philadelphia. That's where I came in. Gordon R. Woodrow Jr. was then Specter's chief political strategist (and a great one), and "Whiskers," as Specter called Gordon because of his beard, had asked me to try to build a street organization for

Specter. We did, and were successful. At the top of the ticket that year was a hotly contested race for governor: Democrat Robert P. Casey (the now deceased father of the current U.S. senator of the same name) vs. Republican William Scranton III. On election day, Specter beat Bob Edgar but Bob Casey beat William Scranton. Why? Partly due to the fact that, while Specter lost the city to Edgar by 60,566 votes, Scranton lost the city vote to Casey by 134,515 votes. By holding down Specter's loss in the city, we ensured his election statewide. Here's how we did it.

Specter wanted to supplement the Republican apparatus where it existed and to field a street organization in the minority wards—and he was prepared to pay to get it done. I was charged with making it happen. We appointed a coordinator for each of a dozen regions and identified every single polling place in those areas. Next, we recruited poll workers for every one of those polling places where there was no Republican committee person; each would be paid $100 for manning a station from 7:00 a.m. to 8:00 p.m. Intercepting voters as they arrived to vote, our recruits would make a special pitch for Arlen Specter. It's pretty basic stuff but not the norm when it comes to Republicans working the minority community. I developed a time-card system in which poll workers would have an identification card that would identify them and their polling place and have three lines for signatures from a supervisor who had checked on them during the day to make sure they were appropriately manning their polls. At the end of the day, they were to present their cards with three signatures to the same person who had signed them, and then they would get the $100 in cash. Simple enough, or so I thought.

Our objective was to minimize Specter's overall loss within the city of Philadelphia. Democrats outnumbered Republicans in the city at that time by a margin of four to one. The thinking was, if Specter could lose the city by a relatively small margin, he would win reelection, because the minimized city losses would be offset by gains in the remaining Republican portions of Pennsylvania. The program seemed like a great success; we covered the polls in the minority wards where the Republican Party had no committee people. There was, however, a relatively major glitch on election night. That afternoon, I had received a telephone call from Channel 10, then the Philadelphia CBS affiliate, asking me if I would be legendary anchor Larry Kane's guest at 8:00 p.m., just as the polls closed. (Funny thing—I had met Larry Kane when I was working as a patio-furniture deliveryman for Mt. Lake Pool and Patio during high school. More on that later.)

Now, back in 1986, the prospect of being Larry Kane's TV guest on election night was a big deal to me. I had done some political interviews, was taken with the Klieg lights, and very much wanted the notoriety that would come from playing a prominent role in a successful Senate reelection. All day long I managed our street operation without incident, but as dinnertime approached I was notified of a problem with the delivery of about $40,000 in cash, our street money for Hispanic poll workers. It seems the guy who was to oversee the delivery never showed up. I had no choice but to serve as the bagman myself. No problem, I thought. The big television debut was not scheduled to come off until the polls closed at 8:00. I could deliver the money to the payment location at about 7:00 and still make it to the live shoot by 8:00.

The Hispanic poll workers were to receive payment in a furniture showroom on North 5th Street in North Philadelphia. A supposed Specter supporter owned the store, hence the locale. I knew there was trouble brewing from the moment I opened the door. Already, our poll workers were assembling (even though the polls were still open for another hour). They were wet from the rain that day and many had been drinking. And in walked El Blanco (me) with a bag stuffed with $40,000. In the back room, I met with our captains, a half dozen Hispanic political operatives with whom I had worked well up until this very moment. They were sitting around a table in the middle of the room where the time cards I had developed to keep track of poll workers were strewn. They had never been distributed! They'd abandoned my method of keeping track of who had worked and which people were owed money for their efforts. I quickly realized that my captains had absolutely no intention of paying the promised $100 to each of the Hispanic poll workers. They wanted me to drop the money on the table and hit the bricks.

Television summoned. I was as anxious to get the hell out of there as they were to have me leave. But I couldn't do it. For the next thirty minutes, we argued. Things got increasingly ugly. And I stayed put as the furniture showroom filled to the point where a crowd was now out the door on North 5th Street. As the clock ticked past 8:00, I sweated through my new Brooks Brothers suit and worried about my safety instead of my makeup. Now, our entire Hispanic workforce was assembled outside the room where we were bickering, and it didn't take a degree from Berlitz to know what they were saying to one another. They knew several things: They were tired, hungry, and wet. Many were stoned. They hadn't been paid. And the lone white guy in the building had all the money.

Suffice it to say I missed the TV hit. I would like to say that I ultimately left the building that night after everyone got paid. That wasn't the case. As the emotion escalated and the clock inched closer to 9:00 p.m. on North 5th Street that night, I was still there and increasingly concerned for my safety. I consulted with Shanin Specter when I finally thought it had reached a point where I had no choice but to leave the money and run. He agreed. I am sure the workers who got slighted with payments of less than what they had been promised concluded that I was the problem. The truth was that I felt I did what I could on their behalf. I remember that the Specter victory party that night was at the University City Sheraton and, when I finally arrived, it was just in time to receive a message telling me to come back with another $50,000 or the furniture building would get torched. I didn't and it didn't. Welcome to Philadelphia politics.

When the Specter campaign ended, I was nearing the second half of my final year of law school and there was a great race on the local political horizon. Frank L. Rizzo, the former mayor of Philadelphia, had changed his registration from Democrat to Republican and was running to get his old job back. I'd had Rizzo as a pen pal when I was in grade school. In 1974, when I was a sixth grader at Doyle Elementary School in Doylestown, I wrote to then Mayor Rizzo and he wrote back. (I still have the letters in my attic!) Frank Rizzo had been elected mayor in 1971 and would be reelected in 1975. Although he would not be elected again, he would continue to dominate every single mayoral election in the city until his death in 1991. We were very close friends for the final fifteen years of his life.

The pen-pal relationship that began while I was in grade school continued into junior high, and then high school. As I was finishing high school, Rizzo was winding down his second and final term. When we finally met in 1980, he had just left office, and I was already in the process of earning my own political stripes. Our initial meeting was arranged in the summer of 1980 by a mutual friend, Bill Snyder. Bill drove me to Frank Rizzo's imposing home in the city's Chestnut Hill neighborhood. Rizzo immediately recognized my name as belonging to the young guy who had been writing him letters for years. A several-hour breakfast ensued and that day would set the stage for me to eventually move from pen pal to political operative in service to the former mayor.

While I had been in college and law school and working on Republican campaigns, Rizzo was busy planning a comeback. First, in 1983 he had attempted to return to City Hall by challenging his successor, Mayor Wilson Goode, in a Democratic primary election. Rizzo lost by 34,105 votes, out of 625,201 cast. (Good trivia: Goode was the only man ever to beat Frank Rizzo in *any* election.) Rizzo then spent the next four years planning a rematch, to occur in 1987. Marty Weinberg, Frank Rizzo's right-hand man and political guru, kept a piece of paper in his suit pocket that summed up the battle plan. Frank Rizzo would have defeated Wilson Goode in 1983, he reasoned, if only the city's 225,000 Republicans had been able to cast a ballot in that election. In other words, if Rizzo could hold his Democratic base and add to it the majority of Republicans who, it was widely believed, were Rizzo voters anyway, he could defeat Goode. The plan presupposed that Rizzo would hold his Democratic base even though he was switching parties, and it sounded plausible to me. In his two terms in office, he had cultivated a relationship with president Richard Nixon and had maintained relationships throughout his career with many Republicans at all levels of government. Weinberg's thinking was simple: It was time for Frank Rizzo to change parties and seek his old office by running as a Republican so that he could face Goode in a general election instead of a primary election. The difference, this time, would be those nearly quarter million GOP voters who did not get a chance in 1983 to pass judgment on Rizzo vs. Goode.

To pull this off, Frank Rizzo, who'd been a Democrat all of his life, now needed some friends within the Republican Party apparatus in the city; and here I was—a guy he had known for years as a pen pal, a young man whom he had once entertained for breakfast at his house, and who had just put together a field organization for Republican Arlen Specter's successful reelection effort. I met with Marty Weinberg and Frank Rizzo and was offered a senior position in the campaign. On the day of the general election, victory was not in the cards. The 225,000 Republicans were not enough for Rizzo to close the gap against Wilson Goode. The race was razor close, but Goode's nearly unanimous showing in the minority community ensured his reelection. The overall margin was 2.7 percentage points. On election night, I remember riding back to Rizzo's house with his wife, Carmella, and then going for a walk with the former mayor and Casey, Rizzo's prized Irish terrier. That's the way it ended. On a chilly November night, we walked in silence through the streets of tony Chestnut Hill, just Rizzo, Casey, and me. Frank Rizzo, as was his custom when we would walk Casey through his immaculate neighborhood, the safest in the city, had a .38 in his rear pants pocket.

Shortly after the campaign ended, Frank Rizzo and I had a falling out that got ugly. Elsie Hillman, a close friend of then Vice President Bush and the statewide chair of his presidential bid, wanted me to manage the city of Philadelphia for the Bush presidential effort. She told me this was because of my bona fides with Bush (the advance work) and the two campaigns I had just engineered in the city of Philadelphia for Republicans. The only trouble was that this was a position coveted by Rizzo in an effort to stay front and center in the Republican Party. The Bush campaign, however, was reluctant to have him running its affairs. Although Rizzo never gave me the credit for doing so, I sold the campaign on the idea of giving Rizzo the title of Honorary Chairman, leaving me to be the nuts-and-bolts chairman/director. It didn't matter. Some guys close to Rizzo convinced him that I'd thrown him under the bus, and I was quickly dead to him.

The headline in the Metro section of the Tuesday, April 19, 1988, *Inquirer* read: "Rizzo, Protégé Part Company over Bush Post."[1] It was embarrassing.

Rizzo and I did not speak for a period of three-plus years, which was painful for me. I really missed the man. By 1991 he had plotted yet another political comeback, and I had continued my political involvement while pursuing radio as a sideline. That 1991 Philadelphia mayor's race was a milestone for me as a radio broadcaster. I had been on the air as a pundit, but this competitive election would give me a chance to wedge my foot firmly in the door of talk station WWDB. In a stunning upset, Rizzo captured the Republican nomination in a three-way race with Sam Katz and Ron Castille, but did not live to see the general election. Had he lived, Philadelphia would have been treated to a Frank Rizzo vs. Ed Rendell general election. Instead, Rendell was easily elected the city's mayor.

Luckily for me, in the midst of the 1991 mayoral race I made peace with Mayor Rizzo, and it happened in front of five hundred people at a debate. Because of my growing radio presence, I was asked to moderate a candidate debate at the Union League of Philadelphia, a private club founded to support the Union in the Civil War. There were five Democratic candidates for mayor and three Republican candidates, one of whom was Rizzo. All but one of the candidates showed up. I controlled the questioning. In an ornate ballroom, here is the first one I put to Rizzo:

"Mayor Rizzo, what was your record while in office as it related to the city's art community?"

These were the first words spoken from one of us to the other in years, and it was in front of a packed room. Now, to the uninformed ear, that would seem like a tough question for the burly former cop. You could easily have thought the question was a cheap shot. But Rizzo and I knew otherwise. He had quite an accomplished record of support for the arts and was, by way of example, very proud of having air-conditioned the Philadelphia Museum of Art. So in the candidates' forum, Rizzo gave a long, detailed answer regarding his record. The question, I confess, was a setup, and it was my way of trying to make peace. Not long after, I was summoned to have lunch with him at the Palm Restaurant.

When we sat down, he looked at me and said, "I loved you like a son."

"And I loved you like a father," I responded, and then it was pretty much like old times.

Rizzo would live only a period of months after that dinner. He died on a Tuesday. We had dinner the Sunday night before he passed. We ate Italian, just like old times. He told the jokes I had heard before, and I laughed as hard as the first time I heard them.

I remember well the day Frank Rizzo died. I had just been appointed by the George H. W. Bush administration to the position of regional administrator of the Department of Housing and Urban Development. That gave me responsibility for all federal housing programs in the states of Pennsylvania, Delaware, Maryland, Virginia, West Virginia, and Washington, D.C. I was only twenty-nine years old. Although I had not formally begun my duties, I was spending some time in the new office in Philadelphia being briefed by staff. On July 16, 1991, I received a telephone message from Jodi Dellabarba, Rizzo's secretary, saying, "The mayor needs to see you." I relayed a reply that I would come to his office at 2:00 p.m. When my schedule unexpectedly freed up sooner, I went to his office and was bullshitting with Mayer "Bob" Cutler, a Rizzo friend, in the reception area of the office when word came from Tony Zecca and David Safronsky, two Rizzo friends and confidants, that the mayor needed emergency medical attention. Cutler and I rode the elevator to the street together and awaited the paramedics. When they arrived, we told them they were about to work on Frank Rizzo. They appeared disbelieving. Who could blame them? No one was more of a personality in Philadelphia at the time.

When they wheeled him away minutes later, I got a look at Rizzo on a stretcher and I knew it was over. Cutler and I did not run, we walked, to Thomas Jefferson University Hospital, where Rizzo would be pronounced dead later in the afternoon. As we walked past strangers on the street, I knew we knew something that would shock and grieve this city—but even I had no idea to what extent.

The funeral for Frank Rizzo was the single largest outpouring and procession that I will ever witness. Thousands of people came to a viewing and then funeral mass at the Cathedral of Saints Peter and Paul to pay their respects, and when the service was ended, many of them drove the dozen or so miles just outside the city to the Holy Sepulchre Cemetery for the burial. The funeral procession turned out to be far more impressive than the outpouring at the church. That was because the cortege traveled north on Broad Street, through the heart of Philadelphia's minority community, and along the entire route, the mourners were several deep. Frank Rizzo got his just due in death.

I rode behind the hearse in a ratty old station wagon that Cutler had used in a variety of campaigns, including the 1987 effort. Cutler was quite a character and that car was kind of a mirror image of him: disheveled, but somehow always able to get the job done. We'd nicknamed it the "Cutmobile." Cutler would advance all of our campaign events, so he'd arrive prior to the mayor's car, in which I would be riding. Invariably, as we would approach a campaign stop, we'd see Cut out front, standing with a finger in the air to direct our entrance. And without fail, Rizzo would say, "Hey, Weinberg, there's your buddy Cutler. Let's run him the fuck over." We'd howl, even though he said it every single night (I'm smiling now as I write this). Cut had told me he thought it appropriate that we participate in the procession by taking the Cutmobile for a final spin and I had agreed. If Rizzo were looking down on us then, I know he'd have said something like, "Weinberg, get a look at those crazy cocksuckers."

Because of these and many other unique political experiences at an early age, I was soon invited to provide political commentary on Philadelphia television and radio. Politics was my foot inside the radio door, and I haven't left the air since.

Chapter 2

Coal Crackers

Immigration: **Our borders are porous. Only when they are closed should we decide what to do with the millions already here illegally. It is impractical to believe we will ship them back; attrition, and ensuring no more friends and relatives join them, however, will probably stem the tide of illegal immigration.**

The United States is on the cusp of an unprecedented population growth. Today, we are a nation of about 305 million. But according to an August 2008 U.S. Census report, we will reach the 400-million mark in just three decades.[1] Left undeterred, this will be the single greatest growth spurt in our history, as we expand by 135 million additional people by 2050.

Try putting aside who's causing the growth, what they look like, and where they come from. Imagine the population pop is being fueled by births by native-born white American women. Don't you think we'd be hearing concerns from environmentalists about the emissions onslaught brought on by more than 100 million additional potential drivers? Wouldn't somebody doubt our ability to educate so many new youngsters? Or treat them in emergency rooms? Or provide them with social services and police protection? But because what's really driving the population growth is significantly higher birth rates among immigrants and the continued influx of foreigners, the conversation gets stifled in political correctness. In the lexicon of American politics, population growth at home comes under the heading of "illegal immigration," which is now perceived to be the concern of only right-wing talk-show hosts and xenophobes.

Well, an outfit called the Center for Immigration Studies (CIS) shares my concern about the data. The CIS is an independent, nonpartisan nonprofit research organization founded in 1985. It is the nation's only think tank devoted exclusively to research and policy analysis of the economic, social, demographic, fiscal, and other impacts of immigration on the United States. Steve Camarota, the director of research at CIS, told me he estimates that one-third of the total increase would be the result of illegal immigration. "In just forty-two years, the United States population will be 135 million people larger. Regardless of the ethnic makeup, that's enormous. That's a growth in just forty-two years of about 44 percent. And that has enormous implications for the environment, quality of life, congestion, pollution, sprawl, traffic and preservation of open space," Camarota said.

Need more proof? There's plenty of information from which to choose. In his book *State of Emergency,* former presidential candidate and President Nixon aide Patrick Buchanan laid it out this way: The number of illegal aliens now in the United States is at least as many as all English, Irish, and Jewish immigrants combined who came to America over four hundred years. Every month, the border patrol apprehends about 150,000 illegal aliens, more than the number of troops in Iraq. One in every twelve people breaking into the United States illegally has a criminal record.[2]

You'd think the numbers alone—135 million more people by 2050!—would demand that our leaders consider and debate how to prepare for such drastic changes. But they won't, because anybody who does is immediately branded a racist touting regressive politics. And politicians know that's no way to get elected.

I saw that axiom in practice in my own political backyard when Pennsylvania was the equivalent of Iowa or New Hampshire in the 2008 presidential primary season. For the first time in decades, our votes in the Keystone State mattered to the presidential nomination process. So for a month and a half, the candidates—John McCain, Hillary Clinton, and Barack Obama—had my home state in their sights.

The Republican race was decided by the time of the April 22 Pennsylvania primary, but Senator McCain nevertheless spent considerable time campaigning there. The Democratic contest was still being hotly contested, and not only did Clinton and Obama spend tons of time in Pennsylvania, but so too did former president Bill Clinton. There sometimes seemed no location to which either Hillary or Bill Clinton and Barack Obama were unwilling to venture.

With one exception: Hazleton, a small city tucked into northeast Pennsylvania's coal-cracker belt. As I joked in a *Daily News* column at the time, it was as if there was a No Fly Zone erected around the city.[3] What did Hazleton have to do with illegal immigration? Plenty. It was tied to the controversy, and I had a personal connection to the city of coal crackers.

My parents are both from Hazleton. My mother is one of the "Grovich girls" from Green Street. Her parents were immigrants from Yugoslavia who settled into mining jobs during the 1920s. I have plenty of cousins still in the area. Mom was once Miss West Hazleton High. Mr. West Hazleton High was a guy named Moose Denesevich. You have to love a name like that, which (along with names as distinctively Eastern European as Smerconish) used to be as common in Hazleton as Smith or Jones.

My dad's family came from Italy and the Austro-Hungarian Empire in the late 1800s. He grew up outside of Hazleton, in a tiny mining town called Audenried. His father was a mine inspector responsible for three hundred men, having risen from the ranks of laborer. Both of my grandfathers had black lung disease; that often came with the territory.

Well, the Hazleton of my parents' upbringing has vanished. It's no longer a hardscrabble Rockwellian community anchored by churches, social clubs, and close-knit neighborhoods. King coal is long gone, and today's new arrivals aren't from Eastern Europe. They are often illegal immigrants from Mexico who have brought with them a host of social problems.

In 2007, Hazleton received national attention when mayor Lou Barletta instituted a crackdown on illegal immigration, which he believed was threatening the quality of life in his town—my parents' hometown. (I didn't know Barletta before the controversy arose, but learned that his Uncle Joe dated my Aunt Melane. You could say we came close to being a butter knife away at Thanksgiving and Christmas.)

Barletta was pushed into action after a May 2006 killing in his city for which several illegal immigrants were suspected. So the mayor tried to stem the illegal influx by punishing landlords who rented to illegals and employers who hired them through what was called the Immigration

Relief Act, which was struck down in federal district court in 2007. He also made English the official language of the city. In the case that nixed the Immigration Relief Act, the ACLU sued the city over the ordinances they deemed unconstitutional. Vic Walczak is the ACLU's state legal director, and in his opening statement at a hearing, he said something significant: "Law regarding immigration can and must be passed only by Congress."[4] Well, therein lies the problem. Congress has abdicated its responsibility, leaving local officials to do the political dirty work.

Where Mr. Walczak and I disagree is over the role of someone like Mayor Barletta, who I credit with having the courage to fill the void left by Congress. Barletta's efforts were rewarded by voters. In 2007, he not only won renomination as a Republican, but was successful in a last-minute write-in campaign to be the Democratic nominee as well.[5] Consequently, he won reelection as both the Republican and Democratic nominee.

During the presidential primary season, Barletta went so far as to invite the presidential contenders to tour Hazleton, voter-rich with its population of more than 23,000, to see the problems he was dealing with and discuss the immigration issue.[6] Nobody accepted, of course. "I believe they're purposely avoiding coming to Hazleton," the mayor told me at the time. "I think this is a very clear indication of how our next president will deal with illegal immigration. Or should I say 'will not deal' with illegal immigration? Everybody knows Hazleton. They know we are at the front line of this issue. What better forum than to come here and tell this country how they feel about illegal immigration and how they will deal with it?"[7]

The presidential candidates were tripping over themselves in the buildup to the Pennsylvania primary in 2008, but not one candidate could find the time for a visit and some pierogies in Hazleton. Nor did the illegal immigration discussion ramp up once the primary season was over; I heard not one word uttered about illegal immigration at the 2008 national conventions, both of which I attended.

Too bad Richard Lamm isn't still in office.

In the spring of 2006, the former governor of Colorado delivered an address entitled, "I Have a Plan to Destroy America." Cyberspace lore held that Lamm, a Democrat, began his remarks by saying to a Washington crowd: "I have a secret plan to destroy America. If you believe, as many do, that America is too smug, too white bread, too self-satisfied, too rich, let's destroy America. It is not that hard to do. History shows that nations are more fragile than their citizens think. No nation in history has survived the ravages of time."[8]

I was sent his speech transcript via e-mail no less than a dozen times. It's one of those things friends keep circulating with captions like "right on," "you won't believe someone had the stones to say this," or "YOU MUST READ THIS." At first, I wasn't sure if it was legitimate.

So what were the elements of Lamm's plan to destroy the country? They included:

- "We must first make America a bilingual-bicultural country. History shows, in my opinion, that no nation can survive the tension, conflict, and antagonism of two competing languages and cultures. It is a blessing for an individual to be bilingual; it is a curse for a society to be bilingual."

- "I would then invent 'multiculturalism' and encourage immigrants to maintain their own culture. I would make it an article of belief that all cultures are equal: That there are no cultural differences that are important. I would declare it an article of faith that the black and Hispanic dropout rate is only due to prejudice and discrimination by the majority. Every other explanation is out-of-bounds."

- "We can make the United States a 'Hispanic Quebec' without much effort. The key is to celebrate diversity rather than unity."

- "I would encourage all immigrants to keep their own language and culture. I would replace the melting-pot metaphor with a salad-bowl metaphor."[9]

Talk about un-muzzled. I tracked down Governor Lamm and asked whether he'd actually uttered these words. He told me he did indeed say those things, and then expanded on them.

"I knew by the impact on the audience that it was a good speech. I really spent a lot of time thinking about how you get the maximum amount of meaning in the minimum amount of words, and how you can compress. I think most politicians speak way too long and I think that conciseness helps focus the mind."[10]

Governor Lamm even had an element of The Plan for those who do not like what he has to say. "I would place all these subjects off-limits—make it taboo to talk about. I would find a word similar to 'heretic' in the sixteenth century—that stopped discussion and paralyzed thinking. Words like 'racist,' 'xenophobe' that halt argument and conversation."[11]

In that regard, it would seem that Governor Lamm's plan is almost complete.

Right about now you are probably saying, Smerconish. S-m-e-r-c-o-n-i-s-h. Hmmmm. What kind of name is that? For starters, it's not an easy one to pronounce. Jackie Mason had the best few lines about my name. I was a guest a few years ago on his television program, which airs on Comcast's CN8 network. To this day, I often use the recording of what Mason said on TV as an introduction for my own radio program: "His name is Michael Smerconish. Michael Smerconish got that name because they were trying to get even with him. I don't know what his parents were trying to do when they picked out Smerconish as a name. Jews have changed their names throughout history when they were called Bernstein or Goldberg and they thought that somehow it was not such a beautiful name. But Smerconish? This is a hit? You couldn't think of another name? When you are trying to get even with somebody, you say 'You look to me like a real Smerconish!'"

Well, speaking of my parents, my father's first name is Walter, or Walt. When I was growing up, and my family of four needed a dinner reservation, we were never "Smerconish," party of four. We were always "Walters," party of four. That saved time and cut down on confusion. Still, a woman whose name actually is Walters once told me I should have changed my own.

In 2007 I was invited to appear on a segment of *The View* to promote my second book, *Muzzled: From T-Ball to Terrorism*, which was being released in paperback. Before the segment began, I was in a holding area outside of the audience view, on the right side of the stage. I was standing, probably pacing, getting ready to go on. Barbara Walters was relaxing in a chair. She asked me how to pronounce my name. I offered it to her, and told her the name was phonetic. She tried a time or two without success. Then she finally asked, "Why, if you are a broadcaster, did you never change your name?" I told her I'd never thought of doing so, but what was really running through my mind was how we had used her surname all of those years when making dinner reservations. I felt like saying to her, what would you recommend, Michael Walters?

Chapter 3

419 People

Michael Smerconish is uniquely qualified to represent Central Bucks in the Pennsylvania Legislature. His lifetime of Bucks County residency, as well as his wide-ranging political experiences, have prepared him to serve our needs in Harrisburg.

Or so I told residents of the community in which I was raised in the spring of 1986. Not enough of them agreed! I was in my second year of law school, and while maintaining a normal load of classes I was also running full-time for the state legislature. That campaign blurb appeared alongside a photograph of me—with hair—in which I was sitting wearing a flannel shirt and pair of L.L.Bean duck shoes, against a backdrop of a leafy glen. This was my bid to avenge my father's loss, but the Hollywood ending was not in the cards. I came up 419 votes shy, and as I like to joke when reminiscing about the race, I have since located 237 of those people!

What qualified me to run for the Pennsylvania state house at age twenty-four? Well, loads of ambition, although I couldn't tout that as a key attribute. I did have some Republican credentials, including: election as an alternate delegate to the 1984 Republican National Convention; having worked as a member of the advance staff for Vice President Bush; serving as an assistant to the Philadelphia Special Investigative Commission, which was a blue-ribbon group of citizens appointed by the mayor of the City of Philadelphia to investigate the infamous confrontation between the radical group MOVE and Philadelphia Police that resulted in a conflagration that decimated an entire city block in 1985;[1] and work as a member of the county Republican Executive Committee, which was responsible for coordinating all GOP activities in the legislative district in which I was now running. My point is that while I was yet to establish a career, I was already knee-deep in party politics.

Mine was a four-way Republican primary for an open seat, and given the composition of the legislative district, victory in the primary was essentially a guarantee of success in the general election. David Snyder, who was only two years older than me, was a commercial pilot and builder. Thomas Scarborough was a forty-five-year-old local borough councilman who received the endorsement of the Pennsylvania State Education Association. Dave Heckler was a lawyer who would later circulate a piece of campaign literature that did a side-by-side comparison of all of the candidates, carefully juxtaposing his age (thirty-nine) and four years of experience in Harrisburg with my twenty-four years and a big fat zero next to "experience." This was an open primary, meaning nobody received the formal endorsement of the local Republican committee. I raised the most money, but it wasn't enough, and in the end the campaign was more about my age than my fundraising.

I remain proud that I ran for office, and nowadays, glad that I lost. I think my radio program, columns, and TV perch give me more of an opportunity to effectuate change than I would have had in the state legislature. But back then, I wanted victory in the worst way. I had good literature, a nice cadre of volunteers, and a campaign office on the main drag in my hometown. I thoroughly enjoyed the crazy pace of attending law-school classes in the morning, then knocking on doors and attending coffee klatches and candidate screenings at night. I remember the night in quaint Newtown Borough when I rang an entrance buzzer only to have a bird crap on my head while I waited for the homeowner to get the door. I was accompanied by a wonderful woman, a campaign volunteer named Rebecca Mammel, who gave me a Kleenex while delighting that this was surely a sign of good luck. Unfortunately she was wrong on election day.

They say all politics is local, and my campaign was no exception. There was only one real issue in the race and it had to do with a proposed water-diversion project called the Point Pleasant Pumping Station. It was intended to take water from the Delaware River and channel it to both suburban residents and the Limerick Nuclear Power Plant.[2] "The Pump," as it came to be known, was a controversy that took on cultural proportions. Environmentalists from all over, including other states, came to Bucks County to contest its construction. One such objector was Abbie Hoffman of Chicago Seven fame, who

I was proud at the time to have campaign *against* me. The environmental position was that the Pump would spur development and the erosion of open space, and might do harm to the Delaware River. The local electric utility, Philadelphia Electric Company (PECO), had a vested interest in wanting the Pump built for its power plant.[3] PECO's political action committee endorsed me and gave me some negligible amount of money (I think it was $250) because of my support for the Pump. The group opposed to the Pump, which called itself Del-Aware, was hatriolic against anything having to do with PECO, including me. ("Hatriolic" is a word I coined, a combination of "hate" and "vitriol." Actually, I once blurted it out on CNN, and *The New Yorker* listed my use of hatriolic as a faux pas. Me, I'm proud of it and wish it would be picked up by *Merriam Webster's Dictionary*.)

Well, one night after I was at a candidate screening with my treasurer, Bill Snyder (the same guy who once introduced me to Frank Rizzo), we stopped at a local bar for a few pops. We then drove home through the community in which I grew up, taking note of my campaign yard signs, which had just gone up that day in front of hundreds of homes. We drove by a few before I realized that they had been defaced. When they left the printer, the yard signs said "Michael Smerconish for State Representative," only now someone or some group had affixed preprinted labels that read "PECO" over the word "State." In other words, now they said "Michael Smerconish for PECO Representative." Well. I was pissed—and tipsy (Bill was driving). We went on a manhunt for the culprits, and lo and behold, we came upon a van that was straight out of central casting for granola eaters. It had all sorts of bumper stickers on the back, including "Dump the Pump" and "No Nukes," the hallmarks of those against the Pump—and me. Outside the van, there was a scruffy guy we both recognized from the Del-Aware group, who was actually in the process of sticking a PECO label over one of my signs. We chased him, but he sped away. We did report him to the police, but it was one of those things a losing candidate—me—had no stomach to pursue after the battle.

Despite months of hard work, on May 20, 1986, I lost to David Heckler. He served in the state house, then state senate, and finally became a county judge. He was a decent fellow, and I have zero regrets about running the race. It was one of the better learning experiences of my life, and when I speak at schools or to student groups, I always urge young people to get involved in politics sooner than later. Not only does the youngest person in the room often get saddled with responsibility they would then find nowhere else in life, but you also develop a political and social network that can last a lifetime. When my race ended, I sent supporters a note that said, "I would be less than honest if I did not admit to being disappointed with the results of May 20. . . . In spite of defeat, I stand proud of our effort to bring *conservative* government to Bucks County." Note my use of the word "conservative." That is not how I would describe myself today.

Not many individuals in their twenties would need to so clearly stake out public positions on controversial political issues. But I did as a candidate, and today, more than twenty years later, I am surprised at some of my early views. What did Neil Young sing in "Old Man"? "Twenty-four and there's so much more." Indeed. The guy who ran for the state legislature would never have bought into the Suburban Manifesto. Not that the issues were the same back then. In 1986, I was focused on the Pump, suburban growth, and ending Pennsylvania's state monopoly on liquor stores. There were times, however, when I had to think about a more expanded menu of issues. As has become the modern norm, during the election we candidates were asked by a variety of civic and special interest groups to answer surveys that could then be disseminated to the group's members. Well, in my attic (of course), I recently found one such questionnaire from a group called the Citizens Awareness Network. I have no recollection of who these "citizens" were, much less why they needed a "network" for their "awareness." But I am fascinated, at age forty-six, to read what I said on seven different issues when I was twenty-four and running for office.

Each issue solicited a yes or no reply. Well, I was seven for seven—I answered each question affirmatively, and was the only candidate with uniformity in my responses (aside from David Snyder, whose failure to answer the survey gave him no answers by default). Here are some of the highlights—a check mark means, yes, I agree.[4]

"Do you favor an overturn of the 1973 Roe vs. Wade Decision which legalized abortion?" ☑

"Would you support a "Right-to-Life" Amendment ,which would limit abortions to cases of rape, incest, or the endangering of the life of the mother?" ☑

"Are you opposed to the use of Government funds to pay for abortions?" ☑

"Would you support legislation which would provide an opportunity for open prayer in public schools?" ☑

"Are you in favor of Tuition Tax Credits for families who send their children to private or Church operated schools?" ☑

"Are you opposed to the sale of alcoholic beverages in supermarkets and convenience stores in the State of Pennsylvania?" ☑

"Would you oppose legislation which would allow gambling institutions such as casinos to operate in the State of Pennsylvania?" ☑

Today I feel like Austin Powers when confronted with that Swedish device in *International Man of Mystery* ("That's not mine!"). Call me a flip-flopper, because I don't recognize many of these views. Clearly, in 1986, in the midst of the Reagan revolution, I was drinking the Kool-Aid. Beyond that questionnaire, I disseminated a written platform that addressed other issues.

Ironically, it is the sort of social issue views I once espoused in that Citizens Awareness Network questionnaire that are symptomatic of where I think the Republican Party has lost its bearings. Republicans lost big in the 2006 elections pushing these types of issues, which no longer resonate with a large portion of the electorate. Looking at the faded, yellowing pages of that survey and my frayed platform from years ago, I recognize that I've come of age politically. Of course, if that is the proper way to describe it, I know that many would like to see me return to my adolescence.

Chapter 4

Straight Talk

Gays: **Homosexuals don't threaten my marriage. As we seek to find some accommodation for same-sex couples, we need to end that false argument.**

I don't get worked into a lather about same-sex relationships. No pun intended. OK, some pun.

Mine is a twist on the Charlie Rich principle. Remember that guy with a full head of hair, who in the 1970s sang, "no one knows what goes on behind closed doors"?[1] Well, my view is that not only does no one know what goes on behind closed doors, but also, that it's only the business of those who are behind the door, assuming they are consenting adults. My laissez-faire attitude (that actually sounds conservative) is grounded in a general inclination to let people live their individual lives as they see fit. Life is short. We all have plenty of obstacles in our quest to lead happy and productive lives, and I don't think it's my business to decide how two adult consenting individuals choose to lead theirs so long as it does not impact my ability to do likewise. I constantly hear people claim that two guys hooking up *does* impact their lives, or the sanctity of marriage generally, but I think it's a canard to assert that my heterosexual lifestyle is impacted by what two consenting adult men or women do with theirs. Marriage may well be in jeopardy in the new millennium, but it's not as a result of guys suddenly being given the societal thumbs up or legal imprimatur to ditch their wives and marry their buddy. Sometimes when I have made that point on the radio, a listener will call or e-mail a name to me that they think disproves my logic: Jim McGreevey. But I've spoken to McGreevey about his sexuality and I think his situation actually supports my view.

Remember August 12, 2004, when New Jersey governor James McGreevey shocked the public when he announced, "I am a gay American" and said he would resign the office three months later?[2] He did, and two years after his resignation came the inevitable memoir and book tour, which passed through my studio on September 25, 2006.

Actually, I hosted him twice: First as an in-studio guest, and second, via the book club I run for radio listeners. I remember it well because it was a difficult sell to my audience. That ticket, unlike those for other book-club events, was not in high demand.

When McGreevey was my in-studio guest after resigning office and leaving his wife (soon before he began a new relationship with a man), we had a respectful and direct dialogue about these matters. For example, he had written openly about the promiscuity with which he had been involved, including looking for sex at roadside rest stops. I took that as my opening to share with the former governor my theory of "the governor" relative to gay sex. This was pretty classic.

I told him I had a go-kart as a kid, and it had a limitation on the gas pedal so I couldn't go fast—a limitation that we called "the governor," although I never knew why. I then explained to him that I thought women were a "governor" in life, because guys are always looking for action, but women are seemingly not. Therefore, if you remove the female limitation—the governor—you'll be left with two willing guys looking for action anytime and anywhere, hence my explanation for the promiscuity he had written about.

The former New Jersey governor said he was unacquainted with my "governor" theory and that he didn't buy it. "I think it's different," he told me, before explaining that he was raised to believe that "this thing called gay was supposed to be evil and horrible," and consequently he didn't want to embrace it.[3] "I thought I would go to hell," he told me. He said he tried to keep it away, deny it, and repress it. "So the only thing I thought was available to me was anonymity." One of the more curious aspects of my interview with him had to do with something he wrote about Golan Cipel, the government employee with whom he claimed he'd had a relationship while governor. In his book, McGreevey said there was a chance Cipel was not gay.[4] I wondered why he wrote that given that McGreevey claimed they were lovers—something Cipel denied when the book came out.

"What did you mean by that? You slept with him," I said.[5] McGreevey answered, "Because I can't say what another person is." I still didn't understand, and I said to him, "But if you sleep with a guy, he's gay. Is it more complicated than that?"[6]

The former governor said, "Clearly it was more complicated than that for me."[7] "For me it was never a choice," he later added. "I don't want to be in a position of judging any other person's heart or intentions or sexuality. That is not the purpose of the book, to say he's gay and everything that proceeds from that. The purpose of book is to say I was gay, I am gay, I was acting out of fear, I made a lot of bad stupid decisions, and if any good comes out of it it's understanding that you act from your own truth, embrace who you are, and follow that passion and also work to live an honest life, and try to do the next right thing."

I appreciated McGreevey's willingness to openly discuss his sexuality even if it was in support of selling a book. I am not defending nor do I excuse McGreevey for hiring an unqualified man for a serious job—one with homeland security responsibilities—only to have a relationship with him while married. I did, however, conclude from my interviews with him that he was a guy who had been through an emotional hell—one partially attributable to having been raised in a culture that ingrained in him a sense of shame for his sexual preferences. No one should have to grow up in such a cocoon because of their sexuality. If society did not then frown on same-sex relationships, I suspect he would never have married his wife, Dina. Ironically, had he come of age in an era more accepting of same-sex relationships, he would arguably have pursued his real sexual interests and would have caused less injury to those around him.

Needless to say, the politics of homosexuality are an area of disagreement between many Republicans and me. Not only do certain conservatives act at odds with the philosophical tenets of self-determinism and independence, they seek to take advantage of visceral anti-gay attitudes at the ballot box. The underlying logic is wrong, and I think driving the base on an issue such as this is fundamentally flawed as a political model. Consider that in both 2000 and 2004, the Republican Party's platform included specific passages affirming that marriage be defined strictly as a union between a man and a woman.[8] In 2004, thirteen states passed ballot initiatives to ban same-sex marriage, including Ohio, the state that determined the outcome of the 2004 presidential race.[9] Those who came out that year to support ballot initiatives, the conventional wisdom holds, probably provided the thin margin by which the president was reelected.

I don't buy it. I think that driving the vote on such push-button issues has a major drawback, namely that while it may be a catalyst for conservative turnout, it most certainly alienates moderates and liberals who, like me, see it as divisive. My home state of Pennsylvania is a great example and lends itself well to such an illustration. Picture the rectangular shape of the Keystone State. Facing the rectangle, Philadelphia is located in the lower right (the southeast) and Pittsburgh in the lower left (the southwest). Both cities, Philadelphia in particular, tend to vote liberal/Democrat. Outside of both are moderate, suburban territories that swing between the parties. In the center part of the state, as well as across the top of the state, are the most conservative regions. This vertical band along with a bar across the top is what we Pennsylvanians call the "T," and what James Carville famously referred to as the Alabama that exists between Philadelphia and Pittsburgh.[10] Hand me a Pennsylvania map in advance of any statewide election, and I can color code it for you according to who will win what geographic area. It's not rocket science. The Democrats win the cities of Philadelphia and Pittsburgh and the GOP wins the central T. The suburbs, meanwhile, are up for grabs, and often determine the outcome of the race. Ed Rendell is the governor of Pennsylvania because he did well in the Philadelphia suburbs. Rick Santorum is not a member of the U.S. Senate today because he lost in the Philadelphia suburbs.

Pennsylvania last went red in a presidential race in 1988, when Bush 41 bested Michael Dukakis. Ever since, the GOP has struggled to find a strategy to return to the win column. In the 2000 and 2004 cycle, Karl Rove's strategy was focused on driving out the conservative vote in the central T of the state, and to that extent it worked. But the focus on push-button conservative issues had the unintended effect of causing a backlash in the suburban areas. I would argue that for every vote driven to the polls by reliance on issues like opposing same-sex relationships, one moderate or liberal vote was lost in the suburbs. I don't think Pennsylvania is unique in this regard—I think that scenario plays itself out in suburbs across the nation. In the end, George W. Bush failed to carry Pennsylvania by small margins in both elections. Who knows—had he been a true compassionate conservative with a more tolerant view of same-sex relationships, perhaps he would have bettered his suburban totals and won the state.

That said, my desire to live and let live on the way to winning presidential elections has limits. I have not fully embraced the idea of calling a same-sex union a "marriage." If thirty years of legal precedent concerning abortion law can be considered settled—and indeed, even Chief Justice Roberts has testified that it is[11]—then thousands of years of precedent that regard the term "marriage" as between a man and a woman should also apply. It's not that I don't believe two men or two women can't have a healthy, successful relationship, or that they should be denied the rights and privileges that come from such a union; it's identifying that relationship as a "marriage" that gives me pause. Maybe it's only a semantic concern I have. I do believe that on matters such as health insurance, inheritance, and hospital visitation, same-sex couples should be treated no differently than heterosexual married couples.

Regardless, I will say this: Politically speaking, sometimes those seeking to advance a gay agenda are their own worst enemies. For a long time, they have needed an image makeover. Long ago, somebody should have reined in the leather crowd at the front of many a gay-pride parade and told them they were too tough a sell in Middle America. Pride schmide. You want to advance the agenda, get to the back of the float!

Of course, it's easy to take sides in the debate concerning homosexuality when it's in the newspapers or part of a discussion with my radio audience. It's quite another issue when that debate is brought to the kitchen table. As any parent knows, perhaps one of the hardest things about raising kids is answering those tough questions they bring home about current events. While these questions often put parents in an uncomfortable place, most of them assume that those sticky queries are a part of the package of having kids, and they, as parents, hold the supreme right to answer those questions in a way they deem appropriate.

This is the exact parental right that was called into question in 2007, when an elementary school in Evesham Township, New Jersey, introduced a video called *That's a Family!* into its curriculum.[12] The video was intended to show a number of different families to promote a greater tolerance for diversity. I talked to parents who were disturbed when their children told them that the video featured a girl with two "mommies." While divorced, mixed-race, adoptive, guardianship, and single-parent families were also shown in the video, many felt that the school was usurping the parents' authority. I was inclined to agree, but it raised the question: Do we need to have a specific conversation about gays and lesbians with our kids?

I said publicly that I believed the school made a mistake insofar as the controversy was predictable and parents should have been advised of the content of the video before it was shown to their children. I used the controversy, however, as an impetus with which to tackle the "gay" topic with my own sons, then ages six, nine, and ten, with whom I had not yet spoken about this issue. My nine-year-old may have offered the most measured analysis of the situation, and, indeed, the issue of homosexuality in general.

His view was that it was unnecessary for the school to display the video, because all of the families featured in the video were covered by the Golden Rule, that unwritten commandment that dictates that we treat others as we wish to be treated. I shouldn't have been surprised. He had grown used to singing about the Golden Rule in Mrs. Schwarz's class at his Montessori school. At school functions, we parents would get teary watching the kids sing, "Do unto others as you would have them do unto you. . . . hmm hmm hmm hmm . . . live the Golden Rule."

In my opinion, he had it right. If you raise your children to treat people well, you don't need to be specific about sexuality, gender, race, or religion. It's amazing how someone so young could form ideas of tolerance and respect that many adults still cannot grasp in this divisive debate. Perhaps those who justify their vitriol on religious grounds should recall this hallmark of morality.

So here's some "straight talk" for the GOP: Time to stop appealing to the fringe by opposing people who want to lead their own lives behind closed doors and stop making a baseless connection between homosexual unions and heterosexual marriage.

Chapter 5

A Face for Radio

How did you end up in talk radio?

When I do public speaking and take questions from the audience, there is always at least one hand in the air seeking an answer to that one. I suspect every radio host has a unique story to tell as to how he or she first got on the air, given that there's really no conventional career path. Mine, as I have mentioned, is rooted in politics. I was very fortunate to have many extraordinary political experiences at a young age, which caused me to be invited onto television and the radio to offer political commentary. I'm probably also distinguishable from many others because I work in a major market without ever having worked in smaller venues. I didn't do overnights in Duluth, then weekends in Cleveland, and finally afternoons in San Antonio before coming to Philadelphia; Philadelphia is the only radio market in which I have ever lived and worked. Still, I think I've paid my dues.

My first appearance on talk radio came on a talk radio station called WWDB (96.5 FM) on May 19, 1990.

On this particular Saturday night nearly twenty years ago, I was asked to be a guest on WWDB to talk Pennsylvania politics. The invitation came while I was helping to raise money for Barbara Hafer, who was then the auditor general of Pennsylvania and Republican candidate running for governor against incumbent Bob Casey. (Her bid didn't work out so well, particularly after she called Casey a "redneck Irishman" in the midst of the campaign—a comment, by the way, that made him more endearing to me.)[1] Brian Tierney, a contemporary of mine who was then setting the world on fire as an advertising entrepreneur, offered me the opportunity. At the time he was regionally famous for his appearances as a weekly panelist on a Sunday roundtable show called *Inside Story*, hosted by Marc Howard, which aired on Philadelphia's ABC affiliate, WPVI. It's funny how life works out. Today, having cashed out of his business (twice), Tierney is the publisher of the *Philadelphia Inquirer* and the *Philadelphia Daily News*, which he purchased with an investment group he assembled. That also makes him my boss, since I am a columnist for both newspapers. Anyway, back then he was filling in for Tom Marr, the host of a weekend show on WWDB. So in my first foray into radio, you could say I was the guest of a guest host on a weekend shift.

I saved the thank you letter that I sent to Brian Tierney the following Monday, complete with some sophomoric scribble at the bottom that says "Howard Stern eat your heart out." That was one day before I sent a different letter to the owner of the radio station, asking that he use me as a political commentator. (This early show of chutzpah will come as no surprise to my agent, George Hiltzik. Or as my mother would tell you, no grass has ever grown under my feet.)

WWDB sported a lineup that included some big names in my hometown—Paul W. Smith, Susan Bray, Irv Homer, Bernie Herman, and Dominic Quinn, to name a few. They were the prime-time talkers. On weekends, Sid Mark hosted his legendary *Friday with Frank* and *Sunday with Sinatra* programs from this location. Sid began his career in Philadelphia with a radio show called *Sounds in the Night,* which aired on Friday nights. At the suggestion of an audience member he began to dedicate an hour block of his show to the swinging tunes of Frank Sinatra. Years later, *Sunday with Sinatra* and the nationally syndicated *Sounds of Sinatra,* which aired on Saturday evening, debuted. Sid's lifelong friendship with the legend himself began with a dinner invitation in 1966, when Sinatra asked Sid to fly to Las Vegas to be his guest at the Sands one weekend. There started a relationship that would give Sid, a kid from Camden, New Jersey, a front-row seat for Mr. S. and the Rat Pack. Many times Sid has regaled me with stories about Sinatra, whom he loved. I'll tell you something else about Sid. On the air, he has a calm and melodic voice. He's a true professional and the best presenter of a live commercial that I have ever heard. You get lost in his promotion of sponsors and forget where programming has ended and advertising begun. But off-air, he is one of the funniest men I have ever met, which might come as a surprise to his vast radio audience. Sid has a deadpan, dry wit. He's also smart as a whip. And when I recently told him he should have been a comedian, I should not have been surprised when he told me he started in stand-up. Sid's unique friendship with Mr. S. has been a blessing for Philadelphia, and my friendship with Sid is something I treasure. Of course, when I was just starting, I was in awe of Sid and dared not approach him, as I was the lowest man on the totem pole. Heck, I wasn't even on the totem pole.

While I was growing up in the Philadelphia area, my parents had often listened to WWDB, and I had become a fan of the station's political dialogue, making my guest spot at the station an important moment for me. This occasion also became a career-altering experience. After sitting behind the microphone for the first time, I knew instantaneously that I wanted to spend time on the air. I'm sure my desire was largely ego-driven. I was pretty comfortable on the air and no doubt enjoyed hearing my own voice. I also thought I had something to contribute to a program about current events.

This was a different era in radio. The era of conservative dominance by syndicated hosts had yet to arrive in Philadelphia. The Rush wave was just commencing and consolidation in ownership had yet to occur. At the time, WWDB was still owned by a local entrepreneur named Chuck Schwartz. I remember having a tough time getting to him and finally enlisted the help of Larry Kane, who said he knew him, to make the connection. I have mentioned Larry previously, but how I met him is a story unto itself.

In high school, I worked stocking shelves and delivering pool supplies and patio furniture for Mt. Lake Pool and Patio, which was owned by Mike and Arlene Stachel. Their son, and my good friend, Michael Jr., who once skipped school with me to go meet Ronald Reagan, also worked for the family business. Mike Stachel Sr. had started as a pool-maintenance guy for Sylvan Pools, and in a classic Horatio Alger move, later started his own pool company.

Every summer, Mike and Arlene Stachel were willing to hire any kids in the neighborhood who wanted to work. I always had summer jobs, and this was the best of them. One day, I came to work and Mike Sr. said that Larry Kane needed a bucket of chlorine delivered to his house. This was a big deal—Larry was quite a local celebrity. In any event, I was excited at the prospect of meeting him. Not only did I ask Mike Jr. to tag along, but, on the way out the door, we also grabbed a

Kodak instamatic camera. It was one of the old Polaroid models where you'd take the picture, it would pop out the front on photo paper, and then you'd stand there holding and shaking it for thirty seconds as the picture developed and slowly come into focus. When we arrived at Larry Kane's house, we were disappointed that a maid answered the door. A photograph of her was of no interest, so we told her that Mr. Kane had to personally sign for the chlorine or we could not leave it. I think we used the words "bill of lading," even though I had no idea what that meant. I should point out that Larry was then anchoring the late news on television, and it was mid-morning, meaning that he was most likely still sleeping. The only thing we had that he presumably could sign was a 3x5 index card with his address on it, but we figured that would suffice. After about fifteen minutes, Larry Kane came to the door—sans makeup, with quite a bedhead, in a pair of cutoff shorts, and with his belt unbuckled. He was quite a sight. As he signed the card in a state of slumber, we snapped the picture. I love the guy and we are friendly today, but I still like to rib him about that scene.

Larry played an important part in launching my radio career. It was he who called Chuck Schwartz and suggested me as a radio host. Schwartz put me in touch with David Rimmer, his program director. After some intense lobbying, David said he'd give me some more air time as a political guest, probably in an effort to get me off his back.

I still have my first radio paycheck. It didn't come until a year after my first appearance and it was for $85.29. I think that was $100, after taxes. The check was signed by Chuck's wife, Susan, who was then the treasurer of the company they owned that controlled the station.

Years thereafter, Larry Kane would again make an introduction for me, this time to Roy Shapiro, who was the vice president and general manager of KYW Newsradio (1060 AM), Philadelphia's perennial radio powerhouse. Just think: Without Larry, Chuck, David, and Roy, I would never have become a broadcaster. Good thing Larry needed chlorine that day.

I had the radio bug from day one. I got my foot firmly wedged in the door as political commentator after that time Brian Tierney had me as his guest, mainly due to the hot Philadelphia mayoral race in 1991, about which I was pretty knowledgeable. From this role, I was invited to be a guest host in odd hours, and finally, I was offered a shift of my own.

If you were to chart my progress in time slots on a graph, it might look as if there was a logical plan, when in reality it was a matter of happenstance. I rarely turned down any offer to be a guest host when I was anxious to land a show of my own. I would get the nod to work Super Bowl Sunday night, or Thanksgiving, or New Year's Eve. That work paid off. *Philadelphia* magazine gave me a "Best of Philadelphia" award in 1993 for my work as a "moonlighter" and wrote at the time, "he's proved to be the only conservative radio voice who makes any rational sense at all. Give this guy his own show already so he won't have to practice law anymore."[2] Well, it finally happened. I was offered my own show. It was Sunday nights, from 8:00 p.m. to midnight.

My first Sunday night as host of my own program was October 3, 1993. In the course of hosting my very first radio show, I responded to a caller who was concerned that traditional viewpoints didn't have a place in the media, to which I responded with a summary of my personal philosophy about the business, which still holds true to this day: "[E]verybody and anybody gets their opportunity to speak their mind. I don't care if they're liberal or conservative, Republican or Democrat, socialist or communist, everybody gets the shot because that's what makes talk radio interesting and that's what's most healthy for democracy."[3]

It was at this stage that I met Mike Baldini, then a young go-getter in sales, who took an interest in my program. Baldini is another of the many characters I have met in radio whom I need to describe so you can fully appreciate the nature of the business. Salespeople are paid mostly by commission, and while others looked at my Sunday-night slot and saw no revenue upside, Baldini saw opportunity. He made an effort to sell my show and I did whatever I could to assist him. But we're not talking Anheuser-Busch beer money. A small computer repair business called TESCO, owned by a man named Frank Faia, was my first advertiser. Entrepreneurs were the economic backbone of talk radio at the time—people like Rich Hoch, who was a jeweler in Ocean City, New Jersey, or a place in Ardmore, Pennsylvania, called the Head Nut, which sold, well, nuts, like pecans and cashews. Baldini would take me out and schmooze clients. Those visits were always a stitch. Baldini is a Philly guy. By the way, not all guys from Philly or who come to Philly are necessarily Philly guys, but Baldini had the credentials. He was born in South Philly, and grew up in the Great Northeast. He went to Father Judge High School, and then graduated from La Salle University.

Like me, he was then in his twenties, but I could already see he was a Runyon-esque guy. Baldini is fun to watch: fast-talking, mind always racing, constantly sizing up people he meets with an innate sense of street smarts. He's perfectly suited for a career in sales because he is a people person. In a previous life, I could see him working as a maître d' at one of the big casino showrooms, making sure that Sinatra had enough Jack in his dressing room while simultaneously deciding who sits where out front. He's now the general sales manager at KYW Newsradio, and is raising his family in a suburban town with "ville" at the end of it. I have a hard time picturing this city guy in the 'burbs.

Back then, WWDB really skewed to an older demographic, something that I think all of talk radio did at the time. In the ratings, we would have huge 12+ numbers, meaning all people who were older than twelve listening to the radio, but we would be weak in the coveted 25–54 demographic. David Rimmer told me he wanted to try to get a younger demo for my show on Sunday nights, which was when Barney the purple dinosaur was taking kids by storm. David's idea was to use the first twenty minutes of my show for Barney storytelling—"Bedtime with Barney"—in the hope that young couples would put their kids to bed with Barney and stick around. It became a bone of contention, but otherwise, Sunday nights were an opportunity for me to get my bearings. In the nascent stages of my radio career, I was having the time of my life.

My Sunday-night show would follow a program hosted by Dr. James A. Corea. "Dr. James A.," "the big guy," was the sort of fellow I have since come to decide you only meet in radio. This former United States Marine hosted a fitness call-in show and a weekly sex show that was cross-your-legs funny. Thursday at 9:00 p.m., Corea would switch roles from the guy you would consult about your sciatica and become "the love doctor," the fellow who could lend advice on luring women to your bed. Usually his advice had to do with taking a shower and wearing cologne. It was the deep inflection of his voice and the locker-room style with which he dispensed his counsel that made it a stitch. That, and the fact that he would wear gym shorts to the studio 365 days a year. He was a bulky guy, with a bodybuilder physique, the kind whose age was always tough to approximate, at least for me. I always marveled at his ability to so quickly respond to listeners' questions about a multitude of health-related subjects. How does he know so much, I wondered? Then one day I watched him do this show. He would sit across from his producer, Tom MacDonald, and flip through an enormous three-ring binder as the listener explained his predicament. The information he offered came from the binders. Corea was not a medical doctor. He had a Ph.D. in something, but I don't know what. He was a nutritionist and weight trainer for the Philadelphia Eagles and owned a sports-medicine practice and gym in New Jersey, which was frequented by many of the Philadelphia Flyers. In fact, I think he sold his gym to Flyers legend Bobby Clarke, one of his friends. Unfortunately, Corea passed away in 2001 from a heart attack, at age sixty-three, after reportedly experiencing chest pains but refusing to go to the hospital until he could arrange for someone to cover his radio show, which was scheduled to debut on a new station that afternoon. He'd been hospitalized only a week or so before for weakness and dizziness, but when doctors recommended immediate bypass surgery, he wanted to go home and think it over.[4] Damn shame. He was a terrific guy, and funny as hell.

In the spring of 1996, longtime broadcaster Dominic Quinn (known as DQ) passed away. DQ had been a prime-time guy, who, before his death, had spent five years doing Saturday and Sunday mornings, 5:30–8:00 and 6:00–9:00, respectively. He built those time periods into immensely popular slots, particularly Sunday morning, when he was followed by Sid Mark doing a highly rated Frank Sinatra–inspired program. When DQ passed, I was asked by new program director Matt Zucker to sit in for him until the dust settled. After a few weekends spent doing nothing but opening the telephone lines and allowing DQ's audience to grieve, his time slot was mine. I vacated Sunday nights and moved to Saturday and Sunday mornings.

Though I was working seven days a week, radio was still my part-time job. I had graduated from law school in 1987, and worked in the real estate business for the next four years. In that span of time, I made a fortune in real estate, and then proceeded to lose a bundle. Then, in 1991, I was appointed by the Bush administration—the George H. W. Bush administration—to serve as the regional administrator of the Department of Housing and Urban Development (HUD). I was a presidential appointee to this sub-cabinet-level post, working under HUD secretary Jack Kemp. When Bush lost to Bill Clinton in 1992, I needed to get another job. I began to practice law with a legendary Philadelphia trial lawyer named James E. Beasley. I was a lawyer Monday through Friday, and then did a talk radio show on Saturday and Sunday mornings. This is the way it would stay for a year, but this double duty wouldn't last for long.

Chapter 6

9/11 + 7

Preventing terror: **We need to implement all of the recommen-dations of the 9/11 Commission, which was entrusted to study what went wrong before the attacks of September 11, 2001, and to recommend how to prevent its recurrence.**

I always saw merit in the creation and work of the National Com-mission on Terrorist Attacks on the United States. I wanted to know everything about the underlying events of 9/11, even if that knowl-edge threatened the reelection of a president I had supported. How can we prevent a recurrence without first fully appreciating what had gone wrong?

So I was terribly disappointed when the Bush administration, con-servative pundits, and Republicans like House majority leader Dennis Hastert tried to stymie the work of what came to be known as the 9/11 Commission. From the beginning, the president opposed the very formation of an investigative body to study the run-up to Septem-ber 11, saying such inquiry should stay within the halls of Congress so it didn't reveal covert U.S. intelligence-gathering methods.[1] The com-mander in chief relented only when the families of the victims of 9/11 pressured him to do so.[2] And even then, some of the 9/11 victims' families questioned the scope the commission had been granted and its ability to provide comprehensive insight into what was happening before September 11, 2001—especially in terms of U.S. intelligence lapses in the run-up to the attacks.[3]

In its five-hundred-plus-page report issued in July 2004, the 9/11 Commission made forty-one recommendations, several of which gave the president pause.[4] He refused, for example, to create the position of national intelligence director if that person would be based in the White House. Some critics expressed concerns that the person in the position would feel pressure to produce intelligence that complied with the White House's political agenda. The president, meanwhile, didn't want that position hampered by congressional oversight.[5]

There remains work to be done. Several of the remaining 9/11 Commission recommendations are still dormant (contrary to some political assertions, all the pending recommendations were not enacted within Nancy Pelosi's first one hundred hours as Speaker of the House).[6] By way of example, the question of who should administer the country's national security efforts in a post-9/11 world remains unresolved—more than seven years after the attacks. Alvin Felzenberg—9/11 Commission spokesman, author of *The Leaders We Deserved and a Few We Didn't,* and a professor at the Annenberg School at the University of Pennsylvania—told me in July 2008 that the most significant unadopted recommendation of the 9/11 Commission is more efficient, defined congressional oversight: "When they created the Department of Homeland Security (DHS) they moved seventeen agencies under its administrative umbrella, but they failed to transfer jurisdiction among congressional oversight committees," Felzenberg told me. "As a result, Secretary [of Homeland Security Michael] Chertoff and his staff must answer to eighty-seven committees and subcommittees, while [Secretary of Defense Robert] Gates and his team appear to answer to no more than two full committees." Requiring those charged with defending America against terrorist attacks, and leading its recovery from natural disasters, to kneel before almost ninety committees and subcommittees only serves to grind the country's response efforts to a dangerous halt.

He further broke it down for me this way: The Secretary of the Department of Homeland Security—formerly Tom Ridge and now Michael Chertoff—spends more than a third of his time entertaining the inquiries of the multitude of congressional representatives monitoring his department. The reason? It's just a matter of "a willingness on the part of the leadership to wrench clout away from colleagues," Felzenberg said. "We also asked that the intelligence committees exert greater authority by sharing in the budget process. Appropriators are the only ones to whom bureaucrats pay attention. House Speaker Pelosi tried a halfway measure—appointing appropriators to the House intelligence committee. Senate majority leader Harry Reid has done little, if anything."[7]

Felzenberg also mentioned a final yet-to-be-enacted recommendation: the creation of a Civil Liberties Board. Congress established it with the intention of creating a check on the extraordinary powers granted to the director of national intelligence, but President Bush was slow to nominate its members.[8] With the two branches of government embattled over who should serve, the entity is still not in operation.

What a sad commentary on how our government works today. When we spoke, Felzenberg insisted that Congress must be a full partner in the implementation of the 9/11 Commission recommendations. Given that the public cannot examine classified materials, it is only fitting that their duly elected representatives do so in their name.

Felzenberg is not the only one to note where all the politics and posturing has gotten us: In the days leading up to the seven-year anniversary of the September 11 attacks, a bipartisan commission headed by former Indiana congressman and 9/11 Commission co-chairman Lee Hamilton concluded that the United States remained "dangerously vulnerable" to a terrorist attack using a nuclear, chemical, or biological weapon. This commission, the Partnership for a Secure America (PSA), gave the federal government an overall grade of C for its progress toward preventing an attack using such weaponry.[9] In 2005, a predecessor to that commission called the 9/11 Public Discourse Project—also established by Hamilton, together with 9/11 Commission co-chairman Thomas Kean, and the 9/11 Commission itself—had given the federal government a grade of D for its post-9/11 weapons recovery and security efforts.[10] That's a far cry from the 9/11 Commission's initial demand for "maximum effort" against WMD proliferation—a fact PSA's 2008 update made note of. And this just months after Hamilton and Kean accused the CIA of purposely obstructing the commission's investigation after reports revealed that the agency had destroyed videotaped interrogations of two al-Qaeda operatives—despite the 9/11 Commission's repeated requests for materials related to al-Qaeda interrogations.[11]

The war on terror lumbers on, stunted by political correctness and legislative games of chicken. And now, more than seven years after the attacks of September 11, what should be an unassailable goal—preventing another terrorist attack by following the advice of the bipartisan commission that spent months studying that terrible day—has been buried by the sort of opposition that almost prevented the work of the 9/11 Commission itself: political and administrative stonewalling.

Chapter 7

He'll Make You Mad

In the late 1990s, I was practicing law during the week and doing my own radio show on the weekends on WWDB. In 1994 I got married, and as my wife, Lavinia, and I started a family, juggling so many responsibilities made for a grueling schedule. Lavinia was always very supportive of my pursuit of my radio goals even when they came at the expense of family (and sleep) time. When I moved to Sunday nights, it meant a portion of the weekend was now shot for any family activity. Next it was weekend mornings. That meant I would practice law during the week, only to set a Saturday-morning alarm for 4:00 a.m. The next day, Sunday, when I would be the lead-in for Sid Mark's highly rated *Sunday with Sinatra* program, the alarm would be set again. So there was never a day when our house wasn't up literally before the crack of dawn. She never complained.

As I was working to establish my radio presence, the station changed hands a few times in rapid succession and quickly gone were the days when a sole proprietor owned such a powerful position on the dial. I soon came to yearn for the days when Chuck Schwartz was the owner and his wife, Susan, would sign my paycheck. With each new owner came a more leveraged radio station, and a management philosophy of willingness to do anything to meet debt service.

One day in 1997, I invited Lisa DePaulo, an old friend then writing for *George* magazine, to be on my show and talk about a story she'd just written about a high-profile murder, the case of Anne Marie Fahey. Through her job as a scheduling secretary in the office of the governor of Delaware, Fahey met a connected Delaware pol named Tom Capano. They dated. After attempting to distance herself from their tumultuous affair, Fahey was brutally murdered by Capano, in what would become one of the most infamous crime cases in the Delaware Valley.[1] Lisa wrote about the case in her typical no-bullshit style, and she was always a terrific interview, but on this occasion I was told by management to cancel her segment because an hour of my Sunday-morning show had instead been sold to a guy pitching some kind of super prostate cream. I told them there was no way I could do that. I had a day job. And what would my legal clients think and say? Unfortunately, the other hosts did not have an option. They did the infomercials, thinly disguised as programming. So I sat out for a few weeks hoping this would pass. It didn't. Across town, WGMP, a station that people derided as "gimp" for its poor ratings, changed format from all sports to talk as WPHT. Don Imus was rumored to be the leading candidate for their new morning man. Once again, it was Larry Kane, the guy to whom I once delivered chlorine, who came to the rescue. He contacted the station and arranged for me to meet Diane Cridland, the program director. We went to lunch and argued the entire time, but at the end of lunch, she said, "So, when do you want to start?" and I said, "This weekend." She agreed, and so I did, on April 5, 1997.

I was already scheduled to have lunch with the manager of WWDB just a few days later, so I kept the appointment so I could tell him face-to-face that I was leaving. I figured that was the honorable thing to do, but he was still pissed. That marked the end of my relationship with WWDB, and I then started on WPHT (1210 AM), a station owned by Infinity Broadcasting, which would later merge with CBS Radio.

WPHT was then a squandered radio signal, but not for technical reasons. It transmits a strong 50,000-watt signal that can be heard as far west as the Rockies depending on the time of year, and sometimes as far south as Florida. I am no technical guru, but I know this: We are a clear-channel signal (that has nothing to do with the huge corporate radio giant of the same name), which means that we do not power down at night. Other stations are powered at a certain level only during daylight, and then they must reduce power at sunset. We do not. Consequently at nightfall, when other stations reduce wattage, our signal is enhanced, and that is when it has greatest reach. During the winter, my father spends a few months in Florida, where he can sometimes pull my show. TC, my producer, is from North Carolina. Her parents routinely listen to the 5:00 and 6:00 a.m. hours of my show from the foothills of that state.

When I joined 1210 AM, which would soon change its moniker to the Big Talker, the station was really struggling. I remember that my first Saturday morning, in the 6:00 a.m. hour, there were no callers

he'll make you mad

and no commercials. The ratings reflected this situation. Radio ratings are expressed in terms of audience share. "Share" is a word used to describe in percentage terms the number of listeners in a particular demographic tuned in to a particular show in a particular time period. So a "12+" measurement refers to all adults aged twelve and above in the Philadelphia marketplace. Whereas I was accustomed to a 6 or 7 share of the 12+ market in my time slot at WWDB, at WPHT, I inherited less than a 1 share. Ouch.

I quickly started to build some audience share on Saturday mornings, but it wasn't easy. During these embryonic stages, the station was experimenting with a variety of hosts during the weekdays and none was able to gain a foothold. One day, Diane Cridland met with me and posed the possibility of wiring my law office so that I could host an hour of afternoon drive after practicing law all day. I was consumed with the radio bug and told her I was interested. That very week, a radio management veteran named Tom Bigby was given the responsibility of consulting at our station. He was then programming an immensely successful sports talk station across town called WIP (610 AM). Cridland shared with Bigby her idea for my addition of one hour of afternoon drive. Bigby said no way. The next thing I knew, Cridland left the station to "pursue other opportunities." At about the minute she left the building, Bigby himself called me for lunch, where he then proposed the same deal Cridland had first suggested. And that is how I made the move to afternoon drive.

Tom Bigby is big. Bodacious. Ballsy. He was very hands-on. We often clashed, which I regret, because over time I came to respect his talk radio instincts. Bigby thought my program was too political. He wanted a more listener-friendly program that had brief calls (he instituted a two-minute limit) and more personal/lifestyle conversation from me, which did not come easy. I was focused on the front-page news, mostly political, and rarely discussed aspects of my personal life. Bigby continued to suggest that I give listeners an insight into my world by talking about my home and personal life. Frankly, I now wish that for the sake of my radio career, I would have listened to Tom Bigby when he first offered the advice, because over time that is exactly what I have done, and I think it has greatly enhanced my program.

On January 19, 1998, I began broadcasting weekdays during the 6:00 p.m. hour. An ISDN line, which enhances a telephone connection so it can then be used for radio transmission, was installed in my law office. My day now consisted of arriving at the office by 7:00 a.m., practicing law all day, and then at 6:00 p.m., from the same desk, throwing a switch and being a talk-show host. The audience never knew where I was located and I never brought it up. Immediately the show worked. Within months, by May 14, 1998, the show was expanded to two hours (5:00–7:00 p.m.). Now this was really a grind. I was burning the candle at both ends and, so far, getting away with it. My law practice was doing very well, and the radio career was showing promise.

I was forever pushing the station management to advertise my program somehow, someway, to no avail. Finally, out of frustration, I decided to do something about it, without consulting management. I called an outdoor advertising firm and bought a billboard for a month. I think my wife designed it at the dinner table. Across the top, in black and white, it said, "He'll Make You Think," and then it had my face, name, and program hours with the station logo. The word "think" was crossed out graffiti-style with red paint and in its place was scrawled "Mad," so it now read "He'll Make You Mad." My face was defaced, meaning I had hair and a mustache and a goatee painted on. Across the bottom, I listed the other primetime hosts on the station—"Imus–Liddy–Grant–DeBella–Bell." The billboard cost me $3,000. How could the station beef if I promoted everybody on my own dime? I then selected a location for the billboard in the Manayunk neighborhood of Philadelphia. I figured if I was going to do it, I may as well make sure the industry knew about it. Manayunk is a trendy part of the city located not far from my radio station and many others, as well as several advertising agencies that buy radio. It is also home to a number of happening restaurants and bars, so I was sure the news of my willingness to invest in my own program would spread fast. It did, and I think it helped create a buzz for the show. No one from management complained, but to this day, when I get contracts from CBS, mine (unlike anyone else's in the country) have a paragraph that says I am not permitted to engage in advertising, even though the company still has not.

The two-hour afternoon show continued to grow as I practiced law by day. Grace Blazer, who was moving up in the ranks of the station and had been a producer of mine, was named the station's program director, meaning she was responsible for the station lineup. She was a hard worker with whom I got along well on a personal and professional level. She was also a great supporter of mine, but when there was a change in more senior management, and a new general manager came on board, my relationship with the station took a tumble. Chris Claus was running my station and an oldies station owned by the same parent. We had a friendship and a good working relationship, but when he left the company he was replaced by a new general manager and things were not so rosy.

In fact, I quit WPHT Thanksgiving week of 2001. My contract was due to expire in a month, but I didn't wait to say I was out. I served notice that week and the station said, If you're leaving, leave now—which is the radio version of, Don't let the door hit you in the ass. What caused me to quit was a lack of support from the station in the face of a bogus lawsuit. Some knucklehead in Philadelphia, whom I would describe as a professional litigant, claimed I said disparaging things about him and his wife. I never did, and had the show tape to prove it. His case was a joke. But even ridiculous cases have to die a death of their own in our civil system. The irony is that this was my area of the law. In other words, the Beasley Law Firm where I practiced law was the preeminent trial lawyer practice in Philadelphia and the state of Pennsylvania specializing in defamation work at the time. Jim Beasley had recorded several of the highest defamation verdicts in the state of Pennsylvania. The expertise of the firm has always been a wonderful training ground for me as a talk-show host—I know the defamation line and never step over it.

I looked into the fellow and learned that although he was not a lawyer, he had initiated no fewer than a dozen lawsuits locally. In addition to me, he had also sued the governor, a state senator, and a city councilman. When, after filing his lawsuit against me, he issued a press release to the Philadelphia news media stating that I had called him a liar and his wife a "whore" on the air, I had had enough. I brought a lawsuit against him for defamation. I made sure the lawyers for the station ownership knew what I was doing, and that they agreed with my action. The station hired a lawyer to defend both the station and me, albeit not as quickly as I had wished. They left me hanging for a few days while the lawsuit of the guy who sued me needed a formal reply within a tight timeline. As I continued to investigate this guy, I learned that he had had his gun permit taken from him in Philadelphia due to an incident where he pulled a gun in public and told everyone "to get the fuck out of the bar." After suing me, he wrote disparaging things about me to people all over town. Consequently, I was not only angry about being on the receiving end of something I perceived as bogus, and disappointed in the lack of support I was receiving from my employer, but also concerned about my safety.

Against this backdrop, the station general manager called me and said he knew the man's lawsuit against me was frivolous, but wanted to settle with him to make him go away, which would necessitate my dropping my countersuit. I said my lawsuit against the guy was the only thing holding him in check and I would have to think it over. His suit against me was without merit, but mine was valid and I was reluctant to give it up. Well, the story then got worse. Not only did the GM expect me to agree to settle the frivolous suit from a non-lawyer who seemed to file lawsuits for a living, he said he wanted me to pay at least a portion of the money.

There had been animus building for a while. I had been doing afternoon drive for four years in addition to my full-time law practice. It was catching up with me. We were building a family and I was not spending enough time at home. To remedy this situation, my wife and I had undertaken a massive renovation to our home, which included construction of a large home office with studio capability (at my expense) so that I could do the show from home and when I signed off the air at 7:00 p.m., still enjoy a late dinner with the family. As construction progressed, the new station GM made clear that he found this objectionable, even though I was funding it and my plans had previously received the station's blessing. The fact that I would broadcast from my home studio was even spelled out in my radio contract, the same one that said I couldn't spend my own money to advertise my program. The new guy didn't like it. He told me he thought it would make me too detached from the radio station.

The prospect of me broadcasting from home wasn't the only bone of contention between the new GM and me. There was also a lengthy profile of me that appeared in a local magazine, and things I said didn't sit so well with management.

The story, written by Richard Rys, appeared in the October 2001 issue of *Philadelphia* magazine. The title was "The Big Talker: Radio host Michael Smerconish has better ratings than Rush Limbaugh—but his own station doesn't want you to know it. That's part of the reason Smerconish is threatening to quit. Is he all talk?"[2] The magazine profile contained photographs taken of me in the home office/studio, which was then under construction. It described my recent success breaking into the top 10 of local radio in the 25–54 demographic, and explained how as my ratings increased (to the point where they passed the station's syndicated hosts such as Imus and Limbaugh), my relationship with the station worsened. I was described as a "buttoned-down maverick" with a "distinctive blend of (mostly) right-wing politics and suburban affability."[3]

To the consternation of the station, I shot my mouth off about those syndicated hosts:

On Dr. Laura: "Laura's a bitch. She's a hypocrite and a faker." Oops.

On Imus: "I can deal with a little bit of Imus." That was a compliment.

On Rush: "Rush's politics are my politics for the most part, but I can't take the Clinton-bashing five nights a week. I thought his 'talent on loan from God' was funny six years go."[4] Yikes.

The GM was quoted in the piece as saying I would never be permitted to broadcast full-time from home, which was pretty tough to take given that I was deep into an expensive construction project that included a home recording studio.

So I quit. When news of my departure reached the newspapers, the *Philadelphia Inquirer* noted: "In the spring rating period, his show outdrew those of Rush Limbaugh and Dr. Laura Schlessinger combined."[5]

So what was the response from management? The GM said I was "mediocre." I took umbrage. I mean, what did that say about the rest of his radio station? So I gave Stu Bykofsky of the *Philadelphia Daily News* a copy of a recent written contract offer from that same GM, which offered me $300,000 for the next year if I would do 3:00–6:00 p.m. weekdays. That's a lot to pay for mediocrity. Not only that, but the contract offer was accompanied by a letter that said my doing so "would be the best thing for the station as a whole." At the very same time the GM said "I wish to build the station around YOU" (emphasis his).

Jim Beasley believed I had a legal action against the station and there was an exchange of harsh, lawyerly communication, but I knew if I filed a case I was done, at least with CBS. Fortunately, I was offered the position of weekly newspaper columnist by Zack Stalberg, then editor of the *Philadelphia Daily News*. And soon thereafter, Roy Shapiro, the general manager at KYW Newsradio, invited me to do daily one-minute commentaries on the news of the day. This was highly unusual. Although Roy would himself sometimes offer an opinion piece, the station was otherwise down the middle with its news reporting, sans any opinion. It's worth noting that Roy was extending this offer from another radio station in the CBS family, which, in retrospect, was either a gutsy thing to do, or a stroke of genius to keep me in the family. Either way, I was and remain appreciative of his help.

So, my new routine became practicing law, doing a one-minute daily commentary for KYW, and writing a weekly column. Meanwhile, CNN came calling, and at the suggestion of my friend Tom Marr, a Baltimore-based talk-show host, began inviting me to appear with regularity on an afternoon program called *TalkBack Live*, hosted by Arthel Neville. Then, something else happened. In the first ratings period after my departure, WPHT took a big hit. As Michael Klein from the *Philadelphia Inquirer* reported, "Big slippage was noted at WPHT-AM 1210. In going from ninth to 15th place overall, the Big Talker saw a stunning drop in its afternoon drive audience. Since the departure of Michael Smerconish, the numbers look, well, mediocre."[6]

One day soon thereafter, Grace Blazer called me. She wanted to come to the house to meet with me. She not only said the station wanted me back, but also that it *needed* me back. Grace said the GM regretted my departure. She wanted to make me an offer. This time, I was being asked to reverse careers. The station was offering to pay me a substantial sum so that I would become a talk-show host who happened to be a lawyer, instead of a lawyer who happened to be a talk-show host. She, the GM, and I went to lunch way out of town and made amends. I thought he was contrite, and truth be told, I welcomed the opportunity to reverse careers. I had no hard feelings against him then, nor do I now. For me to say he was hardheaded would indeed be the pot calling the kettle black. So I approached Jim Beasley, the chairman of my law firm, and sought his advice. Against his interest, he told me to go pursue the radio dream, for which I am eternally grateful. That was classic Beasley, a believer in entrepreneurship and independence. And so on May 9, 2002, a press release was sent out to Philadelphia media. The vice president and general manager said: "Michael Smerconish embodies the pulse and emotion of Philadelphia. He's uniquely dialed in to local issues, politics, and personalities in the community. Michael is a Philadelphia guy with an intellect and curiosity that engages listeners from all walks of life. Philadelphia missed hearing Michael on our airwaves and so did we. We look forward to a long relationship with Philadelphia's Premier local talk show host."[7] You have to say that was pretty big of him, given our history.

I returned to the Big Talker on May 13, 2002, now in an expanded 3:00–6:00 p.m. weekdays time slot, and remained in that time period through the summer of 2003. I was no longer practicing law full-time, and as the contract progressed, I practiced less and less. All the while station management would tell me that someday I would need to move to mornings—"someday" defined as whenever they could get New York's permission to dump morning man Don Imus, who had just never cut it in Philadelphia. Mornings are critically important in radio because they set the stage for the entire day, and the station believed it was handicapped by having him.

Well, just after Labor Day 2003, I made the move to 6:00–9:00 a.m. Nobody wishes to wake up at 3:00 a.m., but after a new contract negotiation, I said I would do it. The program has since been expanded to 5:00–9:00 a.m. What began with guest appearances, then fill-in guest hosting, then Sunday nights, then Saturday and Sunday mornings, then one hour in late-afternoon drive, then two hours in late-afternoon drive, then three hours after Rush Limbaugh, was now finally mornings. As I said, if you charted that progress on a graph it would look logical, but truth be told there was no plan; things just evolved.

Chapter 8

Pakisourced

Bin Laden: **I want a commitment of manpower directed toward finding and killing Osama bin Laden and Ayman al-Zawahiri. I want them hunted, found, and made to suffer a heinous death. The full-court press should never end.**

Nine days after September 11, 2001, President George W. Bush stood before a joint session of Congress and told the assembled members: "[A]ny nation that continues to harbor or support terrorism will be regarded by the United States as a hostile regime."[1]

So it should have been no surprise to see the headline perched on the front page of the *New York Times:* "Bush Said to Give Orders Allowing Raids in Pakistan." After all, the Taliban had been toppled in Afghanistan, and its sympathizers—along with the remaining al-Qaeda militants and camps—had traveled a distance equal to the train ride from Philadelphia to New York in order to find haven in the badlands of Pakistan's largely ungoverned tribal areas. Bush had approved orders that would allow U.S. special ops forces to cross into Pakistan and hunt the criminals who had perpetrated the attacks on 9/11.[2]

Too bad that report came *seven years* to the day after three thousand innocent Americans were murdered in New York, Washington, D.C., and my home state of Pennsylvania.

For much of that seven-year timeline I had been asking questions whose answers slowly emasculated the president's tough talk in the days after the attacks: Where the hell are Osama bin Laden and Ayman al-Zawahiri? And why does virtually no one ask anymore?

I spoke and wrote about Pakistan and the war on terror so incessantly during those seven years that I exhausted my welcome with many conservative members of my own talk radio audience. My editors at the *Philadelphia Daily News* and the *Philadelphia Inquirer* made it clear that I'd published my last column on this issue. Others took note of my preoccupation with bin Laden. When, on the day after Pennsylvania's April 22, 2008, primary election, I told Chris Matthews on *Hardball* that if Barack Obama would focus on Pakistan, he could win support among white male voters, Matthews recognized that it was "[my] issue," before adding, "And I agree with you completely."[3]

I couldn't help myself. So strong was my belief that we've failed in our responsibility to three thousand dead Americans that I started telling listeners in 2007 that I was contemplating voting for a Democratic presidential candidate for the first time in my life. It was the chronology of failure that was leading me down this path.

By the seven-year anniversary of 9/11, the most powerful country in history lacked not only closure with regard to the two top al-Qaeda leaders but also public discourse about any plan to bring them to justice. I believed the Bush administration had, at great cost, outsourced the manhunt to a government with limited motivation to get the job done—and there was a danger of continuing on the same path. Of course, I recognized I might be wrong; I had no inside information. And I often said I'd love to be proven in error by breaking news of their capture or execution. But published accounts of our failures painted an intriguing and frustrating picture.

To begin, bin Laden was presumed to have been in Afghanistan on 9/11 and to have fled that nation during the battle at Tora Bora in December of 2001. Gary Berntsen, who was the CIA officer in charge on the ground, wrote in his book *Jawbreaker*, and told me personally, that his request for Army Rangers to prevent bin Laden's escape into Pakistan was denied, and sure enough, that's where bin Laden went. After Tora Bora came a period when the Bush administration was supposed to be pressing the search through means it couldn't share publicly, and Americans accepted that. But as time went by with no capture, the signs became more troubling, at least to me.

We now know that in late 2005, the CIA disbanded Alec Station, the FBI-CIA unit dedicated to finding bin Laden, something that was reported on July 4, 2006, by the *New York Times*.[4] At the time, I hoped we'd closed the bin Laden unit because Pakistani president Pervez Musharraf was fully engaged in the hunt in his country's northwest territories, where the duo was supposedly hiding. In September 2006, however, Musharraf reached an accord with tribal leaders there, notorious for their refusal to hand over a guest. In doing so, he agreed to give them continued free rein.[5] A report from the BBC detailed what the tribal leaders would grant the army for withdrawing: "Local Taleban [sic] supporters, in turn, have pledged not to harbor foreign militants, launch cross-border raids or attack Pakistani government troops or facilities."[6]

The following month, in October of 2006, I participated in the weeklong Pentagon-sponsored military-immersion program called the Joint Civilian Orientation Conference. This was a unique opportunity for us forty-five civilians who were invited to play military tourist and learn first-hand about the United States Central Command (CENTCOM). Those chosen were a cross section of leaders—very few in media—each of whom had been nominated by a person with a connection to the program. We traveled fifteen thousand miles and spent time in four nations. Our days began at 5:00 or 6:00 a.m. and didn't end until 10:00 or 11:00 p.m. Along the way, we boarded the USS *Iwo Jima* by helicopter in the Persian Gulf, fired the best of the army's weaponry in the Kuwait desert (just ten miles from Iraq), drove an eleven-kilometer Humvee obstacle course (designed to teach about IEDs), boarded the Air Force's most sophisticated surveillance aircraft in Qatar, and even took a tour of a military humanitarian outpost in the Horn of Africa. In addition to hearing from defense secretary Donald Rumsfeld, we were briefed by the vice chairman of the Joint Chiefs of Staff, the vice admiral of CENTCOM, and other high-ranking war commanders. This was arguably the most enlightening week of my life.

I came home with the utmost respect for the men and women throughout the ranks of all five branches of the armed forces who are committed to eradicating the influences of radical Islam. But there was one thing noticeably absent from our jam-packed daily agendas: the search for bin Laden and al-Zawahiri. It was not part of our otherwise comprehensive activities, and when I did probe by asking specific questions, there was no information forthcoming except a generic assertion that, indeed, the hunt continued.

No one told me the search was over, but I came home worried that the days of aggressively hunting bin Laden and al-Zawahiri had ended. Of course, I could fully appreciate that perhaps an aggressive pursuit was underway but that I, a blowhard from Philadelphia, was simply deemed unworthy of any such confirmation. That would have been fine. If true.

But there was another consideration. More than one individual with whom I spoke raised with me the question of what would happen to public support for the war against radical Islam if we were to find and kill bin Laden and al-Zawahiri. They wanted to know: Would the American people then expect the military to pack up and go home? No one ever told me that we're not hunting bin Laden because killing him would cause Americans to want to close up shop in Iraq and Afghanistan, but it was absolutely on the minds of our warriors as support for the war in Iraq dissipated.

To my disappointment, there seemed to be no demand for accountability by our government. The White House and the Pentagon consistently played down the significance of capturing bin Laden and al-Zawahiri, and President Bush offered only superficial responses to the few questions raised on the status of the search. On February 23, 2007, the army's highest-ranking officer, Gen. Peter Schoomaker, said he didn't know whether we would find bin Laden, and "I don't know that it's all that important, frankly."[7] At a May 24, 2007, White House news conference, when asked why bin Laden was still at large, President Bush offered his usual refrain: "Because we haven't got him yet . . . that's why. And he's hiding, and we're looking, and we will continue to look until we bring him to justice."[8]

For me, somewhere between two and four years removed from 9/11 these sort of answers had begun to wear thin—especially because it seemed bin Laden remained active. Unfortunately, the president's standard line was being accepted by the media, whose members rarely asked about bin Laden, and the American people, who were collectively complacent on the issue.

More information was revealed on May 20, 2007, when the *New York Times* reported that we were paying $80 million a month to Pakistan for its supposed counter-terrorism efforts, for a total of $5.6 billion since 9/11, when this program began.[9] So there it was, the money trail confirming the ultimate outsourcing. I wondered what we were getting in return. Then, in July 2007, a National Security Estimate concluded that the failure of Musharraf's accord with warlords in Pakistan's tribal areas had allowed bin Laden's thugs to regroup there.[10] And on July 22, national intelligence director Adm. Mike McConnell said on *Meet the Press* that he believed bin Laden was in Pakistan in the very region Musharraf had ceded to the warlords.[11] I hoped that the presidential campaign would move the issue to the front burner, but despite its 24/7 nature, it failed to stir up a discussion about the failure to capture or kill those who pushed us down such a perilous path. In the first seven presidential debates—four for the Ds, three for the Rs—there was only one question in fifteen hours of discourse that touched on the subject of finding bin Laden in Pakistan, and it came from the audience. Things changed somewhat on August 1, 2007, when Barack Obama delivered a speech at the Woodrow Wilson International Center for Scholars and said this: "If we have actionable intelligence about high-value terrorist targets, and President Musharraf won't act, we will," he said.[12] "We can't send millions and millions of dollars to Pakistan for military aid, and be a constant ally to them, and yet not see more aggressive action in dealing with al-Qaeda."[13]

Finally, I thought, a presidential candidate saying something about this foreign-policy failure. And a Democrat at that.

The reaction? Ridicule.

Joe Biden and Chris Dodd, then presidential candidates, responded derisively. Pakistani foreign ministers did likewise. Across the aisle, John McCain pounded Obama for a perceived lack of seasoning in the realm of foreign relations: "The best idea is to not broadcast what you're going to do," McCain said in February 2008. "That's naïve."[14] (McCain then grew fond of saying that he'll "follow bin Laden to the gates of hell.")[15] Not to be left out, Hillary Clinton said, "You can think big, but, remember, you shouldn't always say everything you think when you're running for president because it could have consequences across the world, and we don't need that right now."[16] To his credit, Obama refused to back away from his insistence on reasserting American control over the hunt for bin Laden. I interviewed him on March 21, 2008, and this issue dominated our conversation.

He admitted that a resurgence of the Taliban had occurred in Pakistan. "What's clear from . . . what I've learned from talking to troops on the ground is that unless we can really pin down some of these Taliban leaders who flee into the Pakistan territories, we're going to continue to have instability, and al-Qaeda's going to continue to have a safe haven, and that's not acceptable."[17]

I closely monitored what Obama said elsewhere on the issue and began to think that he was the only one who appreciated just how clearly we had dropped the ball. When presented with a second opportunity to interview him, on April 18, 2008, I went back to the well of Pakistan. This time he told me that Musharraf, despite being flush with billions in American aid, was not taking counter-terrorism seriously. "That's part of the reason that I've been a critic from the start of the war in Iraq," Obama told me. "It's not that I was opposed to war. It's that I felt we had a war that we had not finished. And al-Qaeda is stronger now than at any time since 2001, and we've got to do something about that because those guys have a safe haven there and they are still planning to do Americans harm."[18]

He also pointed out that the Bush administration had recently shown signs of aligning with the very comments for which he had been roundly criticized. Obama reminded me that a late-January airstrike killed a senior al-Qaeda commander in Pakistan; he called it an example of the type of action he'd been recommending since August. The CIA, it was reported a few weeks after the strike, acted without the direct approval of Musharraf.[19]

Soon after I spoke with Senator Obama, the non-partisan Government Accountability Office, the investigative arm of the U.S. Congress, issued a report dated April 17, 2008, with a title requiring no interpretation: "Combating Terrorism: The United States Lacks Comprehensive Plan to Destroy the Terrorist Threat and Close the Safe Haven in Pakistan's Federally Administered Tribal Areas."[20] The report, undertaken at the bipartisan request of U.S. House and Senate members, minced no words in issuing a conclusion that should have made Americans' blood boil: Six years after September 11, the United States had failed to destroy the terrorist havens in Pakistan's federally administered tribal areas (known in the report as FATA). The GAO confirmed prior reports that al-Qaeda was revitalized and poised to launch an attack, and said that no comprehensive U.S. plan existed to combat terrorism on its most central front.

Seven years later—and still no plan? Everything, it seemed, that I had pontificated about from my armchair in Philly was now being borne out by people with portfolio.

In the days that followed this release, I spoke to Charles Johnson, under whose signature the GAO report was issued. He told me: "With respect to establishing a comprehensive plan, we found that there were some individual plans that had been prepared by the various entities I mentioned earlier [the Department of Defense, Department of State, U.S. Agency for International Development, among others].

"But yet there was no comprehensive plan that integrated all of the key elements of national power that was called for by the 9/11 Commission, by the National Security Strategy for Combating Terrorism, and the United States Congress. And those elements I'm referring to are: the use of military, economic, and development assistance; law enforcement support; intelligence support; as well as political and diplomatic means by which we would want to address the root cause of terrorism in a particular region."[21]

From there the headlines continued to defy the GAO recommendations. "Pakistan Asserts It Is Near a Deal with Militants," read the front page of the April 25, 2008, edition of the *New York Times*.[22] Pakistan's newly elected government was again on the verge of another accord with the militants running amok in the FATA—despite the new government's previously stated desires to move away from Musharraf's policies in those regions. Less than a week later, under the headline "Pakistan's Planned Accord with Militants Alarms U.S.," the *New York Times* reported that the Bush administration expressed concern that the new agreement could contribute to "further unraveling of security" in the region.[23]

The arrangement was tailor-made for bin Laden. It permitted the local Taliban group, Tehrik-e-Taliban, to assist in keeping law and order in the area known as Swat in the northwest frontier province— while not attacking the existing security forces—in return for an exchange of prisoners between the Pakistani army and the Taliban. The army also agreed to withdraw forces from parts of Swat. According to a report from the May 22 edition of the *New York Times*, the

Bush administration was concerned that the deal would "give the Taliban and Al Qaeda the latitude to carry out attacks against American and NATO forces in Afghanistan."[24] Some U.S. officials even went so far as to call it a "victory" for bin Laden, as reported by ABC News.[25]

At about this point, I had a unique opportunity to gain the insights of an amazing American on this important matter of national security. The context was yet another gathering of my book club. This time my guest was Marcus Luttrell. He was the only survivor of Operation Red Wing, a mission that resulted in the worst loss in Navy Seal history. He earned a Navy Cross for his valor and wrote about his harrowing story in the *New York Times* best seller *Lone Survivor*. Unlike most of the bureaucrats from Washington, who have only been able to offer me talking points from a failed policy, Luttrell gave a brutally honest account of the time he spent in the Hindu Kush, a mountainous area located just a few miles from the northwestern border of Pakistan. Luttrell described how his efforts were too often constricted by red tape. "Yeah, we've got some problems with that border . . . because we'd be chasing the bad guys in there and they had a lot of security set up and we have to stop what we're doing while they just run across and if we don't, we'll get engaged by the Paki border guards and that's an international incident."[26]

Luttrell couldn't delve into the details of the prickly international problem that was created by the tension with the border guard, but when I asked him if the Pakistan issue was a problem in general, he wholeheartedly agreed. "Hell yeah, it's a problem. Heck, they're harboring the enemy. It's such a joke, it's so stupid. They come over and do their business, whatever it is, and if it gets them into trouble, all they have to do is sink back into Pakistan and stay there. They say, 'We're good here, we're good here' . . . It's frustrating."[27]

So there you have it. Not from me. Not from some pointy-headed academic or government analyst. Here is a guy who has fought in that region telling us that the real bad guys, the ones who really did cause 9/11, wreak havoc along the Afghanistan–Pakistan border and run for cover across the Pakistan side knowing the Americans' hands are tied in chasing them.

Meanwhile, the presidential contenders remained largely silent in the face of a seven-year timeline moving in the wrong direction. For his part, Ayman al-Zawahiri was apparently so comfortable that he spent time logging into jihad chat rooms and attracting thousands of questions from the peon terrorists prepared to do his dirty work.

This drove me batshit, my frustration so apparent that Will Bunch, a fellow journalist from the *Philadelphia Daily News,* labeled me "fixated" with 9/11.[28] I take it as a compliment, and at least I'm consistent. In 2004, I donated all of my proceeds from my first book, *Flying Blind: How Political Correctness Continues to Compromise Airline Safety Post 9/11,* to a memorial in Bucks County, Pennsylvania, called the Garden of Reflection, created as a place to mourn the Ground Zero victims who were from the county of my birth. Many of my radio listeners bought that book. Ironically, some would later pound out vicious e-mails to me upon hearing that based in part on the failure of Republicans to get justice for those victims, I was of the opinion that Barack Obama was worthy of consideration for president.

By then, I no longer felt any sense of loyalty or obligation to the Bush administration. The administration's failure to orchestrate a successful counter-terrorism plan—one topped off with justice for Osama bin Laden and Ayman al-Zawahiri—left me embarrassed of my party, and angry. And John McCain, a man for whom I had the utmost respect, appeared to offer a continuation of those failed policies.

In a conversation I had with the senator on June 13, 2008, he first attempted to say that our counter-terrorism efforts were working and that remaining on good terms with Pakistan was imperative to our safety. "There has been progress in those areas. Pakistan is a sovereign nation and we have to have the cooperation of Pakistan in order to have these operations succeed. I don't have any classified information, but I do know that there are activities taking place that are intended to counter some of these activities, so all I want to say to you is that if you alienate Pakistan and it turns into an anti-American government, then you will have much greater difficulties."[29]

When Senator McCain attempted to remind me of the fact that the United States also gives a great deal of money to Egypt, which, like Pakistan, could be more helpful in assisting the United States in the War on Terror, I pointed out to him that these guys aren't hiding in Cairo. The people responsible for the atrocities of 9/11 are concentrated in an area in northwestern Pakistan, a fact that I repeated to the senator. He then pointed out the historic difficulty with the region.

"I have promised that I will get Osama bin Laden when I am president of the United States, but . . . you can go on the Internet, and look at that countryside, and there's a reason why it hasn't been governed since the days of Alexander the Great. They're ruled by about, it's my understanding, thirteen tribal entities, and nobody has ever governed them, not the Pakistani government, not the British—nobody, and so it's a very, very difficult part of the world." He added, "I agree with you that we should've gotten Osama bin Laden, but I can't put all of it at the doorstep of the Pakistani government."[30]

I regard John McCain as a bona fide war hero, but I disagreed with him over this issue, something that I let him know would dramatically influence my vote in the general election. For the entirety of my interview, I tried to keep the senator focused on Pakistan, and though he answered all of my questions, at the end of the interview he tried to insert his message of the day, which was about the Supreme Court ruling that granted habeas corpus rights to enemy combatants. I responded, "I hear you, and all I think is that the guys who sent those guys over here are still on the lam and we're writing a big check, and I'm unhappy about it." To my disappointment, the senator said, "Yes, sir, and I understand that, and if you let KSM, Khalid Sheikh Mohammed, and others go, they'll join them over there. Thirty guys, who have been released, have gone back to the battlefield."[31] It wasn't the fact that he once again dodged my clear dissatisfaction with the Pakistan issue that left me dismayed—I'd become quite used to it at that point; it was the fact that I clearly heard an aide mutter the line to him before he delivered it to me and my captive audience. The campaign clearly had a stock answer for me, an answer that I had heard before and had clearly rejected.

Put quite simply, the support for this failed policy drove me to the edge of my long Republican career. And despite having never pulled a lever for a Democratic presidential candidate, I believed the 2008 election presented the chance to relieve this country of the conventional wisdom that President Bush offered for seven years and Senator McCain appeared resigned to advance: that President Musharraf was a friend who did what he could to prevent Pakistan from defaulting towards further extremism; that the hunt for Osama bin Laden is nuanced and U.S. forces are doing everything they can to find him; and that the war in Iraq is a necessary one that hasn't distracted from the fight against those who perpetrated and planned 9/11.

In my opinion, that conventional wisdom has now been proven unequivocally wrong.

My ranting and raving on this issue seemed to register with the Obama campaign; in June 2008 my praise of the candidate on this issue appeared in the fact-check section of the campaign Web site to illustrate the senator's dedication to catching bin Laden.[32] Republicans were also listening but with less satisfaction. The interview I had done with Senator McCain in June 2008 had obviously raised some red flags over at the campaign, and Senator McCain never came back on my program.

When President Musharaff resigned in August 2008 due to political pressure from lingering doubts as to his legitimacy from the previous election, President Bush offered undue praise for the former president. A statement said, "President Bush appreciates President Musharraf's efforts in the democratic transition of Pakistan as well as his commitment to fighting al-Qaeda and extremist groups."[33] Commitment? What a farce. The weeks following Musharraf's resignation brought incremental changes in policy and faint reasons for optimism. The Pakistani military spent most of August launching airstrikes against the Taliban militants attacking American forces from their perch straddling the Afghan–Pakistani border—an effort that resulted in more than 400 Taliban casualties and a shallow retreat by the terrorists. It's "shallow" because the Pakistani government followed up those airstrikes by declaring a cease-fire to coincide with the Muslim holy month of Ramadan. Legislators from the tribal areas promised political support for the top candidate in Pakistan's presidential election in exchange for the truce, which was announced in the days leading up to the country's vote.[34] I know this is a long and fact-intensive chapter, but please go back and read that again. I don't want the point to be lost on any reader that seven years post-9/11, we are relying on the Pakistanis to hunt those responsible for the deaths of three thousand innocent Americans, and how are they responding? By taking a month off for Ramadan!

No wonder less than a week later, though, American forces finally showed signs of taking the central front of the war on terror into their own hands. A *New York Times* report indicated that U.S. special ops forces attacked al-Qaeda militants gathered in a Pakistani village called Jalal Khel. U.S. officials said the move might represent the early stages of a more dedicated and aggressive American presence in Pakistan in the wake of General Musharraf's resignation.[35] And on the day before the seven-year anniversary of 9/11, the *Washington Post* reported that U.S. and Pakistani officials, flustered by their lack of progress in Pakistan and the FATA, had increasingly been deploying Predator drone missile attacks against targets in Pakistan throughout 2008.[36] A day later, the country learned that the president had finally authorized American special ops to wade into Pakistan.

Don't get me wrong, a more sustained U.S. assault against the terrorists squatting in Pakistan was welcome news, and it signified a more urgent effort to hunt down and snuff out the greatest threat to Americans' safety on our own shores.

But it was 2,555 days late, and after $11 billion was squandered. Seven years after 9/11, the country was stoking what was supposed to be a complete and consuming "war on terror" with faint signs of a sustained operation in the country where the bad guys had been hiding for years. How appalling. I doubt the families of the three thousand innocents murdered on 9/11—and the four thousand that followed them in Iraq—are content with it. After all, seven years, thousands of troops, and billions of dollars later, our country had failed to deliver on what we really owe them: Justice.

Nor have we answered the most important question pertaining to our nation's future: Can we really win this war with Islamic extremism? Because if we don't have the fire in our bellies to defend the American troops stonewalled by the Afghan–Pakistani border; to hunt down and destroy the Taliban and al-Qaeda militants camping out on the other side of that border; and do everything we possibly can to capture and kill Osama bin Laden and Ayman al-Zawahiri, I fear we'll be left to deal with another fire—one raging in another building, burning a hole in another American city.

Chapter 9

I Say "Stupid" Things Every Day

It's true. But here's my excuse: Opportunity. I simply have too many chances to shoot off my big mouth. Think about this: I have done talk radio for almost twenty years. You are reading my fourth book. I've authored hundreds of columns, and have appeared on every major television program on which politics gets discussed, from *The Colbert Report* to *Today*. In an average week I am responsible for twenty hours of content on my own radio show, two newspaper columns, and a few television appearances on shows like *Hardball*, not to mention maybe a guest hosting slot on Bill O'Reilly's national radio show, *The Radio Factor*.

Try all that without saying something stupid.

While I have often made a fool of myself by being factually incorrect or using bad grammar—especially of the "I" instead of "me" variety—or by mispronouncing words, I have never said anything on air with undue condescension, anger, hostility, or hatred. So except for the innocent boners, I regret nothing I have ever said on air. If I had otherwise crossed a decency line, you'd know it. Given the strength of the signal of my radio station and the size of my audience, and considering the blog and YouTube world in which we live, somebody would be jumping all over me. Critics jump all over me anyway, that goes with the territory, but usually for things taken out of context. Mostly I get lumped into the right-wing-nut-job category. Bill Maher even assigned his designated seat to me.

I've always liked *Real Time with Bill Maher* on HBO, even if I mostly disagree with his politics. Maher is often funny and the show has an edgy quality that is appropriate for late on a Friday night. My second book, *Muzzled*, contains the sort of defense of free speech with which he has become associated since his former program, *Politically Incorrect*. When *Muzzled* was published in 2005, I know that the publicist working for the publisher endeavored to get me booked on that program, but to no avail. By the spring of 2007, Bill Maher's program on HBO was probably the only remaining TV show for politics on which I had *not* appeared. Still, I was surprised when, completely out of the blue and with no book to promote, I was invited to come to California and do the show. The only date mutually agreeable was Friday, March 30, 2007, which was the end of our children's spring break. My wife and I were already planning to spend the week in Florida with the kids. And I was preparing to broadcast my radio show from there, as I have often done. Then I'd take a flight cross-country in time (hopefully) to grab a quick nap before my appearance on Bill Maher's program that evening. For me to make the only flight that worked, I had to drive (or more accurately, be driven) across the state of Florida so I could catch a direct, nonstop flight from Miami to Los Angeles. A friend named Forrest "Woody" Baker agreed to drive me. It was going to be a long day by the time the show began at 11:00 p.m. Eastern time.

In advance of the show, I was asked by Maher's representatives whether I had any friends whom I wished to invite to the broadcast. Well, the only people I could identify as friends in California were Maureen Faulkner and Paul Palkovic. Maureen is the widow of police officer Daniel Faulkner; she and I wrote *Murdered by Mumia* together. Paul is the man now in her life. Like the good friends they are, Maureen and Paul said they'd love to watch me do the show. They came to the CBS studio that doubles, or did at the time, as the location where Bob Barker hosted *The Price Is Right*. As a matter of fact, I remember seeing the prize wheels for the show backstage before I went on.

The other panelists that night were comedian D. L. Hughley and Catherine Crier from Court TV. I thought I had a good history with Catherine Crier because a few years prior she and I had done a pilot for CNN. I knew little about Hughley other than the fact that our sons watched his sitcom. As you know if you watch *Real Time*, the three panelists sit side-by-side, across from Maher. Other guests may come and go via satellite, but the exchange between the panelists and Maher is the mainstay of the program. I was assigned the seat closest to the audience, which, I had noticed from prior viewing, was where the more conservative of the panelists was always placed. I suspected that was a tip-off to the audience that this person is the foil for the broadcast. During my appearance, when things got a bit ugly between

Maher and me, I dubbed it the "wing-nut chair," and after I drew attention to the location of the designated hot seat, they started rotating the chairs of the guests in subsequent shows.

I didn't expect to win too many friends in Hollywood, but I was prepared to have fun. Unfortunately, Maher's idea was that the fun would be at my sole expense. He had an unmistakable and inexplicable hard-on for me from the moment we went live and very quickly the show became a three on one. After my very first substantive exchange, Bill was quick to tell me that I had made a "dumb-ass" argument. The subject was Iraq. Keep in mind that I, like Maher, favored getting out of Iraq, but I wanted to make the point that things would get ugly when we do so:

> **Smerconish:** *I hope that the very people who say "Get out immediately" are going to have a stomach to watch the footage on television when it all collapses when we're gone. . . . I'm saying, prepare yourself because you're going to watch it. So get American soldiers out of harm's way.*

> **Maher:** *[overlapping] We're watching it now! Every bad thing that could happen is happening now, and it has been happening for years there now. [applause] That's—that's a dumb-ass argument.[1]*

Things went from bad to worse when I made a gratuitous reference to the Ten Commandments. The irony here was—and it shows how little it mattered what I actually said—that I was attempting to make the argument that in the 2008 presidential cycle it would be important for the Republicans to avoid the temptation to drive the party base by pushing social issues, such as opposing same-sex marriages or endorsing the need to post the Ten Commandments in public places and, rather, focus on the non-social issues. That is something in sync with Bill Maher's view of the world. Instead of recognizing our commonality, he used this as a jumping-off point to literally debate me on the merits of the Ten Commandments.

> **Smerconish:** *I think that the message is, I would hope, the party is at a crossroads. And instead of this cycle buying the usual flag-burning amendment or bashing homosexuals or trotting out the*

Ten Commandments—and I believe in them, I just don't believe in using them as a political gimmick—we want somebody who is going to be tough on defense, but more moderate on those social issues. And Giuliani fits that bill. And John McCain, to a certain extent, fits that bill as well.

Maher: *So you—but wait a second—you believe in the Ten Commandments?*

Smerconish: *I believe in the Ten Commandments.*

Maher: *So, like, you can't work on Sunday and you can't swear, and you can't make statues to other gods? [laughter]²*

In the ridiculous exchange that followed, Maher insinuated that I thought things like "no swearing" and "not working on Sunday" were more important than issues like rape and child abuse. The bickering continued until Hughley interjected a moment of levity, saying, "You motherfuckers need to calm down!"

I remember thinking, what a douche bag Maher turned out to be. I flew all the way out here to offer some views and have a couple of laughs, but instead, I was getting the shit kicked out of me on late-night TV. And the only thing the audience knew about me was that I was a skinhead and seated in the chair of evil. Any question about how badly the show had gone for me was answered by the expression on Maureen Faulkner's face afterwards. She and Paul greeted me in the green room, and while her mouth said "You were terrific," her wide eyes told me otherwise.

It's customary for Maher and his guests to go out for drinks after the show. We went to some smokehouse next to the studio and the only thing he said to me was, "You know, you look like a guy who's doing a slow burn." I hadn't heard "slow burn" in a long time, but he was right, I was. That was pretty much all that was said between us. I was friendly to Catherine Crier, who was under the arm of CNN founder Ted Turner, but over a few drinks the person I most enjoyed chatting with was D. L. Hughley, who was funny as hell. I have hosted him on my radio program a few times since, and he was also my guest on one of the occasions when I guest hosted Glenn Beck's TV show. In fact, here is a funny footnote. Hughley and I got along well when

I was the Beck fill-in, but in the course of the segment, he slammed Beck. His comments never made the air. Glenn's producer, Conway Cliff, cut them out of the final product (the show was taped at about 3:00 p.m. for a 7:00 p.m. initial airing). Well, when Glenn got back from vacation, he invited Hughley back on his program. This time, Jon Klein, the head of CNN, was watching. He so enjoyed Hughley that he gave him a show of his own.[3] That happened right about when Beck himself left CNN for Fox News.

The day after the Maher program, as I was flying home to Philadelphia, there began an e-mail correspondence initiated by Maher's booker to my producer, TC, where Maher's person acknowledged the unfairness of the program the night before. "I thought Michael held his own. It isn't easy on this show," the producer wrote. "I cringed a bit when he said 'Well, since I'm in the "wing-nut" seat tonight.' We don't like to have folks ganged up on. It's just so very hard to find conservative folks (or republicans of any stripe) to do Bill's show. Michael made some great points and I am sorry if it ended up being a gang up. I thought Bill went after him for no good reason on the Ten Commandments."

TC had an appropriate reply: "As for your thoughts on the show, I must say that I had to re-read your e-mail to make sure it came from you and not Michael—those were his thoughts exactly. While he can certainly handle political differences and discussions—and was looking forward to it—he was disappointed at Bill's personal animus toward him. Your concern about booking Republicans for that seat is warranted—the 'gang up' as you called it, would certainly give pause. Interestingly, we've also been inundated with hundreds of e-mails that agree—from both regular listeners and Bill Maher watchers who found Michael on the Web. The overwhelming majority took offense at how much Michael was under attack."

Then came this missive from Maher's producer: "One of the executive producers just expressed to me that she was very upset with the way Bill treated Michael. I think everyone was. I'll try to find out how Bill felt (or what was going through his mind) and if I get anymore info on this, I'll let you know. Again, I'm sorry it wasn't very pleasant for Michael."

In retrospect, I think Maher was then filming or getting ready to film his anti-religion screed, *Religulous*. Maybe that gave him a trigger finger when he heard me reference the Ten Commandments. I'd like to think even Maher felt guilty. That's bolstered by the fact that two weeks after my appearance, he injected my name into a discussion with another panel, this time defending me when I was under attack by a group that did not want me replacing Don Imus after he got fired on MSNBC.

I've never met Don Imus, but we've had a few degrees of separation on multiple occasions in our careers. As I mentioned, I was asked to do mornings in Philly when he got the boot. So I replaced him in this radio market, and then, when he was fired from MSNBC, I was the first person to fill his chair. I tried not to call it a try-out when others referenced it that way, but it was. Phil Griffin was then the executive in charge of MSNBC and he was instrumental in getting me the live "audition."

Let me get the essentials out of the way. Don Imus said something indefensible and needed to be punished. On his show *Imus in the Morning,* which was broadcast on more than seventy radio stations nationwide and simulcast on MSNBC, he referred to members of the Rutgers University women's basketball team as "nappy-headed hos."[4] He was suspended and roundly condemned. I took the view that the public flogging he endured, plus the two-week suspension his bosses initially announced, should have been sufficient punishment. I did not believe that MSNBC (where I was doing guest work but without a formal contract arrangement) or CBS Radio (my radio employer) should have fired him, and I said so.

Not only did I say all this on the radio, but I voiced my opinion on this matter in my April 15, 2007, column in the *Philadelphia Inquirer.* At the time, mine was definitely not the popular opinion of the day— particularly amongst the suits at MSNBC.[5] I said publicly that they overreacted. Still, guess who they—MSNBC—then asked to be the first fill-in for the seat formerly held by Imus? Me.

The very day Imus was fired at CBS Radio, I was alerted to a posting on Media Matters for America, a sophisticated liberal Web site instrumental in stoking the flames for Imus's departure. The posting, titled "It's not just Imus," identified seven talk-show hosts in America who bear observation, and I was on the list:

[A]s Media Matters for America has extensively documented, bigotry and hate speech targeting, among other characteristics,

race, gender, sexual orientation, religion, and ethnicity continue
to permeate the airwaves through personalities such as Glenn
Beck, Neal Boortz, Rush Limbaugh, Bill O'Reilly, Michael Sav-
age, Michael Smerconish, and John Gibson.[6]

What the fuck? Me? What did I ever do to warrant making such
a hit list? Needless to say, I was anxious to see which of my words,
among the millions I have offered over all these years, had been documented by these bloggerheads as examples of "bigotry" and "hate."
I mean, what exactly puts me in a category with the likes of Michael
Savage, who once told a caller, "You should only get AIDS and die,
you pig."[7]

Let me give you their evidence of my hatred and bigotry and my
explanation.

Exhibit A: On April 4, 2006, while I was substituting for Bill
O'Reilly on *The Radio Factor*, I discussed the "sissification of America," and said that political correctness has made the United States "a
nation of sissies." I also mentioned more than once that this "sissification" and "limp-wristedness" is "compromising our ability to win the
war on terror."[8]

Guilty as charged, I guess. I mean, I have used the words "sissification" and "limp-wristedness," but if the implication is one of
homophobia, that is just ridiculous. If anything, this assertion was
confirmation of all that I argued in my book *Muzzled*. Those among
us who assert their own brand of political correctness are sacrificing the
rugged individualism that has been the hallmark of our nation. They
seek to mute the words and actions of others and make them conform
to a standard of correctness that is not just silly but also toxic.

Exhibit B: While guest hosting *The Radio Factor* on November
23, 2005, I questioned a move by the New Jersey Sports and Exposi-
tion Authority to create a designated prayer area at Giants Stadium.
On September 19 five Muslim men seen praying near the stadium's
main air duct during a Giants football game had been detained and
questioned by the FBI. Referring to the men's praying in public, I
said, "I just think that's wrong. I just think they're playing a game of,
you know, mind blank with the audience. And that they should know
better four years removed from September 11."[9]

Guilty again. When, post-9/11, five Muslim men in attendance at the Meadowlands for a September 2005 Giants–Saints game that was also a Hurricane Katrina fundraiser, with president George H. W. Bush in the house, saw fit to pray in an area near food-preparation and air ducts, some fans got freaked out. I said I thought it was, at a minimum, a case of mind fuck. Surely they knew they would get a reaction and I suspect that is what they wanted. Well, I say that is a form of terrorism in itself.

Exhibit C: Also on the November 23, 2005, edition of *The Radio Factor*, I spoke with Soo Kim Abboud, author of *Top of the Class: How Asian Parents Raise High Achievers—and How You Can Too*. I said that "if everyone follows Dr. Abboud's prescription . . . you're going to have women who will leave the home and now get a great-paying job, because you will have gotten them well educated. . . . But then they're not going to be around to instill these lessons in their kids. In other words, it occurs to me that perhaps you've provided a prescription to bring this great success to an end."[10]

My favorite—and truly an assertion that shows how asinine and PC our world has rapidly become. Guilty!

Quick background. I've already told you I run a book club for radio listeners. Well, two Philadelphia-area Asian sisters wrote a great book explaining their professional success and attributing it to their traditional Asian upbringing and their parents' hands-on approach and involvement in their lives. I loved the book. I not only hosted them on my radio program, but also honored them at a book club meeting with several hundred attendees. As I considered their thesis, it occurred to me that if their advice were followed, it would create more female "high achievers" with better educational opportunities and job offers, which would, ironically, take those individuals out of the home, where they would've been able to instill those same values in their own children. When I offered that view to the authors, they thought my argument had merit and it became a catalyst for intelligent dialogue on the subject of parenting. But to these bloggers acting on a snippet, my substantive point about parenting was downright sexist.

That's it. Based on those three items, I made the Media Matters McCarthy list of talk-show hosts who needed to be watched. Then, when MSNBC announced on April 20, 2008, that I was to be the first to fill-in for the now disgraced Don Imus, Media Matters took it up a notch and released a statement regarding my new role. It reminded readers of some of my previous comments, as outlined in the "It's Not Just Imus" blog post, and expressed hope that not only I, but all others working in the media, would recognize the important role we play in "shaping the public discourse on the airwaves." It was recommended that in the wake of the Imus controversy we "take this opportunity to elevate the tone, quality, and accuracy of the public debate." Media Matters encouraged MSNBC to consider a broader range of viewpoints in finding a replacement for Imus, and pledged their continued dedication to their mission to bring to the public's attention "bigoted commentary" and "other forms of conservative misinformation in the media."[11]

So who do you think defended me in this firestorm? Bill Maher. Maher's show was on hiatus the week following my appearance, but returned two weeks later with a show on April 13, 2007. During the show there was an exchange with one of his guests, former senator Bill Bradley, where Bill Maher injected my name into the mix in a very favorable way. Here's what he said:

> There's a lot of watchdogs out there now. . . . It's just not like the old days, [to Bradley] even when you were running for president. I don't think everybody had a camera. I don't think there was some group who was always just waiting to go, "Ooh, is this something? Is this something we can fire a guy for? Is this something we can get a guy for?" It's such a "gotcha" culture. And I was reading from this Media Matters for America. I don't know if they're from the left or the right. But they were going after everybody who has ever said anything. They talked about this Michael Smerconish, who was on our show a couple of weeks ago, a very thoughtful guy, and they said, "Michael Smerconish repeatedly discussed the sissy-fication of America, claiming that political correctness has made the United States a nation of sissies." Well, you know what? If you're complaining like this, you are a sissy. [laughter] And Michael Smerconish was right. [applause][12]

In what I viewed as a quasi-apology for the way he had treated me in the previous show, Maher also proved what I have always said. The muzzling of America is neither a liberal nor conservative issue. Sure, as the title of this chapter and statements like those made by Don Imus prove, there is a standard for what is acceptable in our public discourse, but when it becomes a witch hunt, I wonder how long it will be before they start burning my tapes.

Despite the outcry from Media Matters, I was the first outsider to sit in Imus's chair after his firing. What resulted was one of the more memorable weeks I have had as a broadcaster. Instead of getting up at 3:15 a.m. to do morning drive in Philly, I got up at 2:00 a.m. to do morning drive in Philly, simulcast to everyone else from the MSNBC studio in Secaucus, New Jersey. One of the more amazing aspects of the experience was the free rein I was given. Instead of telling me what to do, they simply wanted to know what they could offer to enhance my program. The only real change I made in my show was to get guests who would normally have visited with me via telephone to make the trip into the studio. With the draw of television, that was not too difficult of a sale, even when the guests were people like Rudy Giuliani, Yes lead singer Jon Anderson, or author Lisa Scottoline. Highlights from the week include Andrea Mitchell reminiscing about Frank Rizzo, Jon Anderson (even though he couldn't remember the second verse of "Roundabout"), and Larry Kane, who was promoting his book *Lennon Revealed*. It was cool to interview on TV the man who gave me my start.

Joe Scarborough was my final guest, a fitting end to my week at MSNBC. Guest hosting for Imus was a great opportunity that I will never forget, despite the permanent fill-in spot going to Scarborough, for whom I have great respect. He had paid his dues over at the network and was the natural successor, but I'll admit that I was still disappointed. One vignette stands out from a week full of stories. When the show ended on the morning that Jon Anderson appeared, someone yelled out that Steve Capus was on the telephone. Capus was the head honcho of NBC News and I, basking in the glow of a gaffe-free debut on MSNBC, thought he wanted to congratulate me. "Where can I take that call?" I said to one of the production people. "Oh, he doesn't want you," came the reply, "he wants to talk to Jon Anderson." What a schmuck I am. Turns out Capus, like me, is a huge Yes fan. He just wanted to congratulate Jon after his performance.

Chapter 10

Iraqnophobia

Iraq: We need an end game, and don't call it "cut and run." It's time to articulate an exit strategy to let the Iraqis know they need to stand on their own two feet sooner rather than later.

I guess you could say I was against the war before I was for it, and later wished I had maintained my opposition. For months before the invasion, I questioned the propriety of going into Iraq, but then supported the effort when it occurred, only to later challenge our continued presence in that nation when no weapons of mass destruction were discovered. If I were running for office, I'm sure they'd say I give new meaning to flip-flopping. Confused? Well, an intern of mine, Alex Smith, said she thought my position on Iraq needed to be put on a graph. It looks something like this:

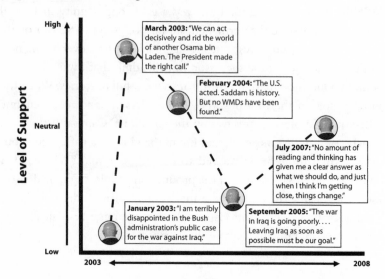

In the January before the March 2003 invasion, I started a *Daily News* column wondering: Where's the beef?[1] I said that no one was asking the questions that needed to be answered prior to committing us to the use of force and to forming an umbilical connection with a deeply troubled country. In a show of blind emotion, understandably resulting from the horrors of 9/11, many Americans unequivocally supported the president when he began making the case for war. Given the political climate in early 2003, my skepticism could have been considered treasonous in the world of talk radio. But I nevertheless aired my concerns both on the radio and in print, where I wrote:

> For months, I have been waiting for a presentation of the evidence of weapons of mass destruction akin to what Adlai Stevenson showed the U.N. at the height of the Cuban missile crisis. And I think the president owes us that before committing American troops.
>
> On a recent day when Hans Blix and company were given unfettered access to a Saddam palace—an inspection that yielded squat—the president was quoted as saying that things in Iraq are not looking so good.
>
> Huh? I'm left wondering what he's talking about. And no one is asking. It's akin to heresy to raise the question.[2]

I was a lonely voice in a sea of flag-waving, causing me to receive many angry e-mails and phone calls in which people questioned both my patriotism and genitalia. Long ago I'd grown accustomed to hearing it from the left. But this heat was coming from the right, where I thought I would be afforded more slack. Initially, the fundamental question for me was not whether Saddam Hussein was a bad guy with an agenda, because there are many of those. The issue was whether he then posed a bona fide threat to U.S. security that needed to be dealt with immediately.

Eventually, just before the invasion, I bellied up to the administration bar and drank the Kool-Aid. What changed? Secretary of State Colin Powell unintentionally poured me a tall glass. The speech that he delivered to the United Nations on February 5, 2003, was a turning point in my thinking on Iraq. The speech was a critical event in the pre-war timeline. For more than an hour, Powell drew on his enormous credibility in the world community as he painstakingly made the case that preemption was needed to rid the world of another Osama bin Laden in the making. The meticulous way in which he outlined the case for war before the world body convinced me that we were doing the right thing.

You know what happened next. The French, Germans, and Russians balked. The United States acted. By the time President Bush announced the invasion in a somber speech delivered from the Oval Office in the evening of March 19, 2003, I had surrendered my original skepticism in favor of a full-throttle support of the commander in chief and the troops. That day, I published—with echoes of Colin Powell in my head—a column that reflected my new view:

"Our President is doing the right thing. I wish it hadn't come to this, but military intervention is now necessary to protect our way of life and the safety of future generations of Americans."[3]

Not only did I write in support of the invasion and speak out on my own radio show, but I also expressed my commitment in a pretty big way in public, when called upon by syndicated talker Glenn Beck. Glenn hosted a number of "Rally for America" events across the country, and I participated in one held in historic Valley Forge, Pennsylvania, just four days prior to the invasion. The outdoor event was sponsored by my radio station, WPHT, and nearly ten thousand people showed up to display their support for the troops.[4]

Recently I pulled out (of the attic) a photo album with pictures of the event, and was not surprised to see what I was wearing that day at the podium. I had on a bomber jacket I had purchased on a family vacation in Arizona soon after 9/11. It has a graphic on the back showing rubble of Ground Zero when an American flag was being raised by the emergency workers in a scene reminiscent of Iwo Jima. On the front the jacket has patches for the NYPD and NYFD. That photograph in my scrapbook reminds me that I was a speaker that day because I believed that the Iraq invasion and the troops who were leading it were fighting the same forces of evil responsible for killing three thousand people on 9/11. I often wore that coat when speaking in public about terrorism. It was a uniform of sorts for me.

A year after I participated in Glenn Beck's rally, I was still convinced that President Bush had made the right call. A conversation at that time with Secretary Powell served to embolden my beliefs. I have always held him in the highest regard and I still do. By then, no WMDs had been found and the chief UN weapons inspector said, "It turns out we were all wrong, probably."[5] The president had reluctantly agreed to establish a panel to examine the intelligence failures. So how did Powell view his own speech a year later? What was running through his mind as he prepared to speak? And how did he respond to those who said we found no WMDs, so the invasion was wrong?

I had the chance to ask him these things point-blank in Washington. The setting was the front lawn of the White House at an event organized by the administration to give big-market radio hosts like me unfettered access to senior members of the cabinet. Frankly, it was a pep rally of sorts for the war effort. I found the secretary of state still comfortable with the message he delivered, resolute in his view of Saddam's history with WMDs, and satisfied that his presentation would stand the test of time. His confidence gave me confidence. I asked him whether he would have changed anything about that UN speech.

Well, you know, a year later, you'd always want to go back and tone it, but for the most part, that presentation was solid. I didn't make it up. It wasn't written in the State Department. It was written with the help of the best intelligence analysts at the CIA.

I spent four days and three nights at the CIA getting the best information, with Director Tenet and his deputy director, all the senior analysts from DOD, from the CIA and elsewhere sitting there with me. And what I presented with Director Tenet sitting behind me, director of the CIA, was our best assessment, and I stand behind it.[6]

Perhaps most insightful was what Colin Powell said to me when I asked him what it had felt like to deliver that important speech to the UN, the one that put me over the top, knowing that literally the eyes of the world were peering down.

What I knew more than anything else was that everything I said would be scrutinized to a fare-thee-well. Anything I said that the Iraqis could shoot down that day, they would shoot down that day. Anything I said that could be undercut that day would be undercut that day. And so I carefully selected what I would say. I made sure that it was substantiated. I gave the presentation for about an hour and thirteen minutes, and nobody was able to come forward and say, 'That's not right, a lie, or that's a miscalculation, or you got that wrong.' In fact, the Iraqis could just fuss and fume for a bit, but that presentation has stood the test of time.[7]

The interview, which I conducted in early 2004, helped (like his original speech) to persuade me to stay on the Bush administration team and to use my radio program to argue publicly that the invasion was the right course of action within the context of the greater war on terror. That is in large part a reflection of the tremendous respect I have for Colin Powell.

At about that time, I received this e-mail from a listener: "While I believe that Saddam absolutely had to be stopped, I think that the only opinions that really matter about the 'misinformation about the WMDs' is that of the parents, the husbands and wives, and the children of the men and women who lost their lives as a result of this 'misinformation.'"[8]

I was intrigued by this perspective, which essentially asked, who are we citizens, those not directly suffering through the service of loved ones, to say whether the invasion was worth it? That is the sole province of the families of the dead. That made some sense to me. It raised the question of whether my opinion should be afforded equal stature to that of a father grieving the loss of a son overseas. What did "he" think we should do?

The same day that e-mail arrived, so too did another I found interesting: "After 9/11, this administration had absolutely no alternative to taking the action it took in both Afghanistan and Iraq. I believe the administration suddenly realized (as well as the administration before it) it had UNDERESTIMATED the threat of terrorism. They also understood it was now better to OVERESTIMATE the threat (i.e., as the old adage warns us: 'It's better to be safe than sorry')."[9]

This too made some sense to me. Hadn't we agreed that never again, after 9/11, would we allow ourselves to be vulnerable to attack by another bin Laden, and wasn't Hussein cut from that same cloth?

So as I often do, I read the two e-mails aloud on the air, and invited people to call and react to either. I didn't have to wait long for a response by someone who unfortunately had the credentials sought by e-mail No. 1, and was calling to weigh in on e-mail No. 2. "Bill on a cell phone" was agreeing with the notion of preemption. In an emotion-packed voice, here's what he told me: "I am a parent who lost a son over in Baghdad, and that e-mail was right on. It is not the soldiers; it is the three thousand killed in the towers. I just hope we all realize we are at war . . . " and his voice trailed off as he lost his composure.

He said his son in the service was thirty-five and a specialist. "He was just over there doing his job like all these soldiers are."[10]

Then he hung up.

The sound of the man's voice hung with me. After the show that day, I Googled the bare information he'd offered: Death of a thirty-five-year-old army specialist in Iraq. Sure enough, on July 28, 2003, William J. Maher III, was killed by an explosive device dropped from an overpass in central Baghdad as he drove a Humvee. He was from Yardley, Pennsylvania, and was the fiftieth U.S. soldier killed in the liberation of Iraq. The stories said he was survived by his mother, Adeline, fifty-nine, and his father, William, sixty-one, who was presumably "Bill on a cell phone."

In reacting to this call, I said at the time that I believed Bill had it right. His son, William J. Maher III, was a casualty of a broader war—not just the conflict in Iraq. I believed that the level of his heroism and sacrifice should not depend upon whether we found WMD. He gave his life in a battle that extends far beyond the border of any one country. Simply stated, the attack of 9/11 demanded that our way of life be defended aggressively. William J. Maher III gave his life for that fight because in the face of terrorism, nothing less was acceptable.

Yet, as time passed, the evidence that Secretary Powell, the president, and then CIA director George Tenet had insisted we would find failed to be uncovered. What did that say about our obligation to William J. Maher III? I wrestled with this. By September of 2005, my original skepticism had returned and I was open about my conflicted views. In my *Daily News* column on September 8, 2005, I wrote about needing an exit strategy:

> *The war in Iraq is going poorly. It is entirely possible that when all is said and done, we will have facilitated the replacement of Saddam with a leadership regime that is beholden to Iran and unfriendly to the U.S., albeit one that does not equal the evil of Saddam nor the type of threat that he could have become. Leaving Iraq now would embolden insurgents and terrorists. Our presence in Iraq provides a rallying point for the insurgency and the radical Islamists. Leaving Iraq as soon as possible must be our goal. It's time for the administration to set a timetable to leave Iraq. It's reasonable to assume that many National Guardsmen who would otherwise have been in America, and in a position to respond to Hurricane Katrina, are instead in Iraq.[11]*

I was now of the view that we were in Iraq based on a false predication and needed to leave sooner than later. What exactly that meant, I wasn't entirely sure, and as I would read or listen to well-informed individuals opine about the situation, there was room to sway my views. How could we get out expeditiously and not leave the place in a worse condition than we had found it? I know what the public has come to expect: He behind the microphone, or with a pen in his hand, is supposed to have everything figured out. But on different days, while I play each of those roles, sometimes the only thing I know for sure is what I don't know.

As I have said, some believed the president lied. I don't. That's just not the core of the man. I also don't believe that Colin Powell was capable of knowingly misleading the United Nations. Do I think the president had a hard-on for Hussein? Sure. Do I think the neo-cons skewed the data? Probably. Were false assertions made about a causal connection between Iraq and 9/11? Sadly, yes.

A few years removed from the Iraq invasion, I had now joined the ranks of those—then almost entirely Democrats—believing we needed a timetable to get out. I thought we needed to light a fire under the asses of the Iraqis to take control of their own situation, and a timeline could do that. Yes, Hussein was gone, but there were no WMDs, and the war was already civil in nature. Then, just as the country had shifted to where I stood, I had second thoughts. Here's why.

I began to think it was entirely likely that the administration's one-time canard about fighting them "over there" so that we don't have to fight them "over here" just might unintentionally turn out to be correct. Not by design, but more like the broken clock that tells the right time twice a day. Maybe we had created a magnet for those who wish to wreak havoc on Americans, orchestrating a sandbox fight with the school bully so far from home that it takes sixteen hours to fly there. The *Los Angeles Times* reported on July 15, 2007, that the greatest number of would-be suicide bombers was traveling to Iraq from Saudi Arabia, the one-time home of fifteen of the nineteen hijackers. It was reported that 45 percent of all foreign militants targeting U.S. troops and Iraqi civilians and security forces are from Saudi Arabia. A full 50 percent of all Saudi fighters in Iraq were believed to have come as suicide bombers.[12]

The article got me thinking. Where would those individuals be if we had not been in Iraq? An estimated sixty to eighty foreign fighters were crossing into Iraq each month.[13] Said differently, how far would they be willing to travel to inflict harm on the United States?

I thought of something Bob Kerrey, a former U.S. senator, Democrat, Vietnam vet, and member of the 9/11 Commission had written in an opinion piece in the *Wall Street Journal* on May 22, 2007: "The key question for Congress is whether or not Iraq has become the primary battleground against the same radical Islamists who declared war on the U.S. in the 1990s and who have carried out a series of terrorist operations including 9/11. The answer is emphatically 'yes.'"[14]

In other words, I was now entertaining the notion that Hussein did not have the WMD that was the basis for the invasion; that Iraq was not a threat to the United States as we were led to believe; and that at the time of the invasion, there was no truth to the assertion (which I freely repeated) that we needed to fight them over there so that we didn't have to fight them here. But now, with jihadists flocking to Iraq to take their shot at the United States, perhaps that statement had become correct. We had created a magnet for the evildoers of the world.

Maybe it was too late for this circumspection. Perhaps things had already gone too far to pull back now. No matter what our foreign policy, we had created a generation of would-be martyrs who would not be deterred by our departure. Now that so many of them were in Iraq, they would follow us home if we didn't stay and eliminate them there. The sand on which I stood was still shifting, and my thoughts continually returned to the escalating number of those who had given their lives in Iraq, men like William J. Maher III. What did we owe them? How about to their parents? And what about those yet to die? Is there a distinction between those two groups? More and more, that was how I framed the quandary we faced in Iraq.

I had long suspected that a similar calculus was going on in the head of the president and that his "return on success" mentality reflects his belief that anything short of total victory dishonors the dead. "Don't let my son die in vain." Those words are often spoken to the president by kin of fallen soldiers.

But is that necessarily the case? Will fallen soldiers have died in vain if we leave Iraq without establishing a stable democracy? I weighed in on this issue and said no with regard to those who had died to date. My rationale was based on how we got into this mess: that notion of preemption adopted against a backdrop of missed intelligence and lost opportunities to kill bin Laden before 9/11. Saddam Hussein appeared to represent a similar threat. (Erroneous, it turned out.) The United States took action. The rest has not gone as any American had hoped. But anyone who died in voluntary service to this country based on those circumstances died with honor, not in vain.

But I think that argument loses steam when we consider those still to die, since we now know the fundamental basis for the invasion was flawed. The more time that goes off the clock since we recognized that a false pretense took us to Iraq, the increased likelihood that soldiers dying there are doing so needlessly.

Chapter 11
Un-Muzzled

My first two books, *Flying Blind: How Political Correctness Continues to Compromise Airline Safety Post 9/11* and *Muzzled: From T-Ball to Terrorism—True Stories That Should Be Fiction,* both dealt with my hatriolic feelings for all things politically correct. In *Flying Blind,* I attacked the refusal of law enforcement in a post-9/11 world to take into account the commonalities of the nineteen who committed atrocities against the United States on that fateful day, namely their gender, age, nationality, religion, and yes, appearance. Others have mistakenly believed they would shut me down by associating me with the deadly "p" word, profiling, but I think profiling is appropriate when it comes to the war on terror.

I followed up *Flying Blind* with *Muzzled,* in which I argued that there was a connection between political correctness at home and the war on terror. I said that PC at home had become so pervasive that it was threatening our ability to defeat terrorism. As I've since outlined on my Web site, I attempted to draw a connection between a number of domestic events and our difficulty in fighting al-Qaeda, including: the Wall Street wunderkind who was fired for having superimposed his face on the photograph of a fully clothed woman for use in a company circular; a military honor guardsman told to stop saying "God Bless You" when handing a folded flag to the next of kin at military funerals; the outlawing of "ladies' nights" at bars in New Jersey; teachers shunning red ink to grade papers and kids being handed trophies just for showing up at Little League; the decline in ratings for the Miss America Pageant; the Ivy League institution that told entrepreneurs not to use the word "maid" in the naming of their room-cleaning business; the dearth of good ethnic humor; and the difficulty in finding a good place to smoke. What was the common denominator in each of these? In a word, I said we'd become *Muzzled.*

The victim-filled society we have created has now invaded and impeded the war on terror. PC is the reason why years removed from 9/11, we still don't look for terrorists at airports and borders by keeping in mind what all the other terrorists have looked like. PC is the reason why in certain quarters there was more interest in and attention paid to the handful of knuckleheads responsible for some truly minor indiscretions at Abu Ghraib than the good work of the 140,000 other honorable service men and women then fighting in Iraq. Why was there more attention paid to whether we played Christina Aguilera music too loud for detainee No. 063 at Guantanamo Bay, than the fact that this same guy would have been hijacker No. 20 on 9/11, had he gotten past customs officials when he tried to enter the country via the Orlando International Airport the month before?[1] PC, of course. It's because we are no longer a country that respects our differences, even when those differences come with rough edges that offend. Instead, we have become a country of kvetchers and apologists, even while at war. The same thinking that says kids on losing T-ball teams should also get a trophy, or that an F grade should be delivered in purple, not red, is what puts interrogators in handcuffs at Guantanamo or precludes our searching airports for terrorists who look like terrorists! We're literally scared to death to offend.

Well, long after *Muzzled* had hit and left the shelves, I was often called upon by my radio audience, or as a television guest, to sort out matters of speech that had caused controversy. Did I think something was truly offensive, or another case of PC like those I had written about? So for use on the radio and occasionally in my *Philadelphia Inquirer* columns, I created the Muzzled Meter to evaluate speech and its possible PC implications. A high score indicates that the speech was highly offensive, regardless of political correctness, while a low score indicates that society needs to just "get over it." A 10 means that a person needs to be "muzzled," and a 0 means no harm, no foul. My determinations are gut-based—there's no science to it. Like Supreme Court Justice Potter Stewart once said about pornography: "I know it when I see it." I think I can distinguish truly offensive hate speech from that which should be shrugged off.

I employed the Muzzled Meter throughout the 2008 presidential campaign and wish to give you a summary of my scoring. Feel free to play along at home. But before I share with you how I analyzed the presidential race, let me first give you some examples of my scoring on the Muzzled Meter based on events that predate the campaign. Each of these is an incident of truly offensive speech, against which you can then compare those events that occurred on the campaign trail:

MEL GIBSON

Gibson sets the gold standard for those needing to be muzzled. We all say stupid things when we're drunk, including yours truly, but no rational person gets tanked and says, "Fucking Jews. . . . The Jews are responsible for all the wars in the world."[2] The guy has issues, especially considering that his blood-alcohol level was a measly 0.12—too high for operating heavy machinery, but insufficient to transform someone into an anti-Semite.

MUZZLED METER

MICHAEL RICHARDS

The guy was funnier as Kramer on *Seinfeld*, wearing a pimp jacket or saying things like, "These pretzels are making me thirsty." Now he's saying, "He's a nigger! He's a nigger!"[3] It's too bad he didn't initiate a serious dialogue about black comics like Chris Rock, who use the "n" word as part of their acts. That would have been un-PC, but worthwhile. Instead he's just a Mel Gibson doing stand-up.

MUZZLED METER

TIM HARDAWAY

This former Miami Heat guard stated publicly that he wouldn't have wanted a gay player on his team. That's a bigoted perspective but not necessarily a high score on the Muzzled Meter. His full statement, however, was indefensible: "You know, I hate gay people, so I let it be known. I don't like gay people, and I don't like to be around gay people. I am homophobic. I don't like it. It shouldn't be in the world or in the United States."[4] That's hate speech, not social commentary.

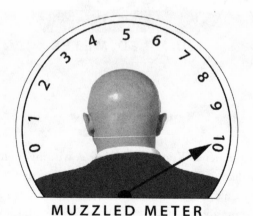

MUZZLED METER

ANN COULTER

This pundit likes to think that she's a part of the serious debate, but she instead extinguishes it. Criticizing the views of those who enter the political arena is fair, but it was outrageous for her to say about the wives of certain 9/11 victims that she'd "never seen people enjoying their husbands' deaths so much."[5] She blew it again by essentially calling John Edwards a "faggot," presumably to make a joke about a TV star that had entered rehab after uttering a similar line.[6] Coulter's not funny, and her comments don't inspire legitimate debate. She's become a caricature of herself.

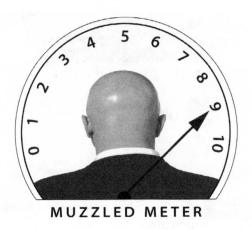

MUZZLED METER

THE MUZZLED METER IN THE 2008 PRESIDENTIAL RACE
BARACK OBAMA AND JOHN McCAIN

Obama in February 2007: "We ended up launching a war that should have never been authorized, and should have never been waged, and on which we have now spent $400 billion, and have seen over 3,000 lives of the bravest young Americans wasted."[7]

McCain in March 2007: "Americans are very frustrated, and they have every right to be. We've wasted a lot of our most precious treasure, which is American lives."[8]

If the basis for invading Iraq was unfounded, what are we to make of the loss of American life? That's a fair question. "Wasted" was, however, a poor word choice. If anyone can say it, it's McCain, the former POW.

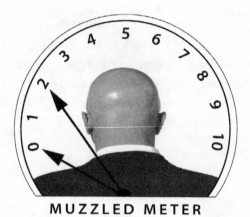

MUZZLED METER

Obama: 2   McCain: 0

JOHN KERRY

People forget that Senator Kerry had clear interest in making another bid for the White House in 2008. One impediment was this statement: "You know, education, if you make the most of it, if you study hard

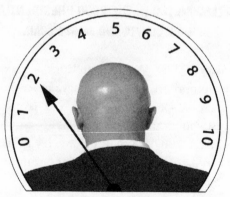

MUZZLED METER

and you do your homework, and you make an effort to be smart, uh, you, you can do well. If you don't, you get stuck in Iraq."[9] I saw it as a poor attempt at humor by a politician so unfunny he couldn't get a laugh when he was a guest on *The Daily Show with Jon Stewart*. This was a dig at the president, not at the troops.

JOE BIDEN

When speaking of Obama, Senator Biden said, "I mean, you got the first mainstream African American who is articulate and bright and clean and a nice-looking guy. I mean, that's a storybook, man."[10]

He was complimenting Obama. How sad we've reached a point where one must apologize for such an obvious accolade. (Obviously we now know Obama was not offended.)

MUZZLED METER

RUSH LIMBAUGH

Army Ranger Jesse Macbeth is a war critic who claimed his Ranger unit perpetrated war crimes in Iraq. He was later found to have failed basic training. Macbeth never made it to Iraq and never saw any of the U.S.-perpetrated abuses he has described.

During his September 26, 2007, radio program, Limbaugh offered the now infamous description "phony soldiers" to characterize Macbeth.[11]

Those condemning Limbaugh in this case reference only his "phony soldiers" utterance. A fair airing makes it clear that Limbaugh was talking about one man who is indeed a phony soldier.

MUZZLED METER

CHRIS MATTHEWS

"They will not silence me!" Matthews assured a crowd at a tenth-anniversary celebration in 2007 for his MSNBC show *Hardball*. Matthews said the Bush administration—specifically the vice president's office—had tried unsuccessfully to influence the content of his program, and had "finally been caught in their criminality" (apparently a reference to Scooter Libby).[12]

Some wondered if Matthews could still fairly moderate a GOP presidential debate coming up a few days later. He did, and no one complained about his treatment of the candidates. Why would they? His comment was about the current administration, not the GOP as a whole.

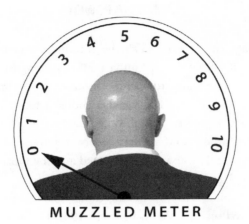

MUZZLED METER

BARACK OBAMA (AGAIN)

Obama told a television reporter in Iowa he doesn't wear an American flag pin on his lapel, as many politicians do, because the pins "became a substitute for, I think, true patriotism, which is speaking out on issues that are of importance to our national security."[13]

He's right, of course, but any mention of Old Glory causes some to thump their chests—hence the controversy.

Wearing my Phillies hat doesn't make me any more of a fan of the Fightin's than the next guy.

MUZZLED METER

SAMANTHA POWER

In a case that exhibits how small the Internet-dominated world in which we live has become, Samantha Power, a foreign-policy aide to Barack Obama's campaign, told a reporter from the *Scotsman* newspaper overseas: "She [Hillary Clinton] is a monster too—that is off the record—she is stooping to anything."[14] Despite Power's after-the-fact request to go off the record, the comment was published on March 7, 2008. By the next day, Power had resigned and the Obama campaign had condemned and disavowed her statement.

Call this Exhibit A of how PC this campaign had become. As Bob Schieffer offered on *Face the Nation*, "In 1952 Harry Truman called Republicans 'a bunch of snolly-gusters'"; President McKinley's opponent said he had 'the backbone of a chocolate éclair'; General Winfield Scott was called 'the Peacock of American politics, all fuss and feathers and fireworks.'"[15]

And then there was labor leader John L. Lewis's description of Roosevelt's first vice president, John Garner, as a "labor-baiting, poker-playing, whiskey-drinking evil old man." "Cactus Jack" Garner, in turn, described the office he held as "not worth a bucket of warm piss."

This 2008 primary campaign was rather timid by historical presidential standards. While Power's descriptor was certainly in poor taste, in the context of a presidential battle this is more whiffle ball than hardball.

MUZZLED METER

GERALDINE FERRARO

Geraldine Ferraro, the onetime Democratic vice presidential candidate, told a local California newspaper, "If Obama was a white man, he would not be in this position. And if he was a woman (of any color) he would not be in this position. He happens to be very lucky to be who he is. And the country is caught up in the concept."[16] When her statements caught fire via the Internet, she revisited the subject and stood her ground: "Every time that campaign is upset about something, they call it racist. I will not be discriminated against because I'm white. If they think they're going to shut up Geraldine Ferraro with that kind of stuff, they don't know me."[17]

I don't mind that she addressed the issue. I just think she is wrong. As Clarence Page of the *Chicago Tribune* said on *Hardball:* "If Barack Obama was white, he'd be John Edwards, and he might right now be in a neck-and-neck contest with Hillary Clinton if he ran a similarly good grass-roots campaign, the way Barack Obama has run his campaign."[18]

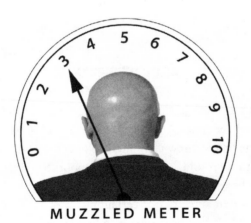

MUZZLED METER

HOWARD WOLFSON

After the losses sustained in Texas and Ohio, the Obama campaign promised to take a more aggressive tack with Hillary Clinton, and began launching criticisms that she was overly secretive and admonishing the senator for failing to release her income tax returns.

Clinton spokesman Howard Wolfson responded by comparing Obama to perhaps the most infamous of Clinton foes from the 1990s: "I for one do not believe that imitating Ken Starr is the way to win a Democratic primary election for president," Wolfson said.[19]

See earlier discussion of Samantha Power.

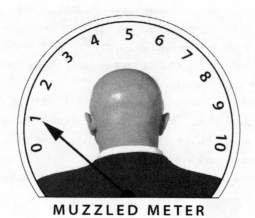

MUZZLED METER

BILL CUNNINGHAM

At a John McCain rally in Cincinnati, talk-show host Bill Cunningham made repeated reference to Barack Obama's middle name, Hussein. McCain immediately threw Cunningham under the bus, causing Cunningham to turn around and pledge his support for Hillary Clinton.[20]

Cunningham was out of bounds. While it is true that Barack Obama has gotten a free ride in certain media quarters, this reference was below the belt. It was intended to fuel Internet lore that Obama is a Muslim when he is not. Using Obama's middle name seemed to align him more closely with the likes of Lee Harvey Oswald or Mark David Chapman than with John F. Kennedy or Ronald Wilson Reagan.

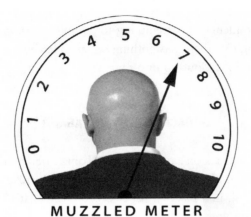

MUZZLED METER

BILL CLINTON

Campaigning in South Carolina, the former president was confronted with this question: "What does it say about Barack Obama that it takes two of you [Bill and Hillary Clinton] to beat him?" "Jesse Jackson won South Carolina in '84 and '88," the former president said. "Jackson ran a good campaign. And Obama ran a good campaign here."[21]

Bill Clinton was factually correct. Jesse Jackson did win South Carolina in those cycles by running a good campaign, as did Obama in 2008. For this comment to register on the MM, one would have to assume that the man heretofore referred to as the nation's "first African

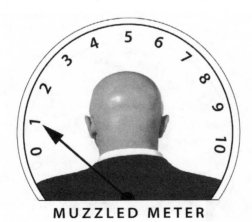

MUZZLED METER

American president" was attempting to diminish Obama's strong run by insinuating that there was nothing remarkable about a black candidate winning down South. I don't buy it.

BARACK OBAMA (YET AGAIN)

"You can put lipstick on a pig," Barack Obama riffed on the old cliché on September 9, 2008, in Lebanon, Virginia. "It's still a pig. You can wrap an old fish in a piece of paper called change. It's still going to stink after eight years."[22]

The McCain camp responded almost immediately, decrying that Senator Obama had called vice presidential nominee Sarah Palin a pig. Why? Because the week before, during her nomination speech at the Republican National Convention, Governor Palin had paused during her remarks to pose a question to her audience of almost forty million: What's the difference between a hockey mom and a pit bull?

Damn lipstick.

Bottom Line: Obama wasn't calling Governor Palin a pig any more than she had called herself a pit bull the week before. Senator Obama's line was a nonissue that got a few laughs when he delivered it and only succeeded in diverting the country's attention for a day or two from the point he'd been trying to make.

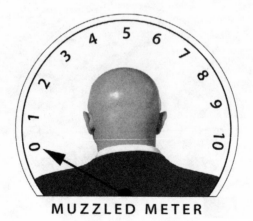

MUZZLED METER

Chapter 12

9–9

Campaign finance: Stop trying to regulate donations. Someone will always find a loophole. Let anyone spend whatever they are willing, as long as there is full and immediate disclosure.

I had never heard of "America's Most Popular Campaign Donor Search Engine" until a radio listener alerted me to www.newsmeat.com a few years ago. I think that listener referenced the site as confirmation that I was a Republican sycophant and offered its contents as the evidence to prove it. When I took a look at what was posted about me, I felt a bit violated—and vindicated. If you visit the Web site, you will learn that (according to these people) since 1980:

Michael A. Smerconish has contributed a total of $18,250 to political candidates (no contributions have gone to special interest groups).

$16,750 has gone to Republicans (92%)

- *Lou Barletta*

- *Arlen Specter*

- *Jim Greenwood*

- *Charlie Gerow*

- *Rudy Giuliani*

- *Stewart Greenleaf*

- *George W. Bush*

- *Jonathan Newman*

- *John Barrasso*

- *Dick Thornburgh*

- *Republican Federal Committee of PA*

$1,500 has gone to Democrats (8%)

- *Bob Rovner*

- *Bill Bradley*

Smerconish has contributed to nine winning campaigns and nine losing campaigns.

Smerconish has a "Power Ranking" of 746.[1]

Frankly, I think their data is a bit light. I'm sure I have contributed to far more candidates than are reflected here, though probably in the same proportion to Rs and Ds as they set forth—meaning my donations have been overwhelmingly Republican. I could be thinking of state races, which are not tabulated at this site. I've made many donations to individuals seeking local office.

The radio listener who called me a GOP Kool-Aid drinker misunderstood my motivations. While it can certainly be said that I have used radio airwaves to advance policy preferences and particular candidates, my own analysis of my donations reveals that the common denominator of my largesse is friendship, not partisanship. I don't like donating money to politicians (who does?), but I do it, particularly when asked by friends who are running for office.

As stated previously, Lou Barletta is a family friend who hails from the place where my parents were born and raised: Hazleton, Pennsylvania. There Barletta has made national headlines as the anti-illegal-immigration mayor.

Arlen Specter is my friend. I also happen to think he has no intellectual equal in the U.S. Senate, and most of the time (although certainly not always) I agree with his voting. I have given him plenty of money through the proper political channels.

Jim Greenwood beat my dad in that 1980 primary for the Pennsylvania state house, but we became somewhat friendly thereafter when he was elected to Congress.

Rudy Giuliani is a friend. I think he would have made a great president, especially if Hizzoner was running, not the former mayor turned security consultant who strayed rightward in the primaries.

Jonathan Newman and I went to law school at Penn and we have been the closest of friends for more than twenty years. We danced at each other's weddings and have traveled together with our wives. Now we split Phillies season tickets. I support him, whatever he chooses to do. The seats are seven rows behind home plate, and I can't run the risk that he cuts me out of the distribution.

John Barrasso is a guy I met during a leadership conference in Switzerland after we were each nominated by a U.S. senator to participate as a "young leader" in an exchange sponsored by the American Swiss Foundation. Now Barrasso himself is in the Senate. That conference was hosted by ambassador Faith Whittlesey, another friend. (If she ever runs for something, I will support her, too.)

Former U.S. Attorney General and Pennsylvania Governor Dick Thornburgh is a friend through our mutual acquaintance with the Honorable Jay C. Waldman.

And so it goes.

The same is true for the Democrats to whom I have contributed. I have known Robert A. Rovner for many years. In 1970, he was the youngest man elected to the Pennsylvania state senate. Until I saw this Web site, I had forgotten he ran for Congress, but when he did, I gave him a donation.

Bill Bradley is not a friend, but when he ran for president my mom and her husband, Gerald Cohn, hosted him at their home for a fundraiser. What was I supposed to say to Mom?

The Web site reports that my federal record is 9–9, meaning I have backed nine winners and nine losers. That gives me incentive to make a donation and break the tie, but I think I'll wait for a friend to ask before risking a losing record.

I get a huge kick out of my power ranking even though I don't completely understand how it's calculated. I assume it fluctuates. As of July 15, 2008, I was number 746 in the country. Amy Grant was in the 745 slot and Annette Bening was behind me at 747. Not bad, especially considering the president (W) came in at 743. Jack Valenti was No. 1. Herb Kelleher was No. 2. Lew Wasserman, Jeffrey Katzenberg, and Donald Trump rounded out the top five.[2]

More than anything, though, the Web site is vindication of my views concerning the way we finance elections. I have long believed that all Americans have an unfettered right guaranteed by the First Amendment to exercise their speech by making political donations to whomever they choose. The only requirement that should exist on such contributions is that they be fully and immediately disclosed online. In my case, if you don't like me, and by extension, one of the friends I have supported for office, then vote against that person, or write your own check. Likewise, if you don't like that somebody benefited from trial-lawyer contributions, welcomed big tobacco money, or received pro-abortion funds, then take some action to defeat that campaign.

In the meantime, enough already with the half-assed attempts to regulate peoples' free speech.

Of course, my view is not the law of the land. In the Watergate era, Congress passed the Federal Election Campaign Act, which required disclosure of fundraising and expenditures and ultimately placed limits on contributions. In *Buckley v. Valeo* in 1976, the United States Supreme Court upheld federal limits on campaign contributions, but struck down provisions limiting how much the campaign itself could spend. The court also refused to limit the amount a candidate could contribute to his own campaign.

In other words, the decision meant that wealthy candidates could spend whatever they wanted to get themselves elected, but an equally wealthy person could not spend what he or she wants to defeat that person by donating to the wealthy candidate's opponent. So while donors were limited at that time to $1,000 per election, and political action committees were limited to donations of $5,000 (the individual amount has since been raised to $2,300), self-funded candidates had no limits with which to contend.

That makes no sense.

I think Chief Justice Warren Burger got it right in his dissent. He lamented the distinction his fellow justices made between how much a campaign could spend and how much a person could contribute to a campaign. Burger wrote, "Contributions and expenditures are two sides of the same First Amendment coin."

Surveying the system, he continued: "All candidates can now spend freely; affluent candidates, after today, can spend their own money without limit; yet contributions for the ordinary candidate are severely restricted. . . . I cannot believe that Congress would have enacted a statutory scheme containing such incongruous and inequitable provisions."[3]

Equally perplexing is the assumption that money is the only currency exchanged between politicians, contributors, and hangers-on. Example: Campaign contribution limits restrict the money donors can give to a candidate, but they still do little to curb non-monetary contributions like legal work or election day "consulting." Is one form of contribution really more harmful than the other? It seems both could later be parlayed into a favor.

So I favor a free-market, no-holds-barred approach. Election laws remind me of the tax code. I say stop trying to regulate the way elections are financed because we're never going to sew every single loophole shut. We should have a flat tax on income, and we should allow anyone to spend anything to influence the outcome of elections—just so long as there is complete and instant disclosure online.

The alternative is the patchwork of loopholes and flat-out goofy regulations in place today. Nowhere was this more evident than the 2008 Republican and Democratic National Conventions. An example: The seemingly sweeping ethics reform that followed the Jack Abramoff scandal and Democratic congressional coup in 2006 included a rule that barred lawmakers or their aides from accepting free meals from lobbyists at the national conventions. The catch? They could accept hors d'oeuvres. So the so-called "toothpick rule" governed the hundreds of parties in Denver and St. Paul in 2008—the point being, of course, that food served with a toothpick constituted hors d'oeuvres and not a full meal.[4]

And with the vagaries of the toothpick rule came all-important questions for the hovering ethics lawyers. Party planners at the Republican convention in St. Paul actually consulted legal counsel to find out if chicken or beef could be added to the quesadillas served at a convention party. (For the record: The line between appetizers and a full meal is drawn at cheese quesadillas.)[5]

Well, the same well-intentioned mindset fuels campaign finance reform—and the same Swiss cheese reality confronts it. There's always a loophole. Still don't believe me? Well, I have a three-numeral answer for you: 527, which refers to largely unregulated, tax-exempt organizations that are known by the section of the U.S. Tax Code that gives them legitimacy. A 527 is not subject to campaign finance limitations so long as it does not directly advocate for the election or defeat of particular candidates.[6] In 2004, we saw how controversial and destructive 527s like Swift Boat Veterans for Truth and MoveOn.org could be.

These 527s were the loophole that ascended from McCain-Feingold, the nickname for the Bipartisan Campaign Reform Act sponsored by Senators John McCain and Russ Feingold, which restricted the types and amounts of money candidates can raise. The 527s have no affiliation with a campaign and do not directly ask anyone to vote for or against a candidate. For the same First Amendment reasons, McCain-Feingold cannot stop a millionaire from spending his own money to further his candidacy. Nor can it prevent an "independent" group from speaking out on issues of the day so long as the group has no connection to a candidate and does not advocate for or against a candidate. McCain-Feingold regulates the content of 527s' message (in prescribing their ability to advocate for or against the election of a candidate) and the timing of their message (preventing them from advertising in the last sixty days before an election), but as we saw in 2004 with Swift Boat Veterans for Truth, these regulations had little effect. The damage has been done.

I know a little about 527s because in 2004 I formed one, largely for shits and giggles. In that cycle, Senator John Kerry came to Philadelphia and made the obligatory cheesesteak stop at Pat's in South Philadelphia. The press coverage at the time noted that when ordering he asked for Swiss cheese, and then daintily ate the notoriously messy delicacy.[7] Swiss? As anybody in the City of Brotherly Love can tell you, the only way to order a cheesesteak is with "Whiz," meaning Cheese Whiz. It was funny, and a sign that Senator Kerry was out of touch. So I formed a 527 called Regular Guys for Bush and created a thirty-second television commercial highlighting Kerry's faux pas, and actually ran it on cable TV during *The O'Reilly Factor*. I think the entire episode cost me about $3,000, and it was worth it. The commercial itself was produced by my friends at Modern Video, Tony Peist and Chris Quin. They did a terrific job. It was funny as hell. In fact, we received an award for it from the Philadelphia advertising community. In 2008, along with my buddy "Liberal" Paul Lauricella, I formed yet another 527. This one was called Waziristan Tourists for Truth, and it too boasted an incredible thirty-second commercial concerning the lack of pursuit of al-Qaeda in the Pakistani tribal regions. I intended to run it the weekend before the general election, but at the time, a Predator strike in Pakistan killed several people and I thought it might be untimely and in poor taste to run it then, and hence counterproductive. As of this writing, the commercial is still posted at our Web site: www.waziristan-touristsfortruth.org. Check it out. It could have been a contender.

Even as I'm writing this chapter, the U. S. Supreme Court issued a decision that strengthened my argument for no-holds-barred fundraising. In a 5–4 decision, the Court ruled that so-called "millionaire's amendments," which raise the prescribed contribution limits for opponents of wealthy self-financed candidates, are unconstitutional.[8]

In other words, millionaire's amendments were an attempt to level the playing field for candidates raising and spending money against self-funded candidates operating outside the contribution limits. That is, until the U.S. Supreme Court struck down such amendments, concluding that they violated self-funded candidates' right to free speech.

The practical effect of all this hand-wringing is to leave candidates for office with a system of campaign finance that gives a distinct advantage to wealthy self-funded candidates. And with no millionaire's amendment to provide them with a degree of flexibility, candidates soliciting funds have been fitted for an even tighter financial straitjacket.

Ethics and campaign finance reform are well-intentioned, but impractical, movements. Scrubbing campaign finance might be all the rage for self-proclaimed reformists and modern-day muckrakers, but in reality all it's given us is a piecemeal collection of loopholes and absurdly specific regulations that miss the proverbial forest for the toothpicks.

Chapter 13

Reverend Wright Was Wrong

During the Christmas holiday at the end of 2007, I read Barack Obama's first book, *Dreams from My Father*. The Iowa caucus and New Hampshire primary were set to officially start the 2008 presidential campaign, and great enthusiasm was already being expressed across the country for the Illinois senator, who had electrified the Democratic National Convention with a speech in 2004. His oratory skills were self-evident, I liked what I saw, but watching his speeches left me wanting more. Did he have substance or was he all style? I wanted to know what made this guy tick. I knew that he had written two books, one when he was thirty-three years old and had not yet run for office, and another after he was in office. I bought the first, hoping it would be a more un-muzzled, personal insight than that which he wrote after becoming a public servant (*The Audacity of Hope*), and my hunch was correct. I was pleasantly surprised to see he'd actually written it instead of having some alter ego, and that it was very revealing.

Obama won the Iowa caucus. Hillary then won New Hampshire. But on Super Tuesday, Obama captured thirteen out of twenty-two states.[1] And as the nation's fascination with Obama grew, I found myself sharing stories on the radio about what I had learned from reading his first book. He was a blank canvas that people were gravitating towards, and I thought I had some good, albeit limited, information to share about him based on what he had written. In March of 2008, I decided to give some framework to my information. I launched what I called the "Obama Project" on my radio show, and every day I took ten minutes or so out of my program to read to the audience a different section of his book. I tried to deliver the good, bad, and ugly. I read passages from the book that covered his accomplishments; I discussed his admission of drug use; I described his first night spent in New York City; his views on race relations (including his discussion of a romance gone south with a white woman);

information about his family in Kenya; and a particular sermon that made an impact on his life, the now famous "Audacity to Hope" delivered by Rev. Jeremiah Wright. My readings were also posted on the radio station Web site. The combination of the two got a strong reaction. My only intention had been to inform and entertain, but people at opposite ends of the spectrum ascribed to me differing motivations. Some who called or wrote said I was giving unfair advantage to Obama by reading from his book and speaking favorably of him. Others said I was reading passages from the book in an effort to embarrass him and undermine his campaign. I only wish I was so sophisticated. Neither was correct.

Suddenly, my "Obama Project" was the beneficiary of an incredible coincidence. Just as I was reading passages about Wright, the YouTube world was exploding with footage of the now infamous sermons that would soon become the political talk of the nation. Sean Hannity had been on this story for months, however it was not until video footage of Wright surfaced in a report by ABC's Brian Ross that the issue catapulted from talk radio into the mainstream media. Perhaps the most repeated was this:

> We bombed Hiroshima. We bombed Nagasaki. And we nuked far more than the thousands in New York and the Pentagon, and we never batted an eye. We have supported state terrorism against the Palestinians and black South Africans and now we are indignant, because the stuff we have done overseas is now brought right back into our own front yards. America's chickens are coming home to roost![2]

I ended my "Obama Project" on a Friday night, and that evening Senator Obama had no choice but to address Wright. He said he'd never been present for the type of sermon that has made his preacher big news. Senator Obama then blogged at HuffingtonPost.com: "The statements that Rev. Wright made that are the cause of this controversy were not statements I personally heard him preach while I sat in the pews of Trinity or heard him utter in private conversation."[3]

I was appalled by Wright's words and believed them indefensible. Less clear to me was whether it was fair to hold Barack Obama accountable for the words of another. Many were saying yes. After all, for two decades, Barack and Michelle Obama made a conscious decision to sit in the pews and listen to the preaching of Rev. Jeremiah Wright at the Trinity United Church of Christ in Chicago. And theirs seemed to go beyond the typical parishioner–preacher relationship. Wright brought Obama to Jesus, presided over Barack and Michelle's wedding, baptized their daughters, and delivered a sermon that was the inspiration for Obama's second book.[4] The Reverend had also served on an Obama campaign committee.[5]

I took another look at what had been my final reading on the air from Obama's first book, *Dreams from My Father*. On page 291, Obama describes a sermon delivered by Wright called "The Audacity to Hope" (itself the inspiration for Obama's second book and its now-famous title, *The Audacity of Hope*), during which Wright recounted the sermon of a fellow pastor that described a painting he had once seen titled *Hope*. The painting depicts a harpist, Obama recalls Wright explaining, who sits "bruised and bloodied" atop a mountain.[6] Chaos in the form of famine, war, and deprivation reign in the valley below, Wright says. Obama quotes Wright: "'It is a world, a world where cruise ships throw away more food in a day than most residents of Port-au-Prince see in a year, where white folks' greed runs a world in need, apartheid in one hemisphere, apathy in another hemisphere. . . . That's the world! On which hope sits.'"[7]

Obama continues: "And so it went, a meditation on a fallen world. While the boys next to me doodled on their church bulletin, Rev. Wright spoke of Sharpsville and Hiroshima, the callousness of policy makers in the White House and in the State House. As the sermon unfolded, though, the stories of strife became more prosaic, the pain more immediate."[8]

I read again the line that said, "white folks' greed runs a world in need . . ."[9]

Those references when Obama *was* in a pew sounded similar to those that caused Obama to distance himself from Wright. The context? He was describing the woman in the painting as looking as if she'd been in Hiroshima, bleeding, bandaged, and with tattered clothing, and yet she had hope. Re-recordings of this sermon by Wright are circulated online and reflect a very measured, thoughtful presentation.

The Obama–Wright story dominated the weekend news. And then came an announcement from the Obama campaign: The candidate would make a major address on the subject of race, and would do so in Philadelphia, at the National Constitution Center. Congressman Patrick Murphy, an early Obama supporter, invited me to attend the speech with him and said he believed he could arrange an interview for me with the senator afterwards. I said I was in.

I'd walked into the National Constitution Center thinking like Howard Baker in the midst of Watergate: What did Barack Obama hear from Rev. Jeremiah A. Wright Jr. and when did he hear it? I wanted to know what kept him coming back to the pew after two decades of toxic diatribes, and I wondered whether he was really taken aback at seeing the now-notorious YouTube clip of Wright, regardless of whether he'd been present for that actual sermon. By now it was widely reported that he had disinvited Wright from delivering the invocation at his campaign announcement.[10] Common sense suggested he knew the man of the cloth was a liability.

Ninety or so minutes later, when I exited the speech, I was thinking that if I ultimately did not vote for Obama it would be for reasons *other* than his minister. I was immediately pleased to have been one of the lucky people in the room that day because while Senator Obama spoke, I knew I was hearing a very significant, historical set of remarks. What I found most refreshing about the speech was Obama's willingness to give it at all—a totally un-muzzled talk about race. In so doing, he made a good effort to distance himself from the angry extremists to his left and right, using something more than just grandiose language: substance.

Most compelling, to me, was this distinction he drew between himself and Reverend Jeremiah Wright:

> *The profound mistake of Reverend Wright's sermons is not that he spoke about racism in our society. It's that he spoke as if our society was static; as if no progress has been made; as if this country—a country that has made it possible for one of his own members to run for the highest office in the land and build a coalition of white and black, Latino and Asian, rich and poor, young and old—is still irrevocably bound to a tragic past.*

But what we know—what we have seen—is that America can change. That is true genius of this nation. What we have already achieved gives us hope—the audacity to hope—for what we can and must achieve tomorrow.[11]

In other words, Wright was wrong. His was a reactionary's dated, disgruntled view of the world, proven inaccurate in the new millennium by the current standing of Barack Obama in the presidential race (and, of course, by his eventual victory in November).

Walking out of the event, I knew I had witnessed history. On the way home from the speech, something else happened. TC had driven me to the National Constitution Center that morning, because she was to handle the sound equipment for my possible interview with Senator Obama, which never came off that day. She's a Harvard-educated Main Line mom, meaning she was at the wheel of—what else—a Volvo. Well, the interview did not happen that day because the Obama campaign wanted the speech to stand on its own. Afterwards, just as lunchtime added bustle to Center City Philadelphia, including the block at Eighth and Race where I stood with my bald white head in my BlackBerry, she was retrieving the car. Picture my lily-white colleague trying to get to her Cross Country wagon in an urban setting. Unfortunately, in her haste to exit the parking lot, she scraped an immaculate SUV in the adjacent space. (Her defense: She herself was on the phone, responding to a request from Fox News for me to react to the speech.) When I went to inspect the damage on the other vehicle, I took note of the Puerto Rican flag on the rearview mirror. A parking attendant responded to the fender bender. He was a black man wearing a bow tie and speaking in an African dialect. I heard him tell my WASP-y producer she couldn't leave the lot until his manager arrived. While she was handling this development, I saw a Hispanic man with close-cropped hair and low-hanging jeans cross the lot and burst into grief upon seeing the damage to his 2007 Suzuki. Manny (as we later learned he was named) was understandably upset to learn what had happened in his absence. The African man with the bow tie did not allow the Mayflower mom to leave the lot until he called his manager, at which point Mr. Tran, an Asian gentlemen, happened upon the scene.

I stood back, watching the WASP, Puerto Rican, African, and Asian amiably sort out a fender bender, and thought, this is *Curb Your Enthusiasm* meets Barack Obama! The scene reminded me of something I'd just heard Obama say: "[W]e may not look the same and we may not have come from the same place, but we all want to move in the same direction towards a better future for our children and our grandchildren."[12]

That night, I appeared on *Hardball with Chris Matthews*. Here is what I said on MSNBC:

> *Well, I was happy to be in the room. And as I was sitting there and I was taking notes—and it was a packed auditorium in Philadelphia at the National Constitution Center—what was running through my mind is, I hope this translates as well on television to the nation at large as it is translating here to this live audience because, like your other guests, I thought it was a stunning speech.[13]*

That was a crazy week for me. Not only was I doing lots of interviews about the Obama speech, but I was preparing to go to Florida for both my annual visit to the Philadelphia Phillies' spring training camp in Clearwater and our kids' spring break. The day I left was particularly hectic, but that night I landed an interview with Barack Obama! I did it from our home in Florida.

This was a Friday-night interview to air the following Monday morning. Again, this was Good Friday, so I thought it appropriate to greet him by wishing him a Happy Easter. He responded in kind, but when I "Zapruder" that tape, I think I hear some hesitancy in his voice. Maybe I am reading too much into this, but my hunch is that he probably thought my Easter greeting was the start of a setup by some right-wing host who wanted to prove he was Muslim. Me, I just wanted to say Happy Easter.

I'd had plenty of time to think about what to ask him. There wasn't much left when it came to Reverend Wright, but what I wanted to know what this: Did he ever tell Reverend Wright behind closed doors that he disagreed with the sermons Wright was delivering in church? That was something I did not think had been asked and I thought it was significant. Obama defended Wright by saying his was not some "crackpot" church. The moment he used the word *crackpot,* a word I love and use myself, but one you don't often hear from presidential aspirants, I knew he was making news on my program. I was right.

So I asked him, had he ever told Reverend Wright that same thing behind closed doors? Here's his response:

I'll be honest with you, I didn't have that many conversations with him over the last year just because I've been so busy. I haven't been going to church. I wasn't hearing a lot of these comments. In fact, the ones that are most offensive are ones that I just never knew about until they were reported on.

I had conversations with him in the past—in fact from the day that I first met him—about some of his views. But understand this, something else that I think has not gotten reported on enough, is despite these very offensive views, this guy has built one of the finest churches in Chicago. It's not some crackpot church. I mean, witness the fact that Bill Clinton invited him to the White House when he was having his personal crises.

This is a pillar of the community and if you go there this Easter Sunday and you sat down in the pew, you'd think, "Well this is just like any other church." You got kids and little girls with bows in their hair and people dressed in their Sunday finest. They're talking about Jesus and the Resurrection.

So I don't want to suggest that somehow this was . . . the loop that you've been seeing typified services all the time. But that's the danger of the YouTube era. It doesn't excuse what he said, but it is to just give it some perspective so people understand.[14]

This, I thought, begged the question of whether Senator Obama believed that his speech would itself have come as a surprise to the former pastor. This was something else I had been wondering that I didn't think had been asked. Obama told me it wouldn't have.

"Some of these remarks first came to light a year ago. And I actually called him and they created some tensions that were reported in the newspapers. He, I think, understood that his perspective on some of these issues was very different from mine. Hopefully we could agree to disagree on some of these issues. Again, I wasn't familiar with some of the most offensive remarks that had come up. Otherwise we probably would have had a more intense conversation."[15]

Carrie Budoff Brown is a terrific reporter at Politico.com. When my interview ended, my producer TC gave Carrie a part of the tape of my Obama interview, and she gave it to a colleague, Ben Smith, who immediately blogged about what Obama had said. The *Philadelphia Inquirer*'s Peter Mucha then followed suit.[16] So immediately, the gist of what Senator Obama had said in the interview was launched into cyberspace. That Sunday, in my own *Inquirer* column, I offered my *Curb Your Enthusiasm* explanation of the Obama speech, complete with the fender bender. My editor, John Timpane, said he thought it was one of the better things I had written. The column was well received, leading me to wonder if the tide was turning. Similarly, polling reflected support for Obama's speech. A national poll released the Friday after the Tuesday address showed that voters who had heard or read about the speech broadly approved of it. I was most pleased to read an opinion piece in the *Wall Street Journal* written by Peggy Noonan, the former Reagan speechwriter extraordinaire, in which she said it was "strong, thoughtful and important. Rather beautifully, it was a speech to think to, not clap to. It was clear that's what he wanted, and this is rare." She noted that the speech assumed the audience was intelligent and educated, a rarity. She concluded by saying, "the speech will be labeled by history as the speech that saved a candidacy or the speech that helped do it in. I hope the former."[17]

That same week, I had nationally syndicated radio personality and CNN Headline News anchor Glenn Beck as a guest on my program. He typically visited every Friday for about five minutes, and we would talk about the day's headlines and promote our respective agendas and projects. It was usually lighthearted. He appeared on my program without incident, and then his producers said he wanted me on his program. His producers told me that Glenn wanted to discuss a decision by the U.S. Court of Appeals for the Third Circuit in the case concerning Mumia Abu-Jamal, the man who executed a Philadelphia police officer named Daniel Faulkner on December 9, 1981. The saga is the subject of my third book, *Murdered by Mumia*, which I co-wrote with Maureen Faulkner, the widow of slain officer Daniel Faulkner.

I have often been a guest on Glenn's show, and I have guest hosted his television show many times. On this particular day, after our conversation commenced and initially addressed the Abu-Jamal decision, it took a turn. Glenn had focused on the Hollywood celebrities who support Abu-Jamal and labeled many of them, like Susan Sarandon and Alec Baldwin, "Marxist." Then he brought up Barack Obama's church. I wasn't sure where we were going. I think he wanted to argue that his church was guided by the same sort of ideology that permeated the Hollywood support for Abu-Jamal. As the conversation continued it became clear that Glenn was familiar with my recent conversation with Obama, and my own refusal to condemn the candidate for the misdeeds and words of his pastor. It was uncomfortable.

At first, I was startled by the abrupt change in the conversation and ultimately he offered the connection between his words and the topic with which we had begun:

"That's how I got to Barack Obama from Mumia . . . I don't think that Tim Robbins is gonna go out and shoot a cop . . . but he is *siding with Mumia* . . . I don't think Barack Obama is going to round up all the white people and say 'whitey's the problem here' . . . but he's hanging with these types of people . . . it must play a [role] when you look at Barack Obama."[18]

It was at this point that I realized that Glenn was implicitly criticizing me for unequivocally condemning those individuals who "enable" or support Abu-Jamal, while I was ostensibly giving a pass to others, like Barack Obama, who enable people like Reverend Wright. I thought the connection speculative at best, as I told Glenn, "I'm not going to vote on this issue. I've made my mind up that—relative to Reverend Wright—I'm not going to hold Barack Obama accountable for the words of another."[19] I didn't find Barack Obama's attendance in the pews of Reverend Wright's church a proper comparison to unabashed advocacy for a convicted cop-killer.

Truth be told, I really didn't want to get into it with him, especially when I was scheduled to guest host Glenn's TV show on CNN Headline News just two weeks later. Soon I would have to confront whether it was appropriate to offer my unbridled views of Reverend Wright and Barack Obama while seated in *his* chair.

Chapter 14

Stem Cells

Embryonic stem cell research: **Pardon my callous nature, but that which exists in a petri dish is undeserving of the full rights that are afforded to a viable fetus.**

On matters of medical ethics, I am fortunate to have Dr. Arthur Caplan, a fellow Philadelphian, as a resource. Dr. Caplan is arguably the nation's foremost bioethicist. He's been the director of the Center for Bioethics and Trustee Professor of Bioethics at the University of Pennsylvania since 1994. He has written or edited over two dozen books. In 2008, *Discover* magazine named him one of the "smartest people on the planet."[1] My many conversations with him on the air have opened my eyes to the perils of medical advance from an ethical point of view. With medical advance comes a series of medically based ethical issues without easy answers. Maybe I've watched *Jurassic Park* too many times, but it seems to me that the debate over stem cells pales in comparison to what is around the corner.

For example, the U.S. House of Representatives has banned all cloning, which also applies to any research with cloned cells.[2] But in the future, Dr. Caplan has told me, the real battle will not be about cloning; it will be about designing better babies. That's genetic engineering, not cloning, and it will drive parents to make better and improved children. Then the key ethical question will be whether society will allow that, or whether it will be seen as too dangerous in terms of equity and fairness to create people who are simply too perfect.

Eradicate heart disease? Sure. Do something about that gene which is pre-disposed toward breast cancer? Marvelous. But, blue eyes, fair skin, even altering male pattern baldness? Now I'm creeped out. Yet that's the dilemma we can look forward to navigating.

For now, though, here's what I see: When we are talking about human embryonic stem cell research, the question for me is simple: What is life? Does life begin at conception, or when you have an implanted embryo? It seems to me that if you have an embryo in a petri dish, you have the beginning of a potential life, but one that isn't real until it gets into a woman's body. That's where I come down: I don't equate something in a dish with a person.

When I recently raised this with Dr. Caplan, our exchange went something like this:

> **MAS:** *Just so I'm clear—we're talking petri dish, we're talking like a thirty-cell mass, we're talking no heartbeat . . .*
>
> **Dr. Caplan:** *We're talking actually nothing bigger than a period at the end of the sentence, we're talking about something pretty tiny, you'd need a microscope actually to manipulate it.*
>
> **MAS:** *And we're talking about something that would need to attach to the wall of the uterus in order to progress in the chain of life.*
>
> **Dr. Caplan:** *Correct.*[3]

Equally important to me is that this debate concerns frozen embryos that would otherwise be discarded were it not for this research. There are about 400,000 embryos frozen in the United States that nobody is going to use.[4] The people who made them don't want them—they either had a baby in the infertility clinic, they moved on, they just gave up trying, they divorced, or they died. These things are just sitting in liquid nitrogen. Nothing will happen to them except destruction.

In addition to Dr. Caplan, I have consulted Dr. Thomas Marino, who is a professor of Anatomy and Cell Biology at the Temple University School of Medicine. I told him I needed a "stem cell for dummies" primer and that I was the chief dummy. He obliged:

"Basically after a sperm fertilizes an egg, we have the fertilized egg that begins the journey down the uterine tube to be implanted in the uterus. That process takes about a week. During that time the cells of the fertilized egg multiply, they divide rapidly, and at about three to five days there's lots of these cells that begin to differentiate a little bit and we have what's called the inner cell mass. That part of the developing, what is called the blastocyst, becomes the embryo," Marino explained in language I could follow.[5]

I asked if that was before it attaches to the wall of the uterus.

Yes it is. So what we have is this group of cells that has an outer group which is going to develop into the placenta and an inner group called the inner cell mass which is the embryo. And it's in this inner cell mass where we get the embryonic stem cells. The way that occurs now is that because of in-vitro fertilization and all the strides we've made there, we can do the fertilization of the egg by the sperm outside a woman's body, it can be done in culture. That fertilized egg then under certain conditions can be allowed to divide and develop normally and then, in the case of in-vitro fertilization, can be reintroduced and hopefully implanted and attached to the uterus and you get a human. So at one point you were a blastocyst, you had an inner cell mass, you were the inner cell mass, you got implanted and nine months later out came Michael Smerconish. So the question really is: When does life begin? That's the hard question.[6]

I asked him what I thought was a threshold question: We're not talking yet about a heartbeat?

"Oh, no, no. At this point the inner cell mass is just about thirty cells. And they will develop over the course of the next two weeks into an embryo, they will develop all the cell types, but at this stage . . . "

I interrupted him: "But this mass cannot go any further unless it is attached to the uterus, correct?"

"That is correct," said Dr. Marino.[7]

No wonder that Britain, China, India, Israel, Australia, Russia, Sweden, Germany, Canada, the Netherlands, Singapore, South Korea, South Africa, France, and many other nations have launched embryonic stem cell research programs.[8] No doubt some will say, OK, but why should federal funding be involved? If there is the prospect of such medical advance in this research, let the pharmaceutical industry pay for the research and development.

Let me quote from one other academic I have found compelling. Assistant professor Aaron Levine from the Georgia Institute of Technology published a study on stem cell funding in the science journal *Cell Stem Cell* that I found insightful. The study revealed that in countries such as Britain, Israel, and China, supportive legislation and public dollars for research help to produce large shares of human embryonic stem cell research in comparison to other fields. And although the United States produces the most embryonic stem cell research in the world, the amount of that research pales in comparison to the work product generated in molecular biology or genetics, for example.[9]

If there's a direct correlation between federal funding and successful amounts of research, then it would seem worthwhile to allocate federal funds to helping produce quality results. Additionally, those who are opposed to having their tax dollars used for stem cell research should consider that with federal funding come regulations and rules about the use of the embryos—something that is lacking when the research is left solely in private hands. There's also an argument to be made for efficacy through federal funding. If federal funding in the European countries mentioned yielded a greater output in terms of research, better research could be generated more quickly by using these funds. Stem cell research is already permitted in the United States. Shouldn't the pro-lifers in the very least favor a more efficient way of going about it?

Yet, as any issue involving life tends to do, stem cell research has become a highly politicized moral lightning rod. This is true of people on both sides of this issue. Who can forget when vice presidential candidate John Edwards ludicrously claimed in October 2004 that people like the recently deceased Christopher Reeve would walk if John Kerry became president?[10] Just as it was absurd to assert that a Kerry administration's support of stem cell research may have yielded a cure for the paralysis that left Reeve wheelchair bound, it is equally specious for pro-life advocates to compare their fight to save unborn fetuses to the cells in question.

On August 9, 2001, however, President Bush announced his "pro-life" position in a televised address when he said what the stipulations would be regarding the funding of stem cell research. They included:

- The derivation process (which begins with the destruction of the embryo) was initiated prior to 9:00 p.m. EDT on August 9, 2001.

- The stem cells must have been derived from an embryo that was created for reproductive purposes and was no longer needed.

- Informed consent must have been obtained for the donation of the embryo and that donation must not have involved financial inducements.[11]

Though the scientists, like Dr. Caplan and Dr. Marino, spoke in specific, factual terms, the president framed the debate as an ethical one, about which he was deeply conflicted:

My position on these issues is shaped by deeply held beliefs. I'm a strong supporter of science and technology, and believe they have the potential for incredible good—to improve lives, to save life, to conquer disease. Research offers hope that millions of our loved ones may be cured of a disease and rid of their suffering. I have friends whose children suffer from juvenile diabetes. Nancy Reagan has written me about President Reagan's struggle with Alzheimer's. My own family has confronted the tragedy of childhood leukemia. And, like all Americans, I have great hope for cures.

I also believe human life is a sacred gift from our creator. I worry about a culture that devalues life, and believe as your president I have an important obligation to foster and encourage respect for life in America and throughout the world. And while we're all hopeful about the potential of this research, no one can be certain that the science will live up to the hope it has generated.[12]

I respect the way in which President Bush's faith guided him in reviewing this as a moral dilemma, but based upon my consultation with scientists, I don't see the need to place such value on cells in a petri dish that cannot become a human being outside a woman's uterus. Not only could research produce cures or leads on any number of diseases that have long stumped scientists, but it has been proven that with federal funds, it may be done more efficiently.

It's time to start rethinking this issue. I see a scientific reality to this debate, not an ethical dilemma. Embryonic stem cells subsisting in a petri dish are alive, there's no doubt about that. But is their "life" equivalent to that of a human being—or even an unborn fetus? My answer is no. A child—properly nourished and sheltered—is going to grow, mature, and change over his or her lifetime. An unborn fetus is going to develop inside his or her mother's womb until it's ready to enter the world. But embryonic stem cells? Without *human* action to put them on the path to *human* life—meaning, unless a doctor attaches them to the wall of a uterus—embryonic stem cells will not naturally progress along the path of life. And to inject a sense of equivalency between stem cells and human life—whether it be a child or unborn fetus—is to introduce a false moral complication to an otherwise scientific process.

Chapter 15

MASMedia

I am very fortunate to be the host of a morning-drive radio program on a powerful station in a large market. Morning drive is the most important part of the day on the radio, because that is when most people are listening— usually in their cars en route to work. More listeners means more advertising dollars, and consequently, greater salaries if you can garner those ad dollars and ratings. As I said earlier, my station, WPHT, which bills itself as the "Big Talker" 1210 AM, is a 50,000-watt clear-channel signal, making it one of the most powerful radio signals in the nation. Philadelphia, while no longer the fourth-largest radio market in the country, is still in the top ten. This CBS station's power is matched only by its heritage. William Paley, who would later build CBS, was fascinated by radio as a child and famously invested fifty dollars a week during the summer of 1925, while his father was away, to sponsor the Miss La Palina Hour on WCAU (the predecessor of WPHT) in support of the family cigar business. When his father returned, he yanked the ads—until he checked the books and saw the fruitful results of the advertising.[1] Paley attended Wharton and, two days before his twenty-seventh birthday, bought the struggling WCAU upon which he built his media empire.[2] Consequently, the station has always been held in special regard by the Tiffany Network.

For many in the business toiling away in second-tier markets or on second-tier stations in primary markets, morning drive for CBS in Philadelphia would be an end game. But I am not satisfied with only doing my own program, and have always sought additional opportunity. Don't get me wrong. I appreciate my perch in Philadelphia, but I would just like to reach more people. My regular fill-ins for Bill O'Reilly on *The Radio Factor* and my repeated guest hosting for Glenn Beck on his TV program, not to mention my countless television appearances on everything from NBC's *Today* to *Hardball*, *The View*, *Larry King Live*, *Real Time with Bill Maher*, evidence my readiness.

At least according to me.

Despite my best efforts, landing a TV show just hasn't happened. There have been so many near misses that I am accustomed to joking with my agent, George Hiltzik, that I am the "bridesmaid" of the business. As in, always the bridesmaid, never the bride. Not only do I fail to walk down the aisle, but I can cause career changes for those who take a shine to me. This, as I shall document, is the Smerconish curse. Woe to those who seek to advance my television career.

In 2002, I was invited by CNN to appear on a daily program called *TalkBack Live*, hosted by Arthel Neville. It aired in afternoons from Atlanta in front of a live audience. The format was the closest thing to conventional talk radio that you would find on television. Indeed, many of the guests were talk-show hosts from across the country. This invitation from CNN was particularly welcome because it came during my radio hiatus after a dispute with management. I was a lawyer writing a weekly column for the *Daily News*, but not someone hosting a radio program. My friend Tom Marr, a talk-show host from Baltimore, recommended me to a producer of this show where he himself had been regularly appearing. Tom's recommendation was somewhat unique. It is not often in this cutthroat business that one person is willing to make an honest recommendation of someone else for air time.

Up until that time, my television appearances had been primarily local. I had done many election nights as a talking head for the Philadelphia network affiliates, and I had appeared regularly with Marc Howard on his weekly television show on the Philadelphia ABC affiliate, WPVI, called *Inside Story*. But this was CNN, and I was elated.

Before long I was making regular appearances on Neville's show. In order to be one of several talk-show hosts on the program, I would go to a satellite television studio in Philadelphia called Modern Video. Little did I know at the time that this was to be the start of a long relationship with Tony Peist and Chris Quin, who own and run the facility. They are the same duo who produced my 527 commercials. Well, soon after just a handful of appearances on this show, I got a telephone call from a producer of the show inviting me on short notice to fly to Atlanta and guest host the program. At first I was not sure they meant guest host—after all, I'd only been on a few times and I had never hosted a program. I was still growing accustomed to being a guest, much less a guest host.

But it happened. By the time of the invite I was back on the radio doing afternoon drive, and my program director, Grace Blazer, decided that she'd carry the CNN show with me as the guest host live on the radio, which made perfect sense. The TV show started at 3:00 p.m. and lasted an hour. Then, the minute that I was off the air on television, I had to hustle up an elevator bank, sit down in front of a radio microphone, and continue my conventional talk show for two more hours.

Two things stand out in my memory about that first day guest hosting, which was September 19, 2002. First, after any number of flawless run-throughs with me reading off the teleprompter, which was a totally new experience, there was an audio failure when we went live and I had no working microphone. Talk about trial by fire. Not only was my chest thumping because theoretically the world could be watching on CNN, not to mention the folks back home who were listening on the radio feed, but also because there was a studio audience of a few hundred. Well, when the red light illuminated, I stood in Atlanta with a dead microphone in front of everyone. I went to bed that night thinking that someday I will die from something other than a heart attack, because if it were meant to be a heart attack that would take me, it would have happened that day at the CNN Center.

The second thing I recall is that after I did just one day on the air, I was summoned to the office of Teya Ryan, who was then running the network. Her office was something out of a movie set, meaning just what you'd expect to see for the office of an executive running the show. She had a bank of televisions from which she could monitor her network and its competition. Additionally, the CNN Center was an office complex that reminded me of a shopping mall, and from her office, she could look down into the interior, which included the set where *TalkBack Live* was broadcast. Teya Ryan was courteous but all business. We'd never met before. In fact, we'd never even spoken before. She said to me, "What would you say if I told you that you could be the host of this program?" I told her that I could never move to Atlanta. She then wanted to know if I could move to Atlanta for a year, and she would then relocate the show to New York City. I told her my radio contract would not permit me to move to Atlanta even for a year. This was one of those events in my professional life where I walked out of a meeting asking myself whether what I believed happened had really just happened. Did she just offer me this show? It seemed I had a friend in Teya Ryan. Soon thereafter, she resigned. This is a pattern that was soon to repeat itself. It was the beginning of my curse.

Teya Ryan's interest did lead to a relationship of sorts with CNN. First, I was engaged for some small sum to appear in weekend segments of a few minutes' duration to comment on legal issues of the day. Then, in June 2003, I was invited to come to Washington to shoot a pilot with two other professionals for a possible legal show called *Attorneys at Law*. Again, I was nervous because this was still pretty new to me, but they told me I'd done fine. Weeks passed and I heard nothing. Then, one day I got a telephone call and was told the show would come on the air the following weekend and it would feature me with Lisa Bloom and Jeffrey Toobin. The show had no long-term commitment. It did not even have a name or dedicated time slot. I was told we would tape on Fridays in Washington, and it would air on either Saturday or Sunday morning. If it gained traction, it would return. If not, it would be history. Well, the show was on the air for a month, but then Saddam Hussein ruined everything. When war broke out in Iraq, CNN covered the invasion 24/7. When the initial phase of the war passed, CNN shuffled its programming, and the legal show was history.

Sometime after that, Phil Griffin took an interest in me. He was then running MSNBC and was responsible for putting me on different shows over there, including Joe Scarborough's *Scarborough Country*, which was airing at 9:00 p.m. My experience mirrored what had happened at CNN. My *Scarborough Country* visits increased to the point where I was often asked to guest host for Joe, who was often missing the show because of a back problem. Then the Smerconish curse kicked in. Griffin was moved from MSNBC in Secaucus to 30 Rockefeller in New York City, where his primary role was to oversee the *Today* show. That was a great gig for him, but it meant that Rick Caplan was now going to run MSNBC on a day-to-day basis. Caplan was the former president of CNN. (Did I mention how incestuous I have found the television and radio business to be?) Caplan soon let me know he liked my appearances, and once brought me to his office for a meeting. I remember it so well. I drove up from Philly. He was sick with the flu.

The meeting lasted ten minutes. He said he was launching a new show featuring Tucker Carlson (formerly of CNN, more incest) and wanted me to be a regular guest. In addition, he said he would give me a show of my own on weekends. I taped a few of Tucker's pilot shows, but was never invited to be a regular. I always suspected Tucker himself had put the kibosh on that. With regard to the weekend show, well, the curse kicked in. Caplan was fired (my curse), but soon resurfaced as the executive producer for Katie Couric's fledgling newscasts at CBS.

Long after Teya Ryan was gone from CNN, there were more close encounters with that network. I was asked by Joel Cheatwood, an executive charged with finding new talent and developing new shows, to come to New York to shoot a pilot with Laura Flanders, a San Francisco talk-show host. The show was described to me as a program with a politically smart man and woman who disagreed on the news of the day but not vehemently. I was assured this was not to be the conventional left/right show, but here I was, a Republican from Philly with a shaved head, and she was a liberal from San Francisco. I knew the day of the taping that we were not onto anything and there was no particular spark between us. I was right; it went nowhere. But Cheatwood continued to be interested in me. Shortly after the ill-fated pilot, he brought me back to CNN to shoot yet another pilot with me as a solo anchor/host. We then exchanged possible dates for the shooting. Alas, that never happened. Cheatwood's boss was canned and a subsequent reshuffling at CNN put all planned projects on hold.

When the dust finally settled, Joel Cheatwood let me know that he liked me, but did not know what to do with me. He told my agent, George Hiltzik, that I should let him know if I had any specific show ideas. Well, I did, and I am sure it was not what he expected from me. My idea was to have a book club on TV.

I am an avid reader, and I'm always into a book. I have greatly enjoyed the book club on my radio show, and the readers have responded well. It was my next-door neighbor and good friend, Pat Croce, who gave me the idea to direct my passion for book clubs into a project. Pat is best known as the former president and part owner of the Philadelphia 76ers. He is also an author and motivational speaker, and in that latter category, he has often been a source of personal inspiration and motivation for me. We sometimes go for a walk around the neighborhood to catch up. One day during a walk, Pat was quizzing me (grilling is probably a better description) about my pursuit of a TV show. I filled him in on the Smerconish curse, and brought him up to speed as to this guest hosting gig, or that pilot. Finally, he asked me what, among the many things I do on my radio show, I am really passionate about. I told him my book club, and just like that, he said, well, there's your TV show. Moreover, he offered to oversee the development of a pitch. He said he would call Timmy Chambers, another Philly guy, albeit one with some Disney credits, and have Tim get some "B-roll" of my book club events. Then we would go back to CNN together and pitch them on a book club–themed show. Within a few months, that is exactly what we did. Tim and Pat created a pitch tape and the three of us, together with George Hiltzik, sat down one day with Joel Cheatwood. Within twenty minutes, Joel said he would shoot a full-blown pilot. The final product is a thirteen-minute tape that is true to my vision of the show. I called in a major chit with Nelson DeMille, the superb writer who has brought us such gems as *The Gold Coast, The General's Daughter, Plum Island,* and many more. Nelson came into New York City from Long Island for a full day of taping as a favor to me.

Joel Cheatwood told me he really liked the finished product and had given it his approval. He envisioned it as a weekly weekend show on CNN. He sent it up the food chain, and said that it was getting good reviews with each viewing. But you can guess the rest of the story. Joel left CNN soon thereafter when he was lured away by Roger Ailes, who recruited him to run Fox Business Network. I was left without a quarterback at CNN and the project simply languished. Never a no, but certainly never a yes. It just sat. I think right now CNN is storing it in the giant government warehouse next to the Ark of the Covenant.

As 2008 began, I was getting more than my fair share of media work in a variety of quarters. No one had offered me a steady TV gig of my own, but I was getting plenty of invites from all sorts of national outlets and had somehow managed to remain a free agent not tied to any one network. In addition to hosting my own radio program, I was regularly guest hosting Bill O' Reilly's *The Radio Factor.* I was also appearing about once a month on NBC's *Today,* and was making weekly appearances on *Hardball with Chris Matthews.* My ability to work when invited was sometimes complicated. O'Reilly is no fan of NBC and its parent GE, and has openly lambasted both. Well, here I was sometimes guest hosting his radio program and then doing a TV appearance across the street. But to his credit, Bill never stood in my way of doing TV across the street.

As the hotly contested Pennsylvania primary drew near, I had more media work than I could handle. I told my wife I would say yes to everyone in one last-ditch effort to find a permanent home for my TV punditry. My involvement came to a head in one intense, incredible week. This now serves as a great record of how hard I have worked—unsuccessfully—to land that TV show of my own.

I jokingly called the week before the Pennsylvania primary "MAS-Media Week" because of the schedule I maintained. I'd been invited a few months prior to guest host Glenn Beck's TV show on CNN Headline News. For that week, my primary responsibility was to do my own radio show, which I did from the CBS studios on West 57th Street in New York City. The plan was for me to host my program until 9:00 a.m., then catch my breath before heading to the Beck studio in the Time Warner Center.

I had guest hosted Glenn's program on several prior occasions and was looking forward to infusing the program with guests from Pennsylvania based on my own contacts because the eyes of the political world were on my home state. I knew this would be a hectic week, but I had no idea just how crazy my schedule would become. Thank goodness I kept notes, which now construct quite an itinerary. Here goes:

SUNDAY, APRIL 13, 2008

CNN sent a car for me in Pennsylvania. On the way to New York, my BlackBerry vibrated. It was an invitation to appear on the CBS *Early Show* the following day. This was potentially complicated because I had been appearing on the *Today* show, but it was unpaid and nothing was exclusive. What the hell, I was already going to be in the CBS building to do my own radio show, so this was literally an elevator ride away.

MONDAY, APRIL 14, 2008

Up at 3:30 a.m., I hosted my own radio show beginning at 6:00 a.m. from NYC. The focus was "Bittergate," which stemmed from Senator Obama's controversial comments about Pennsylvania voters. The home-state callers were against Obama for his statement, which they believed to be condescending. I myself thought his words were flat-out wrong: We don't cling to our guns when we're bitter. We cling to them when we're happy, too. Pennsylvania is a state with a rich hunting tradition. The first day of deer season, traditionally the Monday after Thanksgiving, is a school holiday in much of the state. Pennsylvanians are, proportionately, very gun-friendly, but in my view, that was not dependent upon the state of the economy. In the midst of my own show, I then appeared for a few minutes on the CBS TV program opposite Dee Dee Myers. Harry Smith did the interview.

Harry asked if Obama's statements were "pure poison" in Pennsylvania. I said:

First, it's flat-out wrong and it's kind of funny, Harry, because of how I spent the weekend: our son was in a confirmation retreat and yesterday morning I was shooting skeet with a shotgun. I'm not bitter about anything and I'm a Pennsylvanian and have been for 46 years. It comes at a terrible time because I'm one of those that thought he was poised to win in Pennsylvania and to capture the nomination. But it's condescending and does come across as a form of psychoanalysis. He's not helped by the fact that he offered these sentiments in, of all places, San Francisco; I mean, I can hear the clicking of Chardonnay glasses in the background as I'm reading those words. So I think that it is a potential real Achilles heel for him because 40% of the Democratic base are folks who could say 'Hey, he's talking about me!'[23]

Monday afternoon I taped the *Glenn Beck Program* for airing at 7:00 and 9:00 p.m. that night. The show went very well. Carrie Budoff Brown from Politico.com, Ken Dilanian from *USA Today*, and John Ridley from NPR were guests in a block talking about "Bittergate." That night I also did a segment on Hazleton, Pennsylvania, and made my points about illegal immigration.

I'd been up since long before dawn, but I wasn't finished. That night, I appeared on Dan Abrams' new (and now defunct) MSNBC show *Verdict*, which aired live at 9:00 p.m. from 30 Rockefeller Center. I appeared opposite Pat Buchanan and Lawrence O'Donnell. As I walked in, I wondered if the NBC folks knew that at 7:00 p.m. I had guest hosted a competing show on CNN Headline News, and that while the Abrams show was on live, I would be on again in a repeat of the Beck show. Mystery solved. As soon as I entered NBC, a producer said, "You've had a busy day," which made me feel awfully uncomfortable. Abrams's set was state of the art, and in the adjoining newsroom multiple TV monitors showed live shots of what other networks were then airing. As they seated me on a platform opposite Abrams, it occurred to me that my image would soon be on one of those sets as Glenn Beck's guest host.

And the invitations kept coming.

I can attest to the fact that Macy's wants to sell whatever Saks has on sale—the more I appeared on one network, the more I would be invited to appear on its competition. That seems counterintuitive to me, but it is the case in the TV world. When my Abrams hit ended, and I had finished Beck's shows for the day, I was notified by e-mail that I was invited to be on *Larry King Live* the following night, and that I had an inquiry from *Real Time with Bill Maher* regarding my availability for Friday night. Also, the CBS *Early Show* wanted to know about the following Monday or Wednesday. I continued to say yes to everyone.

TUESDAY, APRIL 15, 2008

On Tuesday, *Hardball*'s Chris Matthews was a guest on my radio show—another uncomfortable moment, because he has had me on so often and his show is live at 5:00 on MSNBC, but replays at 7:00, when it runs opposite Beck's first broadcast. Later that night Chris was having another of his *Hardball* College Tour broadcasts from my home turf of Villanova, Pennsylvania, where John McCain was appearing at Villanova University. In other words, as if things were already not sufficiently complicated for me and my allegiances, I was now having Chris on my radio program to promote his *Hardball* show, which would run opposite my guest hosting of Glenn's TV show!

That afternoon at 3:00 p.m., I taped the Beck show, which featured my interviews with Philadelphia mayor Michael Nutter and Pennsylvania's senior U.S. senator, Arlen Specter. When the Beck show was over, I again returned to the Time Warner Center, now to appear on *Larry King Live.*

This was my first appearance on *Larry King Live,* which is a bit of a surprise given that I had appeared on literally every other program where current events are discussed. As I sat in a green room overlooking Columbus Circle at the Time Warner Center, I was editing my *Inquirer* column for the upcoming Sunday.

I was a guest on *Larry King* for two blocks. The minute he pronounced my name ("Michael Smer-cone-ish") I laughed, because I knew that he would now be added to my radio highlight reel, comprised of those unmistakable voices (including those of Barbara Walters and Katie Couric) who had mispronounced my own name. One of the questions Larry raised was who would make suitable vice presidential timber for both parties. I offered Tom Ridge for the GOP, and when asked by Larry King to identify a Democrat, I offered Bob Graham, the former governor and U.S. senator from Florida. Graham has appeared on my program a number of times and I have always liked him. As a member of the Florida senate he was committed to knowing what a full eight-hour workday was like for various Floridians, so he'd spend a day walking in the shoes of his constituents as they performed their job responsibilities—a feat many politicians later imitated. I told Larry King that given his tenure as governor and senator, his home base in Florida, and his middle-of-the-road status, Graham would be a great pick.

The following week, back in Philadelphia, I got a phone call one day on my cell phone. It was Bob Graham. He said he'd been watching that night by coincidence and gotten a kick out of what I had to say.

WEDNESDAY, APRIL 16, 2008
The following day began with my usual 3:15 a.m. wake-up call, but on this day I had a full agenda and needed not only to shave and shower, but also to file my Sunday *Inquirer* column. I hit the send key at 4:01 a.m., then did my radio show at CBS. This was the day my column appeared in the *Daily News.* Usually it runs on a Thursday,

but tonight was the presidential debate in Philadelphia and I had asked my editor, Michael Schefer, if it could run coinciding with the debate. Not only did he agree, he also allowed me to double my space, giving my column a full page. On the radio that morning, I used the column, which endorsed Barack Obama as the better of the two Democrats, for a lengthy discussion. Many listeners who called were disappointed.

This was a complicated day, even by my standards. Not only was I doing my radio show and Glenn Beck's TV show, but in between I was also doing his radio show. Glenn markets his program as the third most listened to in the United States. I assume he means that only Rush and Sean Hannity have more listeners. By anyone's measurements, he is a huge success in radio.

So here was the issue: Do I repeat on Glenn's radio program my endorsement of Obama as the better Democrat, as I had written in that morning's *Daily News* and as I had outlined in my own program? This was a common dilemma for me when guest hosting Bill O'Reilly's radio show. In other words, is my obligation to mirror the views of the hosts for whom I am filling in? In this instance, I knew Glenn would never offer the kind of laudatory words I was about to offer to Obama. Yet, they were my views and for these three hours, my role was to offer an opinion—my own. On my mind was the dustup I'd had with Glenn on my radio show just two weeks prior, when he linked my opposition to Mumia Abu-Jamal with my kind words for Obama. I decided to give the Beck audience the same thoughts I had offered my own. I went on his national radio show as the guest host and said Obama was the better of the two Democrats. His audience reacted much the same as my own audience had. By the way, in writing this it occurs to me that I have never been invited back to guest host Beck's radio show. Come to think of it, nor does he call in to my radio show on Fridays anymore.

Thursday, April 17, 2008

By the time Thursday rolled around, I was cruising on adrenalin alone. I did my own show and Glenn's TV show. In between the two, I received an e-mail from Barry Nash, a television talent coach based in Dallas. I have never met him, but he has a great reputation in the industry as being knowledgeable with regard to what makes a good TV persona, and so when I would guest host for Glenn I would often ask Barry to watch and evaluate my performance. He never pulled punches. Here is what he had to say:

From: Barry Nash
Date: Thu, 17 Apr 2008 12:34:44
To: MAS
Subject: Beck

Ok, Michael, one question: Can you be just as animated and assertive without being so loud? When you raise your volume you tend to limit your voice to the higher "notes" in your range—a level that can begin to sound shrill if you do not balance with lower notes as well. I'm not saying you should force anything. In fact, I think this results from forcing where you shouldn't have to—your volume.

If you want to mark this, note your level when you ask the question about Lowe misbehaving at the Democratic National Convention. Because you're not speaking so loudly, your voice drops to the pitch you generally use in relaxed conversation. Your goal should be to work at that level, using the higher notes to animate your delivery, but not getting stuck using them almost exclusively.

Lots of good stuff here. I like the way you start with your editorial. It really makes the show feel like it belongs to you. And you manage interviews about as fairly as anyone I know. You just need to be sure that the way you use your voice ranges as broadly as everything else you do.

Tonight I'd go for all of the energy at a lower volume level, letting your voice settle a little lower in your pitch range.

I'm available on mobile this afternoon if you have questions about any of this. Or, of course, by email.

Barry

Anytime Barry has offered me advice, I have tried to keep it in mind during my subsequent appearance. Sometimes I go so far as to write notes to myself on TV scripts, akin to those I wrote on speeches in high school when running for class president. Things like "slow down," or "don't be a deer in HL." But inevitably, when the camera lights go on, I get amnesia.

After the TV show, it was back to NBC to appear on Dan Abrams' show again. This time, while sitting on the set and doing a live shot at 9:00 p.m., I was sure that on the bank of monitors hanging over the adjacent newsroom, I did indeed see myself guest hosting Glenn's TV show. I thought I was dreaming.

FRIDAY, APRIL 18, 2008

That Friday was almost a vacation: I did my own radio show and went back to Philadelphia. The Beck show was largely comprised of elements we had pretaped, and some material from earlier in the week. Then an invitation came from the new David Gregory show on MSNBC, *Race for the White House*. It was the first time I would do this show, and the funny thing is that it is where I would soon find a home—that is, until Gregory objected to my going on *Hardball with Chris Matthews* one night. More on that soon.

What a week it had been! And while I was accustomed to being recognized at home in Philadelphia, something happened at the end of the week that was the funniest of all. That Saturday I was catching my breath, sitting in the kitchen eating, while my wife was on the telephone ordering linens from Pottery Barn. Rita, the operator at a call center in Las Vegas, asked my wife if she was related to me, because she was used to watching me on *Hardball*. My wife handed the telephone to me and we all got a big laugh out of it. I was a bed-linen big shot. That day I also appeared on Roger Hedgecock's nationally syndicated weekend radio show, but still I was not finished.

So how did I relax on Sunday? The Pennsylvania primary was now just two days away, and that night I was offered another interview with Barack Obama. This time, I asked him about a variety of subjects, including (of course) Pakistan and illegal immigration. Again, I found him to be impressive.

On Monday, I was back on the air from my home studio in Philadelphia. Obviously the interest level in the PA primary remained high. I then did an appearance on *Morning Joe* on MSNBC, was interviewed by former Providence, Rhode Island, mayor Buddy Cianci for his new radio show, was interviewed by Ed Schultz, appeared on *Hardball with*

Chris Matthews, and then did Campbell Brown's show on CNN. On election day I did a live shot at noon with CNN's Ali Velshi. Then I took a nap. By the time Tuesday's returns came in, only Hillary and Barack were more tired than I was. I could barely stay awake to hear her proclaim victory.

Postscript: One month later Phil Griffin, the head of MSNBC, called to say he was coming to Philadelphia and wanted to have lunch. He offered, and I accepted, a one-year exclusive television deal, whereby I agreed to appear on that cable network two to three times a week for the next year.

Chapter 16

Choices

Abortion: I want a party with room for pro-life and pro-choice views. Plan B should be available over the counter to anyone at least eighteen years old. I also don't want politicians determining my end-of-life plan.

What would Terri have wanted?

That was what should have determined the end-of-life issues in the case of Terri Schiavo. But some observers—and some elected interlopers—showed that they were more concerned with imposing their own will than honoring that of the woman actually in a permanent vegetative state. The same conservative crusaders who so often decried the role of big government had no problem legislating the federal government directly into one woman's private affairs. Why? To satisfy a high-stakes political agenda. Meanwhile, lost in the shuffle were the wishes of the woman who assumed the role of political football.

Terri Schiavo collapsed without warning in 1990, when she was twenty-six years old. She never recovered, and doctors determined she had fallen into something called a persistent vegetative state. I'm a former trial lawyer, and there is something I always found particularly significant when analyzing the case: Two years after the event, Michael Schiavo, her husband, successfully asserted a medical malpractice action against Terri's doctors for failing to diagnose an underlying eating and nutritional disorder, which led to her cardiac arrest and caused irreversible brain damage.[1] Interestingly, while the jury made financial awards in a number of areas (medical expenses, lost earnings, loss of consortium), they awarded nothing for Terri's pain and suffering. In other words, after hearing the evidence just two years after the tragedy, the jury concluded that Terri was then feeling no pain and was not suffering.

Soon afterwards, there arose an ugly battle between Michael Schiavo and Terri's parents, the Schindlers. The presiding judge concluded that it was a dispute about money from the malpractice action. But that conflict soon morphed into a battle over Terri's end-of-life wishes, given that she could no longer speak for herself. So a court listened to evidence for five days and made a factual determination that Terri's wish was to discontinue her feeding tube. The appellate court process was tested repeatedly and upheld that view.

Despite that fact, many outsiders to the case attempted to affect the outcome. One of those interest groups was the pro-life community, which embraced Terri's parents' cause and opposed removing Terri's feeding tube. Rallying at their side were politicians eager to make inroads with a powerful Republican constituency.

In October of 2003, Florida governor Jeb Bush pushed Terri's Law through the state legislature, essentially giving him the power to order doctors to keep Schiavo alive.[2] Florida's Supreme Court deemed that effort an unconstitutional invasion of privacy, and after fifteen months of further litigation (including an attempt by a U.S. House panel to subpoena Terri Schiavo),[3] Congress frantically passed a law calling for a federal court to review the case.[4] President Bush interrupted a vacation in Texas to fly back to Washington to sign it.[5]

In the midst of all the legal tit-for-tat, a memo written by legal counsel to GOP Senator Mel Martinez surfaced—a memo that celebrated the controversy outside Terri Schiavo's hospice room as "a great political issue." "This is an important moral issue and the pro-life base will be excited that the Senate is debating this important issue," the memo read.[6]

And no doubt the GOP believed it. My friend Senator Rick Santorum visited the hospice and said prayers with the Schindlers.[7] Tom Delay scolded state and federal judges who had defied Schiavo's parents: "The time will come for the men responsible for this to answer for their behavior." Republican Senator John Cornyn went so far as to speculate that "recent episodes of courthouse violence" were a result of judges making "political decisions."[8]

Terri Schiavo left this earth in 2005 after being taken off life support. An autopsy showed beyond any question that she was in a permanent vegetative state, had been for many years, and that the cause of her death was brain damage due to anoxic brain injury. An inquiry by the Florida state attorney found a complete absence of any evidence that Terri's initial collapse was caused by anyone's criminal actions.[9]

I regard Terri's case as one involving the right of a person to die on his or her own terms in the event of an irreparable tragedy. I believe that the affected person should make the decision free of any outside involvement—either from me or the government. Unfortunately, Congress engaged in a game of diversion that subordinated the rule of law to political grandstanding. The interventionists wanted bystanders to ignore the considered decisions of every court that heard evidence from both sides. They wanted the outside community to make decisions based on rhetoric or a perverse sense of principle. So they framed the debate in terms of supporting life or settling for death, when the real issue was whether Terri Schiavo would have wanted to live in such an unresponsive state. And to what result? Uniformity among all of the nineteen judges who played a role in its outcome:[10] Terri Schiavo's wish was not to continue to live in a persistent vegetative state.

Scott Schiavo is Terri Schiavo's brother-in-law. He was a guest on my radio program on March 21, 2005, and told me that he didn't have to speculate what Terri would want. Why? Because Terri had told him, and he had recounted that conversation for a Florida court.

They accepted my testimony. [What happened was] my grandmother was at the old Frankford Hospital. She had signed a DNR—"do not resuscitate." She then took a turn for the worse in the middle of the night. Somebody didn't read her chart and they resuscitated her. They hooked up a respirator, and once they put her on, they could not take her off. They could only withdraw medication. We had to sit there for a full day while the machine blew air in our grandmother, and out of her.

After the funeral, we went to the Buck Hotel on Bustleton Pike in Feasterville. At that luncheon, Terri was seated to my left, we were all discussing this. Terri turned to me, looked me right in my eyes, and said, "Not me. I would never want to

*be left like that. I don't want to ever have tubes keeping me
alive."*

*I can give the same testimony today that I gave five years
ago because it is the truth, and I say it on my mother and father
in heaven.*[11]

That was the version accepted by the Florida courts, and my view
was that if a trier of fact determined that this was Terri's wish, it needed
to be honored.

The Schiavo case had one redeeming quality for me and many
others—it forced us to consider issues in our own lives that would otherwise have been put off indefinitely. In my case, I concluded that I do
not want the government to involve itself in my end-of-life decisions.
My view of abortion follows a parallel track: Let people make their
own decisions until the point when the fetus is viable. While I must
concede as a lawyer that *Roe v. Wade* represents a case of judicial activ-
ism, I acknowledge that it makes logical sense, at least to me.

Obviously it does not make sense to those currently in control of
the GOP. While in St. Paul for the Republican convention in 2008, I
read with some disappointment a *New York Times* story that put some
further distance between the Republican Party and me. The headline?
"G.O.P. Holds to Firm Stance on Abortion." Kit Seelye wrote the
piece. I remembered her from her days at the *Philadelphia Inquirer.*
Here's her lead:

> *ST. PAUL—The Republican Party platform this year will reas-
> sert the party's opposition to abortion. And again it will not
> allow for exceptions in the cases of rape, incest or to save the life of
> the mother, even though Senator John McCain, the presumptive
> presidential nominee, has long called for such exceptions.*[12]

I was flabbergasted. How could the GOP vie for votes in the
center of the political spectrum while embracing a platform that does
not—at a minimum—recognize the usual exceptions for a strong anti-
abortion view? Especially when the presidential candidate to be nominated at that convention had previously argued in support of those
exceptions! Seelye reported that the 2008 GOP platform was at odds

with John McCain's position in 2000, when he argued strongly for a platform that included the abortion exceptions. And Senator McCain himself reaffirmed that position in interviews with *Glamour* magazine in the spring and summer of 2008—months after he had wrapped up the Republican nomination, but before he actually accepted it in Minneapolis–St. Paul.

"My position has always been: exceptions of rape, incest, and the life of the mother," he said in that interview. He also said he would advocate for those exceptions to be included in the platform that would accompany his nomination. "And by the way, I think that's the view of most people, that rape, incest, the life of the mother are issues that have to be considered," he concluded.[13]

So what accounts for his change of heart—and the unchanged Republican platform? I suspect it was the realization that the only way to get the GOP nod was to be unequivocally pro-life. That was the same calculation Senator McCain's rival for the nomination (and later, a potential VP candidate) Mitt Romney had made a few years before. Remember, Romney was elected Massachusetts governor as a pro-choice candidate. It was only after he'd won that election—and a few years before officially announcing he'd run for president—that he became pro-life.[14] In changing his position he joined a long list of public servants who had a similar epiphany, including George H. W. Bush. During the 1980 Republican presidential primary, Bush 41 opposed a constitutional amendment that would have placed restrictions on abortion rights. He tempered that view once he joined Ronald Reagan (another reformed pro-choice candidate) on the Republican ticket.[15]

I can't help but wonder—despite all the bristling and rhetoric, the trips to Terri Schiavo's hospice, and the deification of Ronald Reagan—if Republican presidential candidates actually mean what they say when it comes to life and choice issues. Don't get me wrong, I believe Pat Buchanan meant it when he ran throughout the 1990s. And I think Duncan Hunter meant it when he ran in 2008. They and others like them—Senator Santorum comes to mind—are true believers, and I respect them even when I disagree with their views on this issue. But I have my doubts about those who have been the Republican standard bearers. Think about it: How serious could John McCain have been about his pursuit of a pro-life America if media reports indicated that his first choice for vice president wasn't Sarah Palin, but Joe Lieberman? Some close to the campaign placed Tom Ridge high on that list as well.[16] Both Ridge and Lieberman are pro-choice.

And consider how Republican presidents have left the pro-life community to grovel like a lover scorned—and on its anniversary, no less. Here's how I led off a column in the *Philadelphia Daily News* in January of 2007:

> *As an ex-advance man for Bush 41, I'm convinced that in this president's advance office, the date Jan. 22 is permanently circled. I see it already blacked out as "unavailable" in 2008, just as it was in 2001 through 2007.*
>
> *Unavailable, meaning not able to attend what will be the 35th anniversary of* Roe v. Wade *and the March for Life on the National Mall in Washington, D.C.*
>
> *The president will participate in the nation's premier pro-life event, as he always does. But it will again be by phone, or satellite or CB radio, or some other hookup that allows him to be far from the action.*[17]

That year it seemed particularly obvious that the president wanted no part of the commemoration. He stayed in Camp David. According to the Associated Press, he did so to avoid being in Washington when the event occurred, lest he be asked why he wasn't among the assembled masses.

And it's not just Bush. I wondered the same thing about President Reagan, who also never spoke to pro-life activists in person at their annual rally.

The whole issue has left my party wandering some complicated political badlands. So empowered has the conservative faction become that Republican candidates now feel forced to uphold a clearly half-hearted relationship with the group for the sake of surviving the primaries. Meanwhile, that time spent coddling the base has left the GOP in the hole with the independent voters that increasingly decide U.S. elections, and the Democrats are finding more ways to take advantage of the emerging disparity. The Democratic platform in 2008 left behind what had become standard fare on the abortion issue—that is, ensuring that abortion was "safe, legal, and rare." And when I heard Senator Obama accept his party's nomination at Invesco Field in Denver, I remembered him attempting to be inclusive on this controversial issue: "We may not agree on abortion, but surely we can agree on reducing unwanted pregnancies in this country." The Democratic platform reflected this view.

The GOP could learn from the other side of the aisle on this issue. Republicans need to expand, not contract their tent. The days of revolving all political decisions around the brim and bluster issues should end. After all, not since King Solomon has a political leader displayed the wisdom required to make the absolute right decision with a baby in his hands.

Chapter 17

Things I Wish I Knew
Before I Started Talking

Who is your radio inspiration?

I have often been asked that about my program. I think the questioner anticipates an answer such as Rush Limbaugh, Sean Hannity, or Glenn Beck. Or maybe they think I will stay in the radio realm but offer a name from outside of political talk, like Paul Harvey, or a legendary sports broadcaster like Vin Scully or Harry Kalas.

But if I answer the question honestly, I'd probably mention a guy who's never even hosted a radio show: Larry David.

David was the co-creator of *Seinfeld*. He's also the creator and star of *Curb Your Enthusiasm*. I think I've seen every episode of both. Those who share my fondness for Jerry, George, Elaine, and Kramer will remember when NBC executives asked Jerry and George to come up with a premise for a television show. They settled on a "show about nothing." The genius of *Seinfeld* is that while being a show about nothing, it was really a show about *everything*. That is, all the little nothings in life over which people of differing backgrounds and experiences can universally connect. Today, that same concept is again on display in *Curb*, the best show on television. Too bad that throughout all the years I was watching Larry David's work, I did not recognize that what I was seeing had application to my own.

I wish I had always been comfortable talking about nothing. I've done serious interviews with real newsmakers. Presidents Carter, Bush, Clinton, and Bush, and president-elect Obama, have each appeared on my program. That means five American presidents, plus countless other guests who are household names. Yet I'd be hard-pressed to argue that any of those encounters, even my exchange with U2's Bono, amounted to great radio. They were great for my ego. They probably enhanced my credibility with my audience. But none was anything special when it comes to good radio. Their photographs don't hang over my desk; Larry David's does. (David, whom I have never met, nevertheless inscribed the photograph: "For Michael, Are you My Caucasian?" which any fan of *Curb* will understand as the appropriate greeting and a reference to the episode with Krazee-Eyez Killa.) It serves as a constant reminder of my quest for great talk radio. Identifying the nuggets of everyday life that translate into good radio is how I spend the most time preparing to host my show. I scour every conceivable news outlet, and I reflect on my own life and its daily incidentals. I also consult with my producer, TC, and my technical producer, Greg Stocker. Both play a critical role. TC brings the sensibilities of a mid-thirties, Harvard-educated, suburban wife and mother. She has become a good barometer of what makes good talk radio. Maybe it is her after-hours job at QVC, where she sells flameless candles—we're talking boatloads of flameless candles—that has matured in her a sense of media savvy. Then there is Greg.

I am Greg's favorite morning man—so long as Howard Stern is not in the competition. Greg loves Howard. He tapes Stern's program while my own is being aired, and then he listens to Howard on his way home. I should probably be offended, but I'm not—I used to listen to Howard myself before I moved to mornings. Having said that, Greg's view of what makes good talk radio is often at odds with my own view. His perspective? That of a mid-twenties guy with an earring and bleached blond hair. Many have been the days that I have been involved in what I consider to be a dynamic political conversation, only to look up and see his sour puss through the glass. It's like I have been hit with a Stan "The Man" Stasiak Heart Punch. I rib him constantly about his attitude, but if I did not want to hear a contrarian view I would have parted company with him long ago. The fact of the matter is that I am now closer to fifty than forty, and I want to hear what he has to say even when I disagree with it. This wasn't always my approach.

I used to look only for front-page news to talk about, and I thought that active telephone lines were indicative of a good show. Now I recognize there is little, if any, connection between the two. Just because people are calling doesn't mean I'm entertaining a large number of people; it means only that I have provoked those people who have actually dialed. Conversely, I think there are plenty of worthy subjects I have discussed that didn't lead to any lines blinking. Tom Bigby, a program director for whom I worked, was the first person to point out to me that nobody listens to my show, or anyone else's show, because of the callers. "Nobody is ever going to walk around and say 'Michael Smerconish has the best callers, so I listen to him.'"

He was so right, but I didn't listen to him initially. I found it difficult to talk on the radio and resist the temptation to look at the dozen or so lines in the studio as anything other than a referendum on how I was doing. In the meantime, I overlooked nuggets that were in front of me, and I was often overscripted. Thank goodness there were some notable exceptions.

On a cold December day a few years ago, at a time when I was doing afternoon drive, I remember saying to my program director, Grace Blazer, that I was looking forward to after the show, when my family would stop at a local firehouse and buy our Christmas tree. I repeated that statement on the air. The tradition in my house is to pick out our tree on December 7, my wife's birthday. But I didn't stop with just stating my intention to buy the tree. I then said that if history were a guide, we would take the tree home and wrap it in white lights, matching the way in which we would decorate the outside of our house.

It's one of my favorite family traditions, and one we still maintain each year. But it's a bit different than the Christmas ritual I grew up with. On the street where my boyhood home was located, everybody's tree and porch was decorated similarly, with big, fat, gaudy colored lights. And in truth, I missed those tacky colored Christmas lights—and I said so on the air. As I spoke the telephone lights began to illuminate, unsolicited. I was on a roll. What I was saying had struck a chord, and I kept going, playing armchair psychologist and trying to explain what had happened. I said that each of us got a little more education than our folks. Our jobs were a rung higher on the ladder. We moved into houses that are a little bit larger than the ones in which we had grown up, and once we got there, we somehow decided that we were no longer colored-lights people. No, now we're white-lights people. Petite, non-offensive, uniform white lights. The lights of power and prestige. The lights of suburban panache and urban glamour. And so the colored lights were banished to the basement, or worse.

Having worked myself into a lather, I then told my audience that I, for one, had had enough. This emperor of Christmas present has no clothes and I was prepared to say so. Envisioning myself as Howard Beale in *Network*, ready to run to the window and tell everybody I was "mad as hell and not going to take it," I then said I was prepared to do something about the white-light scourge. I announced that I was finished with white lights. I was tired of being a phony, and I intended to return to my roots. I invited my audience to join me.

The survival of Christmas may depend upon it, I mused.

Well, not only was I stoked, but so too was the audience. I had unintentionally initiated a terrific dialogue about what our Christmas decorations say about us in a status-conscious society. Again, I never set out to do so. If I had intended to have this discussion, it would never have been as effective as it turned out to be. The callers were great. The discussion was spontaneous. The program was at its finest.

Of course, when I got off the air, we bought the family tree and took it home, and when I told my wife my plan to decorate it in color, she told me I was crazy and we wrapped it in white lights as we had every one of our prior years of marriage. But hey, it was great radio. Every December, I attempt to redo my white-light rant. It has never been as good as the first year.

My Christmas-light ravings and the response they garnered were rivaled by another Larry David–esque segment: "The Trial of the Yellow Chair." My wife and I have four children: one daughter who is in college as of this writing, and three (relatively) young sons. One day I came home and discovered that someone had broken a new yellow chair my wife had purchased for our recently redecorated family room. When I asked the boys who broke it, they pointed fingers in one another's direction. (Anyone with kids knows that drill.) So I did what any father would do. Well, any father with recording capability in his home office: We went into my home studio and I conducted a trial. What ensued has come to be known as the "Trial of the Yellow Chair," which I played the following day on the radio. Thankfully, we now have a court transcript. Here is a portion of my verdict and sentencing proceeding:

Judge MAS: OK, *gentlemen, the court is ready to render its verdict. I'd like all three of you to come over here, please.*

(Gavel sounds)

Judge MAS: All rise. *In the Case of the Destruction of the Yellow Chair, here are the sentences. First, my verdict. I find you, Michael Andrew Smerconish Jr.—*

Michael: (mumbling) *It's always me.*

Judge MAS: —*guilty of the crime of the destruction of the left front leg of the yellow chair.*

(Gavel sounds)

Judge MAS: Silence. *In addition, I find you, Michael Andrew Smerconish Jr., guilty of the crime of perjury, lying under oath.*

(Gavel sounds)

Judge MAS: And of the crime of an outburst involving the use of profanity in the courtroom.

(Gavel sounds)

Judge MAS: Lucky, all charges against you have been dismissed with prejudice and the court's apology for the fact that you were charged with a crime to begin with. You are free to go.

Michael: WHAT?!

(Gavel sounds)

Judge MAS: Finally, with regard to Wilson Cole Smerconish. The court finds you innocent of the charge relative to the destruction of the left front leg of the yellow chair.

(Gavel sounds)

Judge MAS: Quiet. However, the court finds you guilty of perjury.

Michael: Perjury. I knew it.

Wilson: No! What does that mean?

Judge MAS: Perjury insofar as you lied under oath and attempted to blame your poor little brother, Lucky, for a crime that the court believes was committed entirely by your older brother, Michael Andrew Smerconish Jr., now a convict.

Wilson: No, Daddy! I DIDN'T SAY ANY OF THAT.

Michael: "Now a convict."

Judge MAS: The sentences: Michael Andrew Smerconish, one hour of chores for the destruction of the chair, thirty minutes of chores for the use of profanity, and thirty minutes for perjury; Wilson Cole Smerconish, thirty minutes for perjury. You're all free to go. Bailiff, take them away.

Wilson: I'M NOT DOING IT.[1]

And that wasn't the last time I let my radio audience into my home. I remember when our house was first overrun by stinkbugs, more scientifically known as *Halymorpha halys*. They were everywhere. Lying in windowsills. Closets. Doorways. They seemed particularly attracted to crashing into my television screen. These things were nasty. They smelled when you touched them, and of course, you couldn't get rid of them without touching them. If you've yet to get acquainted with stinkbugs, know that they're about an inch long, in the shape of a police badge, and come in shades of brown. They're ugly. They're also fat, but they can fly.

Not until I realized that other people's homes were also being overrun by stinkbugs did I finally talk about them on my show, and when I did, I could not contain the audience. I quickly learned that as stinkbugs spread, so do rumors about their origin. When I opened the lines up to callers, one guy told me they came from the Lehigh Valley part of Pennsylvania. Another said no, it was Reading, Pennsylvania. Somebody said that PECO energy, the local electric supplier, imported them so we'd have to close the windows and use air-conditioning. Several blamed exterminators looking to jump-start their economy, and one guy attributed our failure to stop them to Chinese insecticides that break down in sunlight and are therefore useless. My favorite is an e-mail that repeated a rumor suggesting they spread after a lab experiment failed in Lancaster, the heart of Pennsylvania Dutch country. Stinkbugs were good radio.

Speaking of rumors, I'm reminded of a classic sequence of calls that I once entertained. On August 5, 2004, I was interviewing a journalist named Richard Rys from *Philadelphia* magazine. The subject was a story he had just written about Philadelphia-based urban legends. There was something he'd left off his list, and I raised it. Several years before, there was a news anchor in town about whom a terrible rumor spread. It had to do with gerbils. I remember learning at the time that a similar rumor had circulated in other cities about other news personalities. It was out in Hollywood, too, about some actors. I am not going to relate it here and if you have no idea what I am talking about, simply assume the worst. Keep in mind, there was no truth to it. This was pre-Internet. I can only imagine the danger that could be caused today by clicking "send."

By the way, a caller once offered me a great theory as to how the rumor got started. Some poor guy went to the doctor to have a mole removed, the caller theorized, and by the time he left the office, someone in the office blabbed to a friend that so-and-so had come in to have a mole removed. As whisper down the lane ensued, the mole became a gerbil, and "removed" took on a whole new meaning. Not a bad theory.

Anyway, when I was interviewing Richard Rys, and raised the gerbil urban legend, it was only to say what a shame about that poor SOB who had that nasty rumor circulated about him. Well, here are the actual calls that flowed into the radio station unsolicited by me, all individuals who absolutely insisted they had information about the TV personality and that it was true:

Mary: Good Morning, Good Morning, Yea I worked . . . he was brought to Osteopathic Hospital out on City Line Avenue.

Mary 2: My daughter worked at Jefferson and they brought ____ in and they took a gerbil out of his cavity . . . she told me the . . .

Eileen: I almost drove myself off a road listening to this conversation because my girlfriend's sister was going to nursing school.

Michael: Oh Lord . . . your girlfriend's sister . . .

Eileen: Alright! She was telling me that her friend . . .

Michael: Wait! Now her friend . . . time out time out! It's your girlfriend's sister's friend that we're now talking about.

Eileen: Wait . . . just let me finish! I tried to tell her it was an urban legend . . . that this didn't happen but she was completely persistent that her girlfriend was in the emergency room at Einstein when they brought _____ in.

Lynn: Good morning Michael . . . actually Michael, I had heard that it was Hahnemann.

That means four different hospitals were alleged to have been the location where the anchorman was treated. Preposterous.

Christmas lights. Stinkbugs. Gerbils. Good stuff, but for me, the gold standard will always be the letters our daughter, Caitlin, sent from camp. She is now a student at Vanderbilt and doing very well, thank you. But when she was eight years old, she decided she wanted to join her cousin at a camp in North Carolina. Trouble was, her cousin would be on one side of the lake with the boys, and she would be with the girls—over three hundred miles from home. On a Saturday we flew to Asheville, North Carolina, and delivered her to camp. She had cold feet at the last minute, which we believed was normal nervousness. So we dropped her off and flew home.

Initially we believed everything was going well. Monday, Tuesday, and Wednesday passed without a word. By Thursday, we were wondering why no mail had arrived, but still, we were not overly concerned. She must be having too much fun to write, we mused. Then came Friday, when a large package arrived in our mailbox. It contained letters Caitlin had written to us on Saturday, Sunday, Monday, and Tuesday. Sometimes there were multiple letters on a given day.

The first one began, "Camp is fun. At 1 we have lunch. We had today pizza with cheddar cheese, pepperoni, mushrooms, and anchovies (I think)." There must have been some talk at the lunch table about the swimming pool because it ends with, "I'm off to do test swimming and there are snakes in there."

The next letter is where things start to change. "COME GET ME NOW!" "I am having NO fun!" "And know I realized I sometimes take you for granite. I'm sorry." Then it was "I'm having no fun. I miss you too much. I didn't eat lunch today because I missed you too much. Renee my counselor, took me to Ms. Kay (the nurse) and now she thinks I'm a freak. And I was literly going to dye because when I was crying I did not get enough air. The pool has snakes, jellyfish, and frogs."

Then the next read, "Everyday I think of you and cry, like today was raining and you always take me to the movies on rainy days. I cry so much I wouldn't eat breakfast." Then it signs off with "Get me ASAP (Sooner)," and "SWAT," of which we did not know the meaning. Then the last letter finally began to get my wife and me concerned. "I hate it. And I'm sick of the word y'all. Here's your assignment. Get me home or else. Yesterday there was a talent show, and I was an umpa lumpa in Charlie and the Chocolate Factory. Get me out of here right now. I'm never going to sleep over camp again. Here is my mood. So far I cried like 28 times. Get me out of hear."

That day, I read some of the letters on the air. People went nuts. The listeners were evenly divided. In one camp were the men who called and said, "You know, there was always a kid like yours at camp, and if you don't let her tough it out, she's going to be scarred for life." Then there were the women callers, who uniformly were appalled that: 1) I was reading the letters to begin with, and 2) that I was not already on an airplane pulling a rescue mission. Well, my wife was taking care of that. The next day she arrived home with our daughter.

This isn't to say my program is all shits and giggles. My meat and potatoes is still politics, but with a balance provided by the shows about nothing.

I keep in mind some points that were offered to me by a guy named David Hall, a well-regarded radio program director. He came to town as a consultant at the request of CBS when I transitioned from afternoons to mornings. Unlike so many I had met in the business, I believed he understood the medium. He gave me five pieces of advice, and when he finished, I made him write them down and sign the note. Here is what he wrote for me after breakfast, still seated in our booth:

Dear Michael,

1. *What's this mean?*
2. *What's coming next?*
3. *Hope—but never say it.*
4. *Callers are here only to make you look even smarter.*
5. *Guests are tools—you're the biggest thing in your show.*

Love, David

I immediately appreciated his instincts. He was a big believer in adding value, not just reciting the news. David encouraged me to explain the news, give it context, be forward looking, and offer people optimism. He was not one of those who thought you have to be mean spirited to succeed in talk radio. There are many who think you must have an edge or no one will listen to you. I once had a consultant come into my radio station and actually tell me that I needed to hang up on at least two callers per show or I would never get anywhere in the business. I disagreed, and still disagree.

Here's the bottom line: More people have stopped me on the streets in and around Philadelphia to talk to me about my white-light crusade than the controversial things I have written and said about the non-hunt for Osama bin Laden. More listeners wonder which of the three boys at my side broke the yellow chair than pull me aside to discuss illegal immigration. And more folks have asked how Caitlin is recovering from camp than have requested I expand upon why I thought Obama was a better Democratic candidate for president than Hillary Clinton. I guess I shouldn't be surprised. If we've learned anything in these last few years of blogs, Facebook, and user-generated content, it's that people take an interest in the everyday details of the individuals around them. So what have I learned from Larry David?

My show is about everything and it's about nothing. Sure, you'll hear about the front-page news and the critical issues of the day. But the best radio is when I find those rich somethings in nothing. That's what I wish I knew before I started talking.

Chapter 18

Blinking Lights

Global warming: Beats the hell out of me. But given the apparent stakes if the concerns are valid, err on the side of caution.

In the world of talk radio, global warming has joined the rarified stature of abortion and gun control as a subject guaranteed to explode a host's telephone lines. A mere mention, just a passing reference, to any of the three will fill every single incoming line a studio may have. That doesn't necessarily translate into good talk radio; it just means there are always folks on standby willing to stir the pot. So maybe I should not have been surprised by the vehemence that greeted the appearance on my program by Congressman Donald Q. Schwerbitz (R–SD). The purpose of his appearance was to argue in support of legislation he said was pending in the U.S. House, which he was happy to explain to my listeners:

> *Because of our decreasing supply of oxygen on planet Earth, the Schwerbitz-Donaldson Bill would make it mandatory for everyone who exists—everyone—to wear a special respiration apparatus that cuts down our carbon dioxide pollution by 50 percent. Now, according to extensive ecological studies done by the world's leading scientists, we have a maximum of twenty-one years of good air left to breathe on this Earth. In twenty-one years, Mr. Smerconish, at the currently compounding rate of increased use we will run out of oxygen. I know; it's a horrible thought.[1]*

In other words, where certain scientists had calculated that there was only enough oxygen on Earth to last twenty-one more years, Congressman Schwerbitz wished to double the remaining supply by having everyone plug up one nostril, thereby reducing oxygen intake and thereby giving us forty-two more years of breathable life, hopefully enough time for scientists to figure out a permanent solution. He said the diminished oxygen was caused, in part, by climate change. When I expressed concern about people not wanting to wear the apparatus due to vanity, he told me that over time it would become one of the things we all wear every day without a second thought.

"Well, you see, we're not used to it. I suppose you wear neckties, on occasion, and neckties have absolutely no use whatsoever, and yet no one questions what they do or what they're for—they don't do anything, really. But this nose device is saving us—it's saving our lives."[2]

I told my audience I supported the legislation, and that the congressman's alarming news had me worried about my family's future. I ended the call segment with a stern rebuke for the naysayers: "Hey, get out of your SUV, and put in the nose plugs. Do it for my kids, alright?"

The calls came fast and were furious. For this segment, I cherry-picked those I put on the air. I had TC carefully screen them to ensure that those we let through were more incensed. The first call I took was from Karen, a respiratory therapist, who tried to explain how the body would compensate, like it naturally does when we have a stuffy nose. Then came Bob, who told me that the congressman hadn't done his homework, because he hadn't considered the 38 percent of mouth-breathers in the world. Kathy next argued that the device would never fly with OSHA. Cecilia said that global warming was "ridiculous" and that the "insane" congressman was taking advantage of people's fears. Steve told me it was a violation of his civil rights.

Most everyone else on the call board had taken note of the day—April 1, 2008—and recognized the congressman was an imposter, hence the need for heightened call screening. Congressman Donald Q. Schwerbitz was actually my old friend and Philadelphia broadcasting pioneer Les Waas, who graciously agreed to participate. I was simply having some April Fools' fun with my listeners. But that didn't stop the angry e-mails, which were both hysterical and hateful. Just like abortion and guns, global warming really strikes a chord, and everyone who calls has the whole thing figured out. Except me. My head spins from the experts who have come forth on both sides of the debate professing to have proof that man-made climate change is real, or alternatively, nonexistent. The concept makes sense to me—this idea that we are consuming an increasing amount of energy and that our emissions are then trapped in the Earth's atmosphere, thereby warming the planet, especially when I reduce the argument to its lowest common denominator, our homes. I think I can see tangible proof in my own residence that the amount of energy we consume is escalating. Michael Wood was the one who made me think about climate change from a home perspective. Unlike Congressman Schwerbitz, Wood is a real guy. He's the manager of communications for PECO, the utility company that supplies energy to my home. In the Philadelphia area, he's the guy we always see on TV after a storm wreaks havoc and results in a power outage. In the course of a conversation that began with energy and shifted towards global warming, he handed me some talking points (*A Low-Carbon Roadmap*) generated by his parent company, Exelon, which made me think about global warming from a basic level.

Meaning that a knucklehead like me can follow along.

"Take a look around your home," he told me. "How many blinking lights do you see that were not present twenty years ago?"

Well, in my home office I have a computer screen, a modem, and a pair of speakers. Each blinks. I also have a portable TV attached to a VCR. They also blink. I have a MacAir that is plugged into a power strip. It blinks. So too does my iPod.

Then there is our family room, where a big TV sprouts wires attached to a VCR, as well as a DVD player and Comcast VHR. Much blinking. The kids have an Xbox anchoring several blinking controllers. And a Wii. And a Playstation 2. Blinding blinking.

Speaking of the kids, they also have computers in their bedrooms. In the kitchen, the microwave flashes. So does the dishwasher. And the coffee machine. Plus a portable phone. Not to mention my wife's BlackBerry charger.

Many of the things routinely found in American homes—printers, modems, iPod docking stations, digital cameras, stereos, ceiling fans, washers, dryers, personal coffeemakers—are all relatively recent additions, and each requires electricity to charge or function. They not only draw power, they also act as a heat source. No one gadget in itself represents a substantial risk to the environment, but if it's going on in my house and your house and everyone else's house, the sum total quickly adds up to a significant heat source for the planet. That was Michael Wood's point. It made logical sense that all of these sources of heat collectively amounted to something, but I wanted scientific confirmation.

Well, consider this: Back in 2005, British environment minister Elliot Morley reported that Britain emitted around 800,000 tons of carbon per year as a result of electrical equipment like televisions being left on standby.[3] And I'm sure, considering that Britain's population is around one-fifth of ours, that the problem is worse on this side of the Atlantic. Just think: All that wasted electricity—and heat—for a feature that television manufacturers said wasn't even technically necessary.

Indeed, Rebecca Clarren wrote on Salon.com in January of 2008, this so-called "vampire energy loss" sends upwards of ninety-seven billion pounds of carbon dioxide into our environment.[4] In the average U.S. home, the U.S. Department of Energy estimated last year, 75 percent of the juice powering home electronics is used when the gadgets are turned off.[5] And with the size of Americans' houses increasing by more than one-third over the last twenty-five years (from 1,740 square feet to 2,330 square feet), the market for electricity is expanding as there's more space to heat and more outlets to plug.[6]

As Wood said to me, "Essentially, everyone uses more appliances at home, driving up demand for electricity, increasing their own costs, and increasing the need for power generation that results in emissions contributing to global warming. That's the link to our roadmap. And, so we all need to be aware of our power usage and look to improve energy efficiency to reverse these trends."

So what's stopping us from more efficient energy usage? Well, while we've been raiding Best Buy and lighting up our homes like Christmas trees, global warming has become a lightning rod for partisan bickering so fierce it's hard to know what to believe. I read Al Gore's *An Inconvenient Truth* and watched the movie. I found both to be compelling. I find it equally compelling that so many scientists have joined forces to argue in support of reducing climate emissions.

Most notably, in February 2007, the United Nations Intergovernmental Panel on Climate Change for the first time deemed global warming an "unequivocal" occurrence "very likely" fueled by human activity. The IPCC is comprised of hundreds of scientists from numerous countries, but they don't conduct climate research or compile warming data themselves. Rather, they're tasked with reviewing and assessing information, studies, and concepts about climate change from around the world. "The IPCC is a scientific body," the organization's Web site reads. "The information it provides with its reports is based on scientific evidence and reflects existing viewpoints within the scientific community."[7]

At a very basic level, the IPCC study posited, eleven of the twelve years between 1995 and 2006 ranked among the warmest twelve years since 1850 in terms of global surface temperature. Meanwhile, the amount of carbon dioxide emissions grew by about 80 percent between 1970 and 2004. "Atmospheric concentrations of CO_2 and CH_4 [methane] in 2005 exceed by far the natural range over the last 650,000 years," the report acknowledged.

As a result, the study (which was the fourth assessment report released by the IPCC since 1990) cited rising global temperatures, higher global average sea levels, and decreases in snow and ice as physical evidence already manifesting itself on the planet, and noted: "Observational evidence from all continents and most oceans shows that many natural systems are being affected by regional climate changes, particularly temperature increases." Those changes, the panel warned, were very likely a result of the increased levels of carbon dioxide and other greenhouse gases injected into the environment by human activities.

The latest IPCC assessment imparted seemingly dire consequences down the road as well. Not only could sea levels rise between seven and twenty-three inches by 2100, but they will continue rising throughout subsequent centuries. Heat waves, intensified precipitation, and droughts (the effects will be variable—different effects in different parts of the globe) threaten to disrupt natural cycles. Average temperatures could be pushed to highs last seen 125,000 years ago.[8]

Of course, those projections, and the conclusions spawning them, are met on the other side by skeptics raising their own legitimate questions. Some, like Roy Spencer, a former climate scientist at NASA, insist that the oft-cited "consensus" is only that the globe is in fact warming—not that humans are causing those temperature increases.[9]

Others say Al Gore has it backwards—CO_2 increases don't cause rising temperatures. Rather, rising temperatures bring on increases in CO_2 levels.

Some argue that the Kyoto Protocol has proven an impractical, yet expensive, nonsolution to the "problem." Others point to conflicting climate predictions of past decades, especially headlines throughout the 1970s predicting an inevitable global cooling.

With that in mind, perhaps not surprisingly, many resistant to the idea of global warming have accused the media of sensationalizing the issue in an effort to earn more viewers, more readers, or more Web hits. Remember when the *Boston Globe*'s Ellen Goodman said global warming deniers "are now on par with Holocaust deniers"?[10] You get the point.

A few months after the Intergovernmental Panel's latest assessment study, John Coleman, founder of the Weather Channel, published a 966-word mantra in which he called global warming and man-made climate change "the greatest scam in history," perpetrated by research scientists to receive acclaim and research dollars, and to further their careers.[11]

Coleman says, "So when these researchers did climate change studies in the late 90's [*sic*] they were eager to produce findings that would be important and be widely noticed and trigger more research funding. It was easy for them to manipulate the data to come up with the results they wanted to make headlines and at the same time drive their environmental agendas. Then their like-minded Ph.D. colleagues reviewed their work and hastened to endorse it without question."[12]

Coleman's diatribe confirmed my long-held belief that both sides of the global warming debate can lay claim to advocates who would appear unassailable in their expertise. Unfortunately, it also further escalated the political stakes associated with the debate, which leaves me with a single tenable solution: Err on the side of caution. Maybe global warming won't drown all the polar bears—or the Jersey Shore, for that matter—anytime soon. But why not make a few small choices like powering down the computer and TV to reduce emissions anyway? Meanwhile, the federal government works on a larger scale to get us off the crack pipe of foreign oil and onto cleaner energy sources that don't originate in places the terrorists are hiding out.

In other words, at this point, framing global warming as a political debate does nobody any good. Americans should make it a personal goal to reduce our own emissions. And our government should think of clean energy as a national security issue first—one that should be above the post-9/11 partisan fray.

Chapter 19

The Archives

In 2008, I had the pleasure of hosting best-selling author Nelson DeMille in Philadelphia for my book club. We had nearly a thousand people in the audience soon after the release of *The Gate House*, his sequel to *The Gold Coast*. What a night! Not all authors translate in real life—some are better suited to putting pen to paper. Not Nelson—this was the third time I'd had him in town and he is full of personality and rakish insight. I conduct the book club Oprah-style. I spend about ninety minutes questioning the authors about their past and current books. This night was no different. As an added bonus for the audience, I also incorporated some video elements. Nelson DeMille had recorded a brief tour of a mansion on the Gold Coast of Long Island in connection with his new book, and I showed that to the audience to familiarize them (and me) with the book's setting. In addition, I showed the audience a portion of my CNN pilot for a TV book club, which Nelson had graciously participated in filming. The audience seemed to really enjoy that.

And then I had a final surprise. I own every one of his books in hardback, and out of his sight backstage, I had them all stacked on a dolly. As the night was winding down, I got up from my seat, retrieved the dolly, and rolled it out on stage. I held each book up one at a time, and asked DeMille what came to mind for each. He held the theater captive as he recalled a memory or thought about each novel—there was laughter when he asked, "Wait, what is that one about again?"

I have my own "dolly of books," or more accurately, recordings from my radio show. These are items I have saved in my personal archives; items I wanted to be sure I kept for my own enjoyment. These aren't necessarily the best radio moments of my career, only the most memorable. So with DeMille as my inspiration, I have flipped through hundreds of CDs of my radio program looking for memorable moments, and now I offer some of what makes my list. Here we go. . . .

Faux Pas—I talk on-air for twenty hours each week. That is my only excuse for the faux pas that occasionally—OK, more than occasionally—come out of my mouth. I have said plenty of boneheaded things over the years, but two are at the top of any blooper list. First, Barney Frank was my in-studio guest one morning. When I announced his appearance, a friend in our sales department, Neil McKenna, offered to shuttle Congressman Frank from his hotel to my studio and I said sure. Neil later told me he was looking forward to some camaraderie with Frank when he picked him up in his Land Rover Discovery, but to his disappointment, Frank climbed in the back and slept en route to the studio. Upon his arrival, after we'd discussed the issues of the day, I said I wanted to know if he got sick of being asked about his sexual preference given that he was the first openly homosexual member of Congress. That was fine. But here is how I asked: "So, the gay thing, is that just a pain in the butt after a while?" To his credit, and evidencing a great sense of humor, Frank replied, "Well, I better not answer that too literally. . . ."

Wait, my exploits get worse. There was the time I had famed Irish tenor Ronan Tynan on the show. Tynan is a legendary figure, renowned for the role he played at so many police and fire funerals related to 9/11. Others will know him for his singing of the national anthem at Yankee home games. I also remember reading that when Bono's father died, he wanted Tynan to perform graveside. That is the highest of praise. The man can bring an atheist to tears with his rendition of "Amazing Grace." Well, Tynan is also an inspirational figure because he has accomplished so much even with both legs amputated below the knee following a car accident at age twenty. Oh boy, can you see this one coming? Believe it or not I actually said, "Ronan, you've been able to overcome great adversity in your life, will you walk us through that?" Oh man. Walk us through it. The minute I said it, I knew I stepped in it. (Again . . . stepped in it!) He was a gentleman and did not acknowledge my stupidity. Remember . . . twenty hours a week!

George W. Bush—I did a special broadcast on election night in 2000, in front of a live audience at Ruth's Chris Steak House in Philadelphia. Throughout the campaign, I had attempted to get then Governor Bush on my program. No dice. He did not do talk radio during that election cycle. So imagine my surprise when in the midst of the election-night show, with about an hour to go in Pennsylvania vot-ing, Grace Blazer told me, "George Bush is on the line." My first reaction was that I was being pranked, or as my kids would now say, punked. Why would he call now after not having called for the entire campaign? I was half suspecting that if I took the call I would hear somebody say "Baba Booey," in reference to the *Howard Stern Show*. But I took the call, and it really was George Bush. I am tempted to say this was a conversation with a man who that very night was elected our nation's forty-third president, but the counting of ballots would go on for weeks and the Supreme Court would have to get involved before he would be regarded as the victor. The call was brief. He made his final pitch to Pennsylvanians to get out and vote for him and Dick Cheney. They lost the state by a narrow margin.

Al Gore—Speaking of the 2000 cycle, I also remember when Al Gore was a guest on my program—for about sixty seconds! After his presi-dential bid, Gore, of course, wrote *An Inconvenient Truth*, about cli-mate change. In connection with the book release he was offered to me as a radio guest and I was pleased to welcome him. Well, often these high-profile celebrities book shows like mine in major markets one after the other in very tightly controlled time blocks of about eight minutes. There is no time to waste when you finally get the newsmaker on the line because you are only screwing the next guy in line. Gore was one such interview. The only trouble is that he ran late for my interview and when he finally came on the line, one of his handlers held the delay against my interview. So I was still in my preliminary discussion with him when all of a sudden, an assistant to the former vice president burst into the call and said the interview needed to end. Unfortunately, my response was to say, "This is bullshit!" to which Gore responded, "I'll call you back, Michael, I'll call you back." I'm still waiting for that call.

Joe Namath—Broadway Joe was good radio. He released a terrific book, a scrapbook really, called *Namath*. I asked him if he could still hit me deep with a spiral in the backyard. "Sometimes," was his laughing and honest response. The man who went from Beaver Falls, Pennsyl-vania, to Broadway was at his best when imitating legendary Alabama coach Bear Bryant's use of the word "stud."

Jimmy Rollins—Another memorable sports interview, but for a reason I'd just as soon forget. I interviewed the Phillies MVP shortstop from my home studio on a day when the sound equipment was on the fritz. I didn't know this when the interview began, but soon thereafter it became apparent to me that what was being said was not being recorded. I was too embarrassed to tell JRoll that I was not picking up his voice, but reticent to waste his time with an interview that would never be aired. Breaking a sweat, I remember asking myself how long I should question him so it did not appear obvious there was a screw-up, but without keeping him on the line so long that if he later learned what happened he'd be pissed. The one good thing to come out of the interview was a call segment the next day when I told my audience what happened and asked, "What should I have done?"

Deborah Harry—What do you ask Debbie Harry? The onetime hottie from Blondie was promoting a concert appearance, but despite my love of music, the only song I could think of when she was my guest was "Call Me!" I couldn't help myself. I kept interjecting "Call Me!" into the talk whenever the interview lagged. In the end, it was funny because I came off like a radio version of Chris Farley from a hit SNL segment where he is interviewing Paul McCartney, fawning all over the former Beatle, not knowing what to ask. Of course, the difference between Chris Farley and me is that Farley was intending to be funny. I was simply a knucklehead.

Don McLean—In a strange coincidence, I interviewed him on the same day as Deborah Harry. I had the same problem. What do you ask Don McLean about, besides "American Pie"? Seriously . . . that was all I wanted to ask him.

Jimmy Carter—My interaction with this Democratic president did not have such a happy outcome as my interviews with Obama and Clinton. When my morning show ends, I usually sit with my producers TC and Greg and do a postmortem. We discuss what worked that day and what did not, and we plan out a portion of the next day's show. Usually, that means TC is praising what has just occurred and Greg looks like he just got news of his pet's passing. That is just his nature. Unless the show has somehow referenced lesbians, or breaking wind, in which case he is like a boy just handed a puppy. Well, one morning we were in such a meeting when Jimmy Kelly came down the hall to retrieve me. Jimmy is a board operator who runs the transmission for Glenn Beck's program, which follows my own. Jimmy reported, "Amber is on the line with President Carter." Well, TC just about had a heart attack. In a rare lapse for her, she had forgotten to tell me that she had scheduled an interview with President Carter concerning his book *Palestine: Peace Not Apartheid*. I had not seen, much less read, the book, so I was feeling extremely uncomfortable as I literally jogged down the hallway toward my studio. Normally, I read the books of authors who are booked on my show. I have never bought Larry King's explanation for not doing so—he claims he wants to be in the same position as the audience, but I think it is just plain lazy. Anyway, here I was about to speak to President Carter about his brand-new book. As he came on my line, I remembered having heard something somewhere about Harvard professor Alan Dershowitz having a problem with the new book. So I tossed Dershowitz's name into one of my first questions. Jimmy Carter was none too happy to hear that name, and the rest of the interview carried itself. It ended up being a fascinating, OK, rather contentious interview, which I played for Dershowitz the next day and had him critique. I also remember that I told President Carter that the Palestinians would not be happy with a two-state solution and that they wanted a Middle East rid of Israel. The interview ended abruptly with the former president responding curtly, "Well, I think you are mistaken." I replied, "Maybe, and maybe not, sir." Surreal.

Senator Barack Obama—I interviewed our new president three times by telephone when he was running for the office. The interviews were each memorable not only for the dialogue but also for what was going on at my end of the line. The first occurred on Good Friday 2008. I was with my family at our home in Florida for a long weekend. We go to Florida for the kids' spring break, but that is historically an important time of year in the radio business and I am loath to miss work. So I broadcast from our home there, and I have the ability to record interviews from this location too. The first Obama interview was particularly important because it came on the heels of the revelations concerning Reverend Wright. So on this Friday night, my producers TC and Greg had come back into the studio to facilitate the recording. I think they were nervous that I would fumble the recording. Either way, I appreciated their commitment. Down in Florida, I suggested to my wife that perhaps at the time of the interview, she should take our three sons, then eight, ten, and twelve years old, out of the house. The walls have a fair amount of soundproofing, and normally our children sleep through most of my morning show. But for this evening interview with Senator Obama, I could not take the risk that our three boys would start roughhousing. So I asked my wife if she could time a pizza pick-up while I was doing the interview. I had a pre-arranged time, and I knew that I would only have him on the line for ten to fifteen minutes. She readily agreed. I'm not going to tell you where our home is, but if you know a terrific Chicago-style pizza joint called Aurellio's, you're in the right neighborhood. Well, I mention this because the Obama campaign ran late, and the interview kept being postponed. First by ten minutes, then fifteen, then thirty. Meanwhile, my wife was circling our building with three boys and a delicious-smelling pizza. So in addition to my angst over getting what I needed out of the interview, I had the added guilt about feeding the kids. It was yet another Larry David moment. Finally I told my wife to come on home, the kids ate and behaved, and the interview went well.

Joe Lieberman—Lieberman has been on the program a number of times, but one occasion stands out. After the Phillies won the 2008 World Series, the City of Philadelphia planned and executed a fabulous celebration, complete with a parade attended by more than two million people. I am a huge Phillies fan and my radio station is the broadcast home of the Phillies, so this was a significant time in my personal and professional life. The day of the parade, I worked double-duty. In the morning, I broadcast my program from a second-story restaurant on Broad Street, which offered the perfect perch to watch parade-goers assembling for the noon kick-off. Later that day, I co-hosted an unusual second program that featured me and Angelo Cataldi, he of sports radio fame, each providing commentary on the end of the Phillies' celebration as it wound its way inside Citizen's Bank Park. It was a lot of ego and testosterone in one show with both Cataldi and me, but we worked very well together. He has a tremendous wit and sometimes, when discussing sports on his own show, hides the depth of his intellect. Before I moved to mornings, I used to split my listening time between him and Stern. Back to Lieberman. Well, the night before the parade, the McCain campaign offered me Joe Lieberman as a guest and said he was in town. I told them to have him walk on over from his hotel to my makeshift broadcast booth and join my parade show, and he did. In fact, he even arrived wearing a red sweater, and completely got caught up in the spirit of the broadcast that day. My mother is married to a man named Gerald Cohn. Jerry was then very supportive of John McCain and terribly disappointed in my kind treatment of Barack Obama. He is also a huge fan of Joe Lieberman, with whom he has a relationship. So during a commercial break, I dialed Jerry's number and handed the phone to Lieberman. Ever the good sport, he ribbed Jerry about how I had gone off the deep end politically and the two had a private laugh—no doubt at my expense.

Denise Brown—Like much of America, I was fixated on the OJ Simpson trial when it occurred and horrified by the outcome of the criminal case. When Denise Brown was offered to me as an in-studio guest to discuss a foundation named after her late sister, Nicole Brown Simpson, I was happy to oblige. The trial had been years prior by the time she walked into my studio. I figure she'd been asked every question and I would break no ground, but I was wrong. See, I know OJ got away with murder, two murders, actually. So I asked Denise if she'd ever thought of hiring someone to off OJ. I was sure this was a question she wouldn't touch, but she answered it. She said candidly, yes, of course . . . but she didn't because she didn't want to end up in jail. Can you imagine living with that for all these years? She is a woman of enormous class and courage.

Chris Moneymaker—One morning I had the Texas hold 'em champion in my studio. Unfortunately, my good friend Jonathan Newman, the former head of the Pennsylvania Liquor Control Board and a wine connoisseur, had Chris out drinking and playing cards the night before. I know I'm skewed in what "early" is, as my alarm goes off at 3:15 a.m. each weekday, but Moneymaker really took the night to an extreme. Rumpled, reeking, and barely knowing what he was supposed to be promoting, he fell asleep on the floor of the studio waiting for his segment. But when it was showtime he rallied, and gave me great tips on playing poker.

Ted Nugent—I love Uncle Ted and have often been in his company. Like the night I went to interview him in his hotel suite accompanied by "Liberal" Paul Lauricella. The recorder, an old-fashioned piece of crap with cassette tapes, started spooling out on the hotel rug, right on top of Uncle Ted's stocking feet. When he saw it, he pulled out something the size of what Clint Eastwood carried in *Dirty Harry* and threatened to blow my device to smithereens. Speaking of that "Uncle" Ted moniker reminds me that once I took our sons to meet him and I introduced him as Uncle Ted. They weren't sure what to make of the Motor City Madman. When we were walking away, my eldest, Michael Jr., said "Dad, is he related to us on Mom's side of the family or yours?" ("Your mother's," I said without missing a beat.) But what I most remember about Nuge and his many visits to my program was the day he came in studio and played an electric-guitar version of "The Star-Spangled Banner." As he played, a bunch of listeners who had e-mailed and said they wanted to meet him were waiting in our studio kitchen, anxious to show Uncle Ted their antlered deer heads or just break some, er, venison jerky. It was complete chaos and fabulous. And his rendition of our national anthem is one of the most inspired I have ever heard.

Chevy Chase—Either TC or Greg had mispronounced Chevy's name moments before he was calling in. So here I was set to interview the star of *Caddyshack*, one of the best movies of all time, something I have watched two dozen times, and all I could think about was whether it was CHevy or SHevy? SHevy or CHevy? No matter—I loved Chevy Chase in *Caddyshack*, and got him talking about his interplay with Bill Murray in the famous scene with the bong ("Cannonball!!"). He told me that he and Murray came up with that scene at lunch and delivered it largely unscripted.

From Auschwitz—I'm one of a half dozen Philadelphia friends who regularly travel after New Year's to historic sites about which we have read. One year we wanted to study the Holocaust, so we read Anne Frank's *Diary of a Young Girl*, Sir Martin Gilbert's *Auschwitz and the Allies*, and Elie Wiesel's *Night*. Then we traveled to Berlin to see the

Wannsee villa, where on January 20, 1945, officials of the Third Reich plotted the Final Solution. Next it was on to Track 17 in the fashionable Grunewalt section of Berlin; the former station was a point of departure for Jews from that area being sent to camps. It is a terribly sad but important historical site. Listed next to the tracks are the dates, number of passengers, and destination of the railcars. We next went to see the ends of those tracks—in Poland. There, on a raw, dark, rainswept day, we spent four hours walking the grounds of Auschwitz I and Auschwitz II–Birkenau. At Auschwitz I, we walked through the infamous gate ("Work Brings Freedom"). We toured the surviving crematorium. We saw the ghastly displays of human hair, personal effects, suitcases, even shoe polish, all confiscated from the prisoners who'd packed in haste under the ruse of "resettlement." Also there: empty canisters that had held pellets of Zyklon B, the agent used to exterminate human life in the crematoriums. In the midst of the visit I was an extended caller to my own program, which on that day was guest hosted by Dom G. I knew I could capture for my radio listeners only some of what I had seen. Still, it was an unforgettable broadcast.

Buzz Bissinger—Pulitzer Prize–winning journalist and author of *Friday Night Lights*, Buzz is an old friend. When *Friday Night Lights* was made into a movie, I had him in studio with the director, Peter Berg. I had been invited to a private screening of the movie a week before and had taken my father with me. My father loves football, especially high school football. For years he was a high school and college referee, and then stadium announcer for my alma mater, C.B. West, when they were perennial state champions. Well, Dad did not like the movie. He thought it was a negative portrayal of high school athletes and high school athletics in general, and I thought he made some valid points. So I invited him to come into the studio when Buzz appeared and share with Buzz his concerns, on the radio. I thought it would be a good conversation. I had no intention of ambushing Buzz with my seventy-year-old father, but I did not tell Buzz in advance, which was probably a mistake. Well, Buzz didn't take kindly to Dad's appearance, dressed in his C.B. West football letterman jacket. And I didn't take kindly to Buzz's treatment of my dad. While we were on air, Buzz ripped off his headphones and stormed out of the studio, with at least twenty "Fuck that," "I don't have to fucking sit here," and "Fuck yous" as he went out the door. Berg was gentleman enough to finish out the interview. Philly is a small town. Months later, I was at a bar mitzvah for my friend Larry Ceisler's son Danny. At the next table, I saw Buzz. The room was relatively small. There was no way to avoid crossing paths. So I walked up behind him and asked him if he wanted the "salmon or the filet." He said salmon, I think, and when he turned around, perhaps recognizing my voice, we shared a laugh.

Steve Lopez—I try not to let my grudges get in the way of a good interview, but I'm not about to leave past injustices off the table. Not long ago, a friend asked if I would interview former *Philadelphia Inquirer* and now *Los Angeles Times* columnist Steve Lopez about his best-selling new book *The Soloist*. I said I would, but this was calling in a major chit because of my disdain for the writer. After all, I almost sued the man. About fifteen years had passed since he wrote something nasty about me when he was with the *Philadelphia Inquirer*. I was then a young presidential appointee working in the administration of Bush 41. Lopez questioned my honesty and I was super pissed. I wanted to sue him. To investigate if a claim existed, I contacted a legendary trial lawyer named Jim Beasley. Beasley had just recorded the largest libel verdict in Pennsylvania history against the very same *Inquirer* on behalf of another Philadelphia lawyer named Richard Sprague. Sprague is often credited with the victory, but it was actually Beasley who litigated the case to verdict—twice. The verdict was for $4 million in the first case. In the second trial, the verdict was for $34 million. Clearly, he was the man for the job. In the end, Beasley said he would take the case, but we never filed the lawsuit. Instead, he hired me. I practiced law at his side for ten years, and it was a wonderful and prosperous relationship. Which, I guess, explains my willingness to have Steve Lopez in my studio. Of course, I began the interview by telling him all of this. Then we discussed his book, which happened to be terrific and is being made into a movie. By the way, my friend who asked if I would interview Lopez? The aforementioned Buzz Bissinger. I told you, Philly is a very small town.

Best Friend of the Phillie Phanatic—I love the Phillie Phanatic— there is no greater mascot in all of professional sports. Tom Burgoyne has worn the suit—I mean, has been the best friend—of the Phanatic for fifteen years. His big, green, furry body language says it all! The Phanatic came into the studio one day on the way to the Phillies World Series Championship. By the end of the morning, the costume was partially off and Tom gave me a classic interview about what it's like being *that* close to a pro mascot. Busy, hot, and never dull!

Bernie Parent—The Philadelphia Flyers great, and my boyhood hero back when "only the Lord saved more than Parent," has become a great friend of the show. One morning we had a Man Show—a remote broadcast at an upscale grooming spot called Shaving Grace—complete with segments on all the things that interest guys: beer, whiskey, hot dogs, cigars, Sinatra, and sports! Why at Shaving Grace? Well, it began as my idea that we needed to encourage balding men to shave their heads, and many with classic male pattern baldness did so for the first time that day. Bernie did not shave his mane, but he held court that day as a man among men. As he is fond of saying, "It's a beautiful thing."

Cheryl Hines and Teri Hatcher—I always say that Cheryl Hines is my TV wife, which I guess makes Teri Hatcher my TV girlfriend. I love Cheryl as Larry David's wife on *Curb Your Enthusiasm*—my favorite episode featuring my TV spouse is #38. Wandering Bear, the Native American gardener, gives Larry some herbs to help heal Cheryl's nether regions, which were numbed by an inside-out condom. On *Curb*, Cheryl is shocked by Wandering Bear asking her the next day, "How is your vagina?" So I felt it only appropriate to ask her the same question when I got her on air. She laughed uproariously . . . clearly I was right to have her as my TV wife. Now if I'm asking Cheryl about her vagina, obviously I have to ask Teri Hatcher about her breasts. Who can forget the *Seinfeld* episode where she storms out on Jerry, leaving him with the killer line about natural vs. implants. I interviewed Teri about her book *Burnt Toast* and she played along when I asked her by repeating, "They're real and they're spectacular." By the way, on a one to ten Greg Stocker scale, both of these segments get a ten. The Bush, Clinton, and Obama interviews? Probably a collective five in his book.

Cybill Shepherd—Cybill, Cybill, Cybill! I suppose my morning-drive show could be considered early for some folks, especially those from the West Coast. Cybill was in town raising awareness for some sort of bladder or kidney disease or some such thing. . . . I know . . . Irritable Bowel Syndrome. I kid you not. She had a syndrome that morning alright, but not of the bowel type. She arrived fully made up but somewhat disheveled, and that fantastic Southern drawl was slurry and unfocused, but what a great interview! I asked her about Elvis. (The answer is yes.) And she swooned over Yul Brynner and Bruce Willis's current look, saying she found bald men incredibly sexy. I told her to look at me when she said that! I kept her for a full segment even though she was almost falling off her stool in the studio. Stool . . . no pun intended. . . . She attributed her speech impediment that morning to jet lag. Sure.

Yes—I played a role in having August 7, 2002, designated as Yes Day in Philadelphia, and later that day I also had all five members of the band in my studio—not the usual fare for so-called "conservative" talk radio! Jon Anderson, Chris Squire, Steve Howe, Alan White, and Rick Wakeman were all cramped in my tight space for a full hour regaling their many fans and me with what you might call Tales from Topographic Oceans. And when the show ended, they all came to a cookout in my backyard. Someday I will write an entire book about that one day.

Kenny Gamble—Speaking of music, I once had the legendary producer, one half of the Rock and Roll Hall of Fame Philly team Gamble and Huff, which supplied us with so much of the soundtrack of our lives, in my studio. It was July 3, 2008, and Gamble was set to debut a new song, "I Am an American," for the conclusion of fireworks over the Philadelphia skyline the very next night. We relished playing a clip of Patti LaBelle's soulful voice singing this patriotic tune, but my favorite story of the morning was how Gamble and Huff came up with their classic "Me and Mrs. Jones." You know—"we got a thing, going on." Kenny told me that he and Leon Huff used to frequent a particular Philly lunch spot where every day they would see a distinguished older man in the company of a beautiful young woman. They wondered if the two had a thing going on, and so Gamble and Huff spun a story around the two that eventually they put to music as the incomparable "Me and Mrs. Jones."

Wild Bill Guarnere and Babe Heffron—You will never find two more heroic men, two better friends, or two more exceptional radio guests than Wild Bill and Babe. They are two of the men of World War II's Easy Company, immortalized by Stephen Ambrose in *Band of Brothers*. They are also Philly guys. They are classic. They are bawdy. And they are national treasures. I am honored every time they step into my studio.

Maya Angelou—I interviewed the captivating and melodious Dr. Angelou to promote her book *Letters to My Daughter*. Her voice is intoxicating. As she spoke, I recalled her reading poetry at the inauguration of President Clinton and I wanted very much for her to read something to me from her new book. I picked something out and asked if she would indulge me. She told me she had something better: a gospel song she had written in honor of her grandmother. Dr. Angelou proceeded to sing to me, a cappella:

> *You said to lean on your arm*
> *And I am leaning*
> *You said to trust in your love*
> *And I am trusting*
> *You said to call on your name*
> *And I am calling*
> *I'm stepping out on your word*

Chapter 20

The "P" Word

Profiling: Let's look for terrorists who look like terrorists. In virtually every instance, they have age, race, gender, ethnicity, religion, and appearance in common. Those characteristics should be considered in seeking to prevent strikes against us. Everyone must be screened, but some more than others.

If you haven't seen this list, or one like it, you should:

Takeover of the U.S. Embassy in Iran, November 4, 1979: A group of militant Iranian students ambushed the U.S. Embassy to show their support for the Iranian revolution. The revolutionaries had been opposed to Mohammad Reza Pahlavi, the Shah of Iran, whom the United States had supported in the CIA-generated coup of 1953. The students took fifty-two diplomats hostage for a total of 444 days before releasing them as Ronald Reagan was being sworn in as president.[1]

Bombing of U.S. Marine Barracks in Beirut, October 23, 1983: During the Lebanese Civil War, two truck bombs struck buildings that housed members of the Multinational Force. Out of the 241 Americans killed, 220 were Marines, constituting the worst single-day loss for the Marine Corps since the Battle of Iwo Jima in World War II. In addition to the Americans who were killed, fifty-eight French servicemen were killed, along with six civilians. The identity of the attackers is still unknown, though the U.S. government has long suspected that Imad Mughniyah, a terrorist thought to be involved in an early incarnation of Hezbollah, was responsible.[2]

Hijacking of the *Achille Lauro*, October 7, 1985: Hijackers from the Palestinian Liberation Front took control of the *Achille Lauro*, an ocean liner sailing in Egypt from Alexandria to Port Said. As the hijackers directed the vessel towards Syria, they demanded the release of fifty Palestinian prisoners in Israel and murdered a wheelchair-bound American named Leon Klinghoffer. After days of negotiating, the hijackers agreed to abandon their mission, and were flown out of Egypt on a commercial airliner that was intercepted by U.S. fighter jets.[3]

Bombing of Pan Am Flight 103, December 21, 1988: A New York–bound Pan Am flight that originated at London Heathrow Airport was destroyed by a bomb over Lockerbie, Scotland. Libyan nationals were to blame for the disaster that killed 270 people, including more than 180 Americans and eleven people on the ground in Scotland.[4] The U.S. State Department later characterized the bombing as "an action authorized by the Libyan Government."[5]

World Trade Center Bombing, February 26, 1993: A truck packed with explosives blew up in a garage below the World Trade Center in New York, leaving six dead and more than one thousand injured. It was the first instance of Middle Eastern terrorism making its way to American shores. Ramzi Yousef, the mastermind of the attack who is serving a life sentence for his role, is the nephew of Khalid Sheikh Mohammed, operations planner of 9/11.[6]

Bombing of U.S. Embassies in Kenya and Tanzania, August 7, 1998: More than two hundred people were killed when two bombs exploded within minutes of each other at the American embassies in Nairobi, Kenya, and Dar es Salaam, Tanzania. The United States retaliated two weeks later with airstrikes targeting al-Qaeda training camps in Afghanistan and Sudan.[7] Ali Mohamed, an Egyptian-born U.S. citizen and former sergeant in the U.S. Army, was the first to plead guilty to the bombing, telling a U.S. court that bin Laden had personally reviewed his surveillance work and suggested places where the explosives-laden trucks could do the most damage.[8]

Attack on USS *Cole*, October 12, 2000: Two suicide bombers steered an explosives-laden boat into the USS *Cole* (then refueling at the Yemeni port in Aden), killing seventeen U.S. sailors and injuring almost forty more. Six al-Qaeda terrorists were charged in a Yemeni court in connection with the attack—two of them were sentenced to death in 2004.[9] In 2007 a federal judge ruled that the Sudanese government also bore responsibility for the attack, agreeing with a lawsuit brought by the families of the seventeen victims that alleged that Sudan allowed the terrorist network to host training camps within its borders.[10]

Attack on the World Trade Center and U.S. Pentagon, September 11, 2001: Nineteen suicide militants, most of them Saudis, hijacked four planes and flew them into the World Trade Center in New York City and the Pentagon near Washington, D.C. A fourth plane, thought to be headed towards the Capitol in Washington, crashed in a field in Somerset County, Pennsylvania. More than three thousand Americans were killed. Six weeks later, the United States launched attacks against al-Qaeda and the Taliban in Afghanistan.

"Shoebomber" Richard Reid, December 22, 2001: Nearly four months after 9/11, a British convert to Islam, Richard Reid, boarded American Airlines Flight 63, which was flying from Paris to Miami. Reid's explosives, which were hidden in his shoes, went undetected by airport security. After a flight attendant smelled something burning in the cabin, she noticed Reid attempting to light a fuse on his shoes. The would-be bomber attacked her, but was quickly subdued by other passengers. The flight was diverted to Boston's Logan International Airport, and Reid was found guilty on terrorism charges in Massachusetts on January 30, 2003.[11] Intelligence documents later indicated that Reid was an al-Qaeda operative who reported to Khalid Sheikh Mohammed.[12]

Bali Bombing, October 12, 2002: Two bombs exploded in a busy nightclub area on the Indonesian island of Bali, killing 202 people, most of whom were foreign tourists (seven Americans were among the victims). A third bomb exploded near the U.S. consulate, but no one was injured as a result. Authorities believe a Southeast Asian militant network with ties to al-Qaeda was responsible for the attack, which was the deadliest terrorist strike in Indonesian history.[13]

Madrid Bombing, March 11, 2004: Ten bombs exploded on four crowded commuter trains in Madrid, killing almost two hundred and leaving more than eighteen hundred injured. It was the deadliest terrorist attack in Europe since the Pan Am Flight 103 bombing, and was orchestrated three days before Spain's general election. The subsequent investigation revealed that the perpetrators comprised a network of Islamic extremists inspired by al-Qaeda.[14]

London Bombing, July 7, 2005: Four separate bombs exploded on three London trains and one bus during the morning rush hour, killing fifty-two people and wounding more than seven hundred—a day after it was announced that London had been selected to host the 2012 Olympic Games. A video recording and last will left by one of the bombers offers that the attacks were meant as retaliation for "atrocities" committed by the West against Muslims.[15]

Mumbai Attacks, November 2008: At least 173 people were killed and hundreds were injured in coordinated machine gun and grenade attacks in the Indian commercial and financial capital of Mumbai in late November of 2008. In the days after the assault, Indian authorities claimed the ten attackers were Pakistani militants between the ages of eighteen and twenty-eight, which reportedly matched claims by Ajmal Amir Qasab, the only terrorist apprehended alive. Qasab told Indian police he and his co-conspirators had trained for six months in camps operated by Lashkar-e-Taiba, a militant group based in Pakistan.[16]

So. . . . Notice any commonalities among these thirteen incidents? All acts of terrorism. And all committed by young male Middle Eastern Islamic extremists. But of course, saying such things is politically incorrect if you are a public servant.

Not even the 9/11 Commission, which I thought did an otherwise comprehensive job, had the courage to say that in a war being waged against young Arab males who are religious fanatics, the United States ought to be on guard against young Arab males who are religious fanatics.

The closest it came to recommending adequate terrorist-targeting was to recognize the need to trust "subjective judgment."[17] Maybe that's code for "profiling," because those words are used in connection with the case of a "potential hijacker who was turned back by an immigration inspector as he tried to enter the U.S."[18]

I know what episode the commission was talking about: the road-block to martyrdom that Jose Melendez Perez threw in front of Mohammed al-Kahtani. Melendez screened Kahtani, who was being met at the airport by Mohammed Atta, in Orlando on August 4, 2001. Taking into account Kahtani's Saudi nationality, his grooming, military appearance, dress, and physique, as well as his attitude, Melendez refused to let the would-be twentieth hijacker into the country. That's why Flight 93, which crashed in Pennsylvania, had only four hijackers—one less than each of the three planes that reached their ultimate destinations.

When Melendez testified before the 9/11 Commission, commissioner Richard Ben-Veniste correctly concluded, "Taking into account that the only plane commandeered by four hijackers, rather than five, crashed before reaching its target, it is entirely plausible to suggest that your actions in doing your job efficiently and competently may well have contributed to saving the Capitol or the White House, and all the people who were in those buildings, those monuments to our democracy, from being included in the catastrophe of 9/11, and for that we all owe you a debt of thanks and gratitude."[19]

To the commission, Melendez exercised "subjective judgment." To me, he engaged in profiling, and his willingness to do so saved either the White House or the Capitol. I wish Melendez's heroism figured more in the 9/11 Commission's conclusions, because no doubt it would have inspired a recommendation like this: "While the United States government still values civil liberties, protecting our homeland in the midst of a post-9/11 reality should demand that we err on the side of national defense."

My hunch? This is purely speculation, but I believe the commission was intent on issuing a completely unanimous opinion, and that former U.S. naval secretary and then 9/11 commissioner John Lehman just couldn't muster the votes on this issue. I say that because I know he gets it. "The fact is that Norwegian women are not, and eighty-five-year-old women with aluminum walkers are not, the source of the terrorist threat," he told me in 2004. "Our enemy is violent Islamic extremism, and the overwhelming number of people that one needs to worry about are young Arab males."[20]

Unfortunately, instead of Lehman's blunt understanding of the situation, we got more Norman Mineta–speak when it came to targeting terrorists. Mineta, who was secretary of transportation from 2001 until 2006, refused to heighten security concerning young Arab males because he carried with him the scars of his own internment in a Japanese-American camp in World War II. Typical of his statements was this: "The terrorists have used our open society against us. In wartime, government calls for greater powers, and then the need . . . recedes after the war ends. This struggle will go on. Therefore, while protecting our homeland, Americans should be mindful of threats to vital personal and civil liberties. This balancing is no easy task, but we must constantly strive to keep it right."[21] I respect the personal experiences that shaped Mineta's views—but they are views that overlook the fact that we have street smarts and profiling to thank for the fact that the White House and Capitol were not struck by Flight 93 on 9/11.

There's also this: A two-hundred-page study released in July 2008 by Rand Corporation examined terrorist groups and activities between 1968 and 2006, and determined that terrorists were defeated by local law enforcement and policing efforts more than four times as often as by military action.[22] In other words, Rand's historical analysis determined that terrorists like the ones who perpetrated the 9/11 attacks are more likely to be caught or killed when they are deemed criminals and their captors act like police officers.

It's appalling, but here's the truth: Even the horrifying dose of reality that was 9/11 didn't inspire our country to pursue security *the right way*. Don't get me wrong, we're looking out for the bad guys. We're just not using the most effective, efficient strategies to do it.

It's an itch I've been trying to scratch for years now. I wrote my first book, *Flying Blind: How Political Correctness Continues to Compromise Airline Security Post 9/11*, after my eight-year-old son was singled out—twice—for secondary screening in March of 2004. An inefficient but necessary price to pay after the airport security breakdowns of September 11, I thought initially—until the 9/11 Commission hearings revealed that the U.S. Department of Transportation (DOT) actually *limited* the number of young Arab males who can be pulled aside for secondary questioning. In April of 2004, Secretary Lehman told me that the DOT *fined* airlines that were "caught having more than two people of the same ethnic persuasion in a secondary line for questioning, including and especially two Arabs."[23]

In other words, while operations like the Israeli-owned El Al put their passengers through tougher questioning with the objective of sniffing out actual terrorists (rather than the bombs and weapons they might use), those tasked with airline security in the United States are bound by a quota. The message to potential terrorists is clear: Flood that quota, and U.S. airlines' hands are tied.

The result is the pre-9/11 mindset that threatens to lull us away from the realities of the dangers we face. I don't believe airlines are still being fined, but that is probably because they are reluctant to do anything that could be considered profiling. I'm not saying we should only screen young Arab men, or that we should screen every young Arab man that gets onto a plane. But we cannot ignore the commonalities in age, gender, nationality, religion, and appearance of the nineteen men responsible for 9/11 and other acts of terrorism. Some types of people simply need to be screened more than others, and once our lawmakers can swallow that reality, the more effective we can be in working to keep our skies safe.

Chapter 21

Talking Points

Time for another *Seinfeld* moment. In season five's "The Opposite," George takes a lonely walk on the beach and comes to the realization that "every decision I've ever made, in my entire life, has been wrong." So of course, when Jerry goads him into doing the opposite ("If every instinct you have is wrong, then the opposite would have to be right"), George starts by ordering chicken salad on untoasted rye with a side of potato salad (instead of his usual tuna on toast with a side of coleslaw). Next he goes for tea instead of coffee. And a minute later, instead of shrinking from the chance to start a conversation with an attractive woman, George sidles up to her and tells her: "My name is George. I'm unemployed and live with my parents." He ends up dating her—and her uncle sets George up for his infamous stint with the Yankees.[1]

I love that episode. And after I referenced it a few times on my radio program, I was delighted to get an e-mail from the man who wrote the script, Andy Cowan. It turns out his father is a listener and alerted his son that I admired his work. Maybe I have such an appreciation for Cowan's work because there are so many days when I leave the radio studio feeling a bit like George Costanza. In other words, I feel as if I have done the opposite, by taking the route contrary to that deemed to be good talk radio. Anytime anyone in a prominent talk radio position deviates from the conventionally held, and almost uniformly repeated, conservative talking points, they are doing the opposite. And yet, like George, I sometimes feel like the circumstances demand such an approach. I work in a medium dominated by ideologues and doctrinaire types who are loath to acknowledge any middle of the road; in fact, they portray compromise as a sign of weakness. And they have conditioned talk radio listeners to expect to hear only the right-wing perspective, so that the listeners themselves become intolerant of anything shy of that standard.

My interview with Lieutenant Colonel Orson Swindle is a perfect example. Col. Swindle is an awfully impressive man. He is a veteran of the U.S. Marines with over two hundred fighter missions and twenty military decorations for valor in Vietnam. He visited my radio program as a surrogate for his friend, John McCain, on October 9, 2008. There was no mystery as to why he would be my guest. Ten days later I would publicly declare my support for Barack Obama, but I gladly welcomed Col. Swindle to the airwaves and made a conscious decision not to cross swords with him.

Col. Swindle met Senator McCain in a Vietnamese prison in 1971, and as Col. Swindle told me, the two slept side by side in a cell for eighteen months. Senator McCain's former cellmate provided my audience and me with a unique window into the Republican presidential candidate's character and honor, a glimpse into a time when he probably felt farther away from the White House than most of us could ever understand. Col. Swindle described an honorable and courageous friend whose memory and love of history served him well in prison, where embarking on "projects" like reconstructing the history of the world or reciting the development of the American novel would serve to keep imprisoned troops' minds occupied and sharp.

Truly, I intended to yield the floor for as long as Col. Swindle wished to talk about his friend's candidacy. But as the interview progressed and Col. Swindle spoke increasingly about Senator Obama and less about Senator McCain, I found it necessary to challenge—as deferentially as possible—some of his assertions.

When I tossed one underhand to Col. Swindle—what do voters in Pennsylvania, New Jersey, and Delaware need to know about the Republican nominee for the presidency?—he told me about the sense of duty and love of country Senator McCain had displayed in the Hanoi Hilton. But then he went a step further: "I think that experience in prison pushed all these qualities which are necessary for great leaders—intellect, intelligence, courage, and character—pushed them all together and tested them," Col. Swindle told me. "And he came out of it experienced and totally committed for the rest of his life to giving back to his country and doing what he thought was best for his country, and that's why he'll make a great president. Barack Obama has none of these qualities."

Eager to avoid a politically charged discussion, I attempted to steer the conversation back to their time in the Hanoi Hilton. I asked Col. Swindle about his friend's decision to forgo early release when offered it by his North Vietnamese captors, but here again, his answer included an Obama reference:

He knew the damage it would do to the POWs that were there before him, who by all rights of international standards would be released before him. He knew the harm it would do his father, his family, his Navy, our efforts in South Vietnam. And he just said, you know, I can't do this. Honor tells me I have to stick this out and pray for the best. Not many political figures would do that. That is an act that Barack Obama cannot begin to even fathom. And this is the kind of act—this single act is probably the most dramatic illustration of why John McCain needs to be our president.

The negative reference to Obama made me cringe again.

We elect presidents for the things that we have not yet seen. Who would have imagined that President Bush would be confronted by the 9/11 tragedy? It's things over the horizon. Because we don't know what those things are, we want people who are tested and qualified and have the attributes that we feel comfortable can cope with those things we have not yet seen. That's why it's important to elect John McCain. Barack Obama has never done anything in his life—he's been on the take most of his life from public funds. You know, you're known by the friends you keep. I can list you five hundred people who are great admirals, generals, secretaries of state, great business leaders, great enlisted leaders in the military, hundreds of POWs who would talk to you for thirty minutes about the character and courage and qualifications of John McCain. Can you name one person who can do that for Barack Obama?

Now I had to say something. I knew Col. Swindle had witnessed firsthand the sense of honor and valor with which Senator McCain had conducted himself in Hanoi, but I couldn't allow him to take what I regarded as a cheap shot at Barack Obama in the process of discussing those experiences. So I answered Swindle: Yes, I could name many people who could attest to Senator Obama's character and love of country. But I also told him that I admired him and Senator McCain, and didn't want to engage him in a political discussion. The colonel was persistent and soon reasserted: "[Obama] has been the recipient of public funds most of his life. He has never done much of anything to serve his country. His accomplishment is winning the Democrat nomination, which is extraordinary. But he did it by . . . we don't know who he is. . . . Hillary Clinton was by far the more qualified candidate."

I took particular umbrage with the idea that Americans "didn't know" Senator Obama, because I believed that to be a tacit way of fueling the anonymous online slurs that had dogged his candidacy for months, and that's exactly what I told Col. Swindle. What he meant, he explained, was that despite being "wrapped" in the mantra of change, some of Senator Obama's relationships—Tony Rezco, Reverend Wright, Bill Ayers—were cause for further investigation into his life and associations. I conceded to my guest that part of the reason he felt that way was the free ride Senator Obama had received from the media throughout much of the primary campaign. But matters like Reverend Wright? Fully litigated, I asserted.

To which Col. Swindle responded by recounting the two so-called "change" elections in his lifetime, 2006 and 1976. Since 2006, he said, "things have gone to hell in a hand basket." As for 1976, replacing president Gerald Ford with Jimmy Carter "was a disaster if you recall. Obama is less qualified and less intelligent and experienced than President Carter."

Obama less intelligent? Here's how our conversation ended:

MAS: The man was president of the Harvard Law Review. *Colonel, you're making it so hard for me to maintain my sense of decorum. He was the president of the* Harvard Law Review, *and you're going to tell me he doesn't have the intellect?*

Col. Swindle: No, I didn't say he didn't have the intellect. I said he does not have the intellect of President Carter. He's obviously a very smart guy. He's a very attractive candidate. For crying out loud, he's an extremely attractive candidate. He's one of the best speakers I've ever heard in my life. But I didn't say he didn't have the intellect. I didn't say that.

MAS: *I honor your service, and I mean that most sincerely. It's a privilege for me to have you here. I've yielded the floor and I'm anxious to hear whatever you have to tell me and I hope you feel—*

Col. Swindle: *You've been very kind, very generous. I appreciate that.[2]*

OK. I have just offered a straightforward presentation of what transpired in the interview. I remember that when the call ended, I was pleased with how I had handled it. I had given an American hero the opportunity to say whatever he wanted about his good friend who was running for president. In a manner he described as "kind" and "generous," I questioned only those gratuitous slaps he took at his friend's opponent. But when I looked up from the microphone at my computer screen of callers, I had a surprise waiting for me. The lines were full. And people were pissed. The colonel may have been pleased with his treatment on my show, but the callers were outraged that I would have done anything but fawn all over him—even when he was cheap-shotting Obama. The e-mail messages were similar and unrelenting.

Of course, lost on those who decried my "mistreatment" of Col. Swindle was the list of evenly divided guests I had hosted on the radio that very week: Pennsylvania (nonpartisan) pollster Dr. Terry Madonna; Obama spokesman Bill Burton; Ted Nugent, the rarest of breeds, a conservative gun-toting rock star; McCain surrogate and former governor Tom Ridge; former U.S. senator (and Obama supporter) Bill Bradley; former Republican presidential candidate and housing secretary Jack Kemp; and Senator Obama himself.

Aside from hosting a presidential aspirant a month before the election, that was a very typical week on my program—an even split between the two sides of the aisle and my best effort to present all sides of an issue fairly without surrendering my own point of view, no matter what side it happened to fall upon. But the presence of certain of those guests had fallen on deaf ears attached to the heads of conservative listeners. It occurred to me that because of the knee-jerk conservatism so prevalent elsewhere along the talk radio dial, they had grown accustomed to hearing only viewpoints with which the host, and they as listeners, agreed. In my case, because people know I'm a lifelong Republican or assume I'm an unwavering conservative, they expect to hear only those perspectives becoming of an authentic right-winger. But that's just not the way I have ever run my program.

As I carried my mantra deeper into the 2008 presidential election season, I encountered more and more e-mails and calls from listeners claiming they'd "had enough" and would no longer be tuning in to my program. Some said they couldn't understand how I could *even consider* voting for a Democratic candidate for president. Others said my slow but sure movement toward liberalism was nearing completion. Many more complained that I had sold my political soul to the mainstream media and MSNBC in the hopes of furthering my career.

The implication is clear: Airing different sides of an issue isn't being fair or covering all your bases, it's waffling. Practically speaking, in today's talk radio world, being "fair and balanced" actually only requires showing fairness to the right side of the political spectrum. The shame of this state of radio is that these attitudes only serve to shut down the informative debates we need to be having about the important issues of the day. Let me be clear—the last thing we need is the reintroduction of the Fairness Doctrine, which essentially required broadcasters to balance controversial subject matter with opposing views. That's a dated and ridiculous notion.

What we need instead are hosts who do not feel obliged to repeat only the talking points. A host like, Tim Russert.

To the extent I have ever had a role model in the talking-head business, I would look to Tim Russert before anyone on the radio. He didn't become the preeminent political journalist in the nation by browbeating, condescending, or stifling debate. Which doesn't mean he asked guests to check their partisanship at the door, or that he was devoid of strong views. To the contrary, Russert's was a forum where clear differences would emerge, but minus the edge that has otherwise become commonplace. Through direct discourse, not shouting and cross talk, he guaranteed that all sides would be represented, and not in a carnival atmosphere. He was forceful, yet deferential. He'd ask the tough questions, and then afford an opportunity for a response. Had he been a radio man instead of a TV personality, I wonder if Russert's approach would have survived in this climate.

I interviewed Russert twice—once after the publication of each of his two books, *Big Russ and Me* and *Wisdom of Our Fathers.* He was as impressive on the receiving end of questions as when he was the questioner. Perhaps his greatest gift, I found in our interactions, was his humble, down-to-earth nature, no doubt a mindset he gleaned from his dad. When we last spoke, almost a year to the day before he died, Russert told me he admired the "quiet eloquence" of his father's hard work. Well, like father, like son.

One funny story. Not long after I interviewed Russert about *Big Russ and Me,* I selected that title for reading by a small, informal book club to which I belong, the same guys with whom I went to Auschwitz after we read extensively about the Holocaust. Not only do we read, but we also drink and eat, and generally enjoy one another's company. Sometimes the books are an excuse for the other activities. Well, I asked Russert if he would mind calling us while we were gathered and chatting with the group for a few minutes about his book. There was no upside in his giving us his time, but the host of *Meet the Press,* the most esteemed talk show in America, obliged. That night, in a small private dining room in a French restaurant outside Philadelphia, his call arrived. He was on a cell phone from his car, and we lost the connection soon after. But the guys were thrilled, and Russert seemed to get a kick out of their interest in his book. Months later, I met him at an NBC party in the Rainbow Room high atop Rockefeller Center, where we spoke for a few minutes. I was anxious to talk politics; he wanted to know more about my gathering of guys he had called. I painted the picture of our end of the call, especially the camaraderie he had inspired. Tim Russert seemed to genuinely enjoy the fact that for one night, he'd been the catalyst for such friendship.

What a shame that listeners, viewers, and fellow journalists, so many of whom feted the *Meet the Press* host after his tragic death, don't follow his lead in his absence.

Chapter 22
Torture

Torture: **Once we identify the bad guys, we have to get the information from them on impending attacks by any means necessary, and that includes torture. If you believe it not to be efficacious, tell me: Why do our best interrogators continually seek to use it as a technique? Answer: It works.**

How do you debate the propriety of torture with a guy who has been tortured? Say, John McCain, for example? I had such an exchange with the senator on this subject when I hosted him for my radio book club on December 2, 2005. Senator McCain was with me in front of a group of several hundred to discuss his book *Character Is Destiny.* I had also read his memoir, *Faith of My Fathers*, which offers an incredible recounting of his twenty-third bombing mission in Vietnam. It began aboard the carrier USS *Oriskany* on October 26, 1967, and ended when he took enemy fire, had his wing shot off, and ejected from his A-4 Skyhawk while traveling at 550 miles per hour. The force of the ejection smashed McCain into his aircraft, breaking both his arms (the right in three places) and his right knee. He was briefly knocked unconscious.

"I landed in the middle of the lake, in the middle of the city, in the middle of the day," he wrote.[1]

When he came to, he was being hauled ashore on bamboo poles by a group of angry Vietnamese. Someone smashed a rifle butt into his shoulder, breaking it, and another stuck his ankle and groin with a bayonet. That was only the beginning of the constant torture that McCain experienced during more than five years as a POW.

Offered early release, McCain deferred to the Code of Conduct that obliged him to refuse freedom until it was given to those who had been captured earlier than he. When asked to identify the members of his squadron, McCain dutifully obliged by reciting the offensive line of the Green Bay Packers. When instructed to diagram an aircraft carrier, his sketch included a swimming pool on the fantail. He also painfully recounts submitting to a confession on the fourth straight day of a particularly horrific series of beatings. Heroic doesn't begin to describe his ordeal.

Fast-forward nearly forty years. The Senate twice voted in support of a McCain-sponsored measure that would prohibit the "cruel, inhuman, or degrading treatment or punishment" of any person in U.S. custody regardless of location, a direct response to a *Washington Post* revelation that al-Qaeda detainees are being held in Eastern European locales called "black sites," where we take prisoners so the gloves can come off.[2]

So I thought Senator McCain was the perfect person to ask why, if torture is supposedly an unproductive tool of interrogation, some experts still use it as a technique to obtain information. I knew we were headed for disagreement. I had heard him say this on *Face the Nation*: "If we are viewed as a country that engages in torture . . . any possible information we might be able to gain is far counterbalanced by (the negative) effect of public opinion."[3]

Well, just as I was aware of the senator's strong opinion on the subject, it became apparent that he also knew of my feelings. Not long into our discussion, he made reference to my position, indicating that he had seen my columns on the issue. In fact, I had written one just three weeks before he arrived for my book club, in which I said that I particularly disagreed with him on the subject of torture. When the topic was raised during the book club event, he said, "I'd be glad to talk about this whole torture issue, which Mike and I have a mild disagreement on—" and I interrupted him by saying, "You've read the clip files, I see." Now that I knew that the senator was aware of our difference of opinion, I was eager to hear his thoughts. I asked him why we still use torture if it is supposedly a useless tactic. Here's what he said:

"[T]here is a near desperation in the Pentagon to try to get intelligence to try to foil these attacks that are so insidious and so awful and so terrible and tragic that are inflicted upon young Americans."

He went on to say that torture damages a unique reputation that America has carefully built in its short history: "I can tell you that the image of the United States in the world is not good. [A]bu

Ghraib . . . those films were shown on Al Jazeera 24/7 for weeks and weeks and weeks. We're in two wars . . . but there's also a war of ideas and ideals and image, and I believe that the United States of America still remains the greatest hope of oppressed people throughout the world. We are a beacon of hope and freedom. We are the example they want to follow, and we hurt that image when we do the kinds of things that we've unfortunately found out have been done. Sorry, Michael."

John McCain is compelling but not persuasive with me on this subject, and we can ruminate about the case of Sajida Mubarak al-Rishawi to further the argument. She's the thirty-five-year-old Iraqi woman who walked into the Radisson Hotel in Amman, Jordan, in 2005, hoping to kill celebrants at a wedding party with the bomb strapped to her belly. Her bomb didn't go off, but her husband's did, sending him to hell and killing people whose only crime was going to a wedding.

She was believed to be the sister of a man with ties to Abu Musab al-Zarqawi, the former al-Qaeda leader in Iraq, who was killed in a bombing raid in 2006. In a TV confession, she offered details of the Radisson bombing plot.[4]

But let's take it a step further. Let's assume she knows a significant piece of information—Zarqawi's whereabouts or the target of some future terrorist attack—but won't flip for a piece of quiche and a warm blanket. Now what? I say do whatever is necessary to get her to talk. Waterboard her. Strap her to a pig. Whatever it takes.

And guess who agrees with me in such an instance? In a "ticking time bomb" scenario, I think even John McCain would agree with me. Senator McCain told *Newsweek* in 2005 that presidents have an obligation to step over the bounds of the "cruel, inhuman, or degrading treatment or punishment" limitations and get the information necessary to save American lives. "You do what you have to do. But you take responsibility for it," McCain said at the time.

Maybe our views aren't so divergent after all. Let me be clear: I am not in favor of giving military interrogators a free hand in all circumstances—or with all prisoners of war—to use any means they believe necessary to procure information from enemy combatants. But I do believe that in certain instances, most notably those in which we have captured a murderous terrorist or a person who has knowledge of an imminent act of terrorism, that harsh methods of interrogation are appropriate. That includes waterboarding. I also note that for all of the hullabaloo over torture since 9/11, the published record suggests that we have waterboarded exactly three al-Qaeda members.[5] That suggests to me that America has not presided over a situation out of control.

Nonetheless, the debate about the efficacy of harsh tactics has raged for years now—both in public and behind the scenes of the highest-level U.S. intelligence agencies. In June of 2008, the *New York Times* reported a detailed account of how the use of harsher coercion tactics evolved in CIA interrogations:

Senior Federal Bureau of Investigation officials thought such methods unnecessary and unwise. Their agents got Abu Zubaydah talking without the use of force, and he revealed the central role of Mr. Mohammed in the 9/11 plot. They correctly predicted that harsh methods would darken the reputation of the United States and complicate future prosecutions. Many C.I.A. officials, too, had their doubts, and the agency used contract employees with military experience for much of the work.

Some C.I.A. officers were torn, believing the harsh treatment could be effective. Some said that only later did they understand the political cost of embracing methods the country had long shunned. . . .

In about two-thirds of cases, C.I.A. officials have said, no coercion was used.

If officers believed the prisoner was holding out, paramilitary officers who had undergone a crash course in the new techniques, but who generally knew little about Al Qaeda, would move in to manhandle the prisoner. Aware that they were on tenuous legal ground, agency officials at headquarters insisted on approving each new step—a night without sleep, a session of waterboarding, even a "belly slap"—in an exchange of encrypted messages. A doctor or medic was always on hand.

The tough treatment would halt as soon as the prisoner expressed a desire to talk. Then the interrogator would be brought in.[6]

I recognize the split in opinion even amongst interrogators as to the propriety—and yes, the effectiveness—of these harsh methods, but that debate misses the point. In the most urgent situations where a piece of information could mean saved American lives, the question we need to ask ourselves is this: Does torture *have the potential* to work? The answer is yes.

Published accounts hold that Khalid Sheikh Mohammed, the self-described mastermind of the 9/11 attacks, started talking only after he was waterboarded. KSM held out for more than two minutes (most who are waterboarded last an average of fourteen seconds)[7] before breaking and subsequently confessing to the murder of Daniel Pearl during a long conversation with CIA interrogators. One CIA official told reporters that Mohammed said his admissions were spurred specifically by the waterboarding.[8]

Need more? In his book *Why America Slept,* Gerald Posner wrote that "false flag" methods—convincing a detainee that individuals from a country other than the United States are interrogating him—induced bin Laden henchman Abu Zubaydah to detail KSM's role in 9/11 and Jose Padilla's quest for a "dirty bomb." And when CIA officials felt it necessary to accelerate the pace of Zubaydah's interrogation in late 2002, interrogators began torturing him. That willingness reportedly earned U.S. intelligence officers additional information about Abd al-Rahim al-Nashiri, an al-Qaeda recruiter, and Abu Turab, who helped train the September 11 hijackers. In 2007, a former CIA officer named John Kiriakou, who helped capture Zubaydah and later reviewed classified reports that detailed his torture, said that treatment "probably saved lives."[9]

So here's what we know: Torture has worked when our intelligence officials felt urgency sufficient to employ it. We also know that those intelligence officials sought and received approval for each step towards harsh treatment of detainees. Even then, it has been used sparingly. So why not continue to reserve the ability to torture in those situations where grave threats to American lives arise? Or at least, as Senator McCain put it, prepare to take legal responsibility for harsh methods when they're deemed necessary? I understand the argument that these harsh detainment methods lead to a darkened U.S. standing around the world and provide Islamic extremists with propaganda opportunities. But haven't we learned yet that our enemies—no matter the motivation for their hatred—are content to ignore the rules of engagement and the Geneva Conventions the United States trips over itself to obey? It seems to me that in these ticking-time-bomb scenarios, we need to remember one truth: No matter what Al Jazeera shows on the evening news, there is no moral equivalency between those who killed three thousand innocent victims and a few knuckleheads (out of 140,000 troops) at Abu Ghraib.

While I respect the views of Senator John McCain, as his experiences in captivity have certainly qualified him to pass judgment on the issue, we're fighting in a new age of warfare, in which the enemy is not always clear and the tactics used against us are both cruel and ruthless. If more aggressive techniques can yield information necessary to prevent the loss of life, there is a clear moral imperative to employ them.

Chapter 23

Sticks and Stones

For as long as I have been a radio talking head, or played one on television, people have always tried to label me. Usually the bookers, the folks who extend the invitations to appear on shows, are the labeling type. I do not buy into the prevailing view that in order to hold an audience's attention, you need to supply them with a left-versus-right battle. I think my success in Philadelphia, where I do not play that game on my own show, is proof of that fact. But my approach remains the minority view, especially in the cable TV world in which we live. When I am identified in a word, it is usually as a "conservative" talk-show host. I am certainly more conservative than I am liberal, but that has never been my way of describing myself when it comes to my work as a pundit. In fact, on many occasions I have tried to talk people out of labeling me as such, not because I would be embarrassed to be identified as a conservative, but rather, because I think the people who listen to me on a regular basis and know me best would cry foul. In other words, they know the label does not apply, and I never want them thinking I have tried to market myself under a false flag.

This labeling thing is all the rage, and becomes a self-fulfilling prophecy. People are quick to ascribe labels to others and to themselves, as if not fitting neatly under some umbrella is evidence of being uninformed or lacking resolve. I don't see it that way, and if I had my druthers, the way I would like to be introduced is under the heading of "reasonable" or as a "scourge of all things politically correct." I guess that doesn't fit on a chyron, the banner that appears under guests on television, but just once I would like that kind of truth in advertising.

A related thought occurred to me as I sat down to write about my forays into the brave new world of political punditry: There's probably something to be said for the appearances I *didn't* make, as well as the ones I did.

Over the past few years, there have been several invitations I've declined because I was not comfortable with the role I had been prescribed. Take for instance a Fox News producer's invitation to appear with Neil Cavuto in the heat of Pennsylvania's primary election in 2008. He had initially called me to discuss the segment, and I asked that he e-mail me the specifics of what he had in mind. Here's what I received:

From: Christopher _____
Date: Tue, 1 Apr 2008 10:10:02
To: Michael Smerconish
Subject: Fox News - Your World

Hi Michael,
Like we just talked about, wanted to see if you're available today at 4:05 for Neil's show today. The topic is on Obama and his cockiness. We're looking for someone who will say yes he's cocky and his cockiness will hurt him, if not in the primary, definitely in the general election against McCain. It seems like whenever he goes up in the polls, ego takes over and he slips.
What'd you think? Thanks!
Chris
Your World w/ Cavuto

In other words, I was invited to the party—so long as I was willing to say Obama's cockiness would catch up with him. The problem? That wasn't my view.

-----Original Message-----
From: Michael Smerconish
Sent: Tuesday, April 01, 2008 10:51 AM
To: Christopher _____
Subject: Re: Fox News - Your World

Thanks for the clarity, I am not your man.
Sent via BlackBerry by AT&T

But that did not end our exchange. Later that same day came this overture: "What about a debate off the top of the show on whether or not Hillary is trustworthy? We have someone who says she is and we're looking for someone who says she isn't. It would be straight up at 4pm. If not, there's later this week. Thanks!"

But I similarly had no interest in going on TV to say that Hillary was untrustworthy. That did not dissuade yet another message from the same fellow three days later, after Hillary had made a verbal gaffe and then went on Leno and joked about her mistakes. Now I was invited to appear as long as I was willing to call Hillary Clinton a liar. Again I declined.

Look, I don't mean to single out this producer or the show he works for. I like Neil Cavuto. He has been very good to me when I have appeared on his program. I doubt he knows that e-mails like these were sent on behalf of his program, although he certainly knows how to manage the incessant cross-talk they invite.

I just have a real problem with the prep that goes into the three-minute sound-bite exchanges that are fueling talk radio and cable television these days. No, not the huddles between PR pros and communications gurus before their clients sit for a tough interview. I'm talking about the off-the-air back-and-forth between producers and pundits. The mindset in the cable world is a base one: Good TV means bickering between right and left, red state and blue state, Republican and Democrat. It's so pervasive—and so pressurized by our warp-speed news cycles—that producers and bookers try to fit each guest and every segment into a prescribed formula.

That might make for controversial television. But if I wanted to read a script, I would have been an actor.

And the minutia of it all gets even more absurd. I have often been put in the position of negotiating with bookers over how I will be introduced. My experience on CNN's *Larry King Live* on May 29, 2008, stands out. En route to Modern Video to appear on *Race for the White House* on MSNBC, I received a telephone call from a booker inquiring about my availability to talk presidential politics. I was free later that night. (A night that also stands out because in the interim between the two shows, I joined my friend Larry Ceisler for dinner at a Pennsylvania Society for the Prevention of Cruelty to Animals fundraiser thrown by Chase Utley of the Phillies.)

I went through an exhaustive pre-interview with a producer and answered all of her questions about the political news of the day, which was particularly easy because I was already well read in anticipation of appearing on *Race*. When she had asked what she needed to know of my views, I wondered how they would introduce me. She said as a supporter of John McCain. I replied that I wasn't sure I would be voting for John McCain. This was met with silence. Then she asked if she should say I was a conservative. I said, "Well, if somebody who wants us out of Iraq, doesn't care much if two guys hook up, and believes we should legalize pot and prostitution is conservative, fine."

Now she was speechless. I asked why they didn't just introduce me as a radio-show host, columnist, and author. She said that wouldn't fly (but didn't specify why), telling me she'd have to check with some people to see if I was still needed. What was totally bizarre is that the other guests booked that night were Lanny Davis, a Hillary supporter; Congressman Robert Wexler, an Obama supporter; and Kellyanne Conway, a Republican strategist. In other words, they already had their neat little boxes filled—and still, it was important that I fit into one of them.

Ultimately, with no further conversation, I did appear on that night's show, where I was introduced by Larry King as follows: "And in Philadelphia is Michael Smerconish, talk-radio host, columnist for the *Philadelphia Daily News* and the *Philadelphia Inquirer*. He is a Republican."[1]

At least that's all true. Most often, I get introduced as a conservative, and I have a theory as to why. There's no doubt I'm more conservative than I am liberal: long-time Republican, sub-cabinet appointee in Bush 41's Department of Housing and Urban Development, emcee at a Bush 43 rally in 2004 . . . but I don't think the people who do TV bookings know any of that.

Here's what I think they do know: I have a shaved head (which in the television world means I'm a wing-nut) and I'm supportive of profiling terrorists at airports. Show a television producer a guy with a shaved head willing to speak in support of profiling, and they put that guy in the address book under C for conservative—regardless of how he may see any other issues. In this case, I have never seen the profiling issue in ideological terms. Still, I am continually surprised when critics raise my past writings or commentaries on the need to profile post-

9/11, thinking I will be embarrassed by what I have written or said. I don't wish to retract a single thing.

Here is a great example: On August 29, 2007, I appeared on *Today* opposite Hussein Ibish, who is the executive director for the Hala Salaam Maksoud Foundation for Arab-American Leadership in Washington, D.C. The issue that day was the refusal of newspapers like the *Washington Post* to print an installment of Berkeley Breathed's *Opus* in which a character (Lola) appears in a headscarf and tells her boyfriend (Steve) she wants to be a radical Islamist. This same cartoon had taken a shot at Rev. Jerry Falwell just one week prior with no backlash. But now, the *Washington Post* and other newspapers said they would not run it in print.[2]

Cue the skinhead who supports profiling.

Matt Lauer presided over the discussion. I said, "We are so scared to death to offend one another, particularly Muslims, and that PC impacts the way we do or don't protect our borders and our airports and in the end, it impacts our safety." (That was just about the time the chyron under my live image said "Conservative Talk Radio Host.")

Ibish responded with what I regarded as a cheap shot. He said, "[T]he political correctness is Mr. Smerconish demanding that everybody runs a cartoon because he doesn't like Muslims." He then referred to me as "Commissar Smerconish of right-wing thought police."

Really? Just because I believe we need to contemplate the similarities amongst terrorists, I am against Arabs? That is ridiculous. And I believe that sort of rebuttal is intended to chill speech. Nobody wants to be called a racist, including me. When Matt Lauer gave me the chance for a final word, I said, "Remove it from funny pages, you'll deal with it on the front page." Ibish got off a final volley of his own. He said, "You may not have standards on your radio show, they do."[3]

So I emerged from that encounter as a conservative racist, which I'm sure would be especially interesting to some of my radio listeners who chastised me due to my interaction with Barack Obama's campaign throughout the 2008 election cycle. I interviewed Senator Obama three times in the spring and fall of 2008 and hosted countless of his surrogates and spokespeople as well. And with each interview

I encountered an increasing level of hostility—and even confusion—from folks wondering how a perceived "conservative" or "Republican" could even entertain an Obama candidacy. My third interview with Senator Obama comes especially to mind.

It was Thursday, October 9, 2008, just before 5:00 p.m. I had been anxious to speak again with Senator Obama, and had found out earlier that afternoon I'd have the opportunity for a quick eight- to ten-minute conversation at 4:45. Which was fine, because I was slated to appear on *Hardball with Chris Matthews* at the top of the 5:00 p.m. hour, then I could go watch baseball. It all worked. Our ten-year-old son, Wilson, was with me as I interviewed Obama. He sat spinning in a desk chair at my side in the radio studio, and then he watched me participate in a discussion with Chris Matthews and Pat Buchanan. I wore a bright-red Phillies jacket for both.

The Fightin's were opening a seven-game National League Championship series with the Los Angeles Dodgers that night, and Wilson and I were headed to the game afterwards. By the time I got home from the game (a 3–2 Phils victory), my interview with Senator Obama had already begun launching its way across the country. And I suspect not just because the Democratic nominee had "endorsed" the Phillies to win the series.

Given the time restraints I was operating under, I decided before the interview to move quickly through a range of topics instead of focusing on just one or two, as I had in my prior conversations with Senator Obama. Perhaps most notable was our exchange about William Ayers, the cofounder of a 1970s domestic terrorist organization responsible for the bombing of several government buildings.

Little more than a month before the November 4 election, John McCain and Sarah Palin had begun making a big deal of the Obama-Ayers connection. Although it seemed Obama attempted to downplay his relationship with Ayers, it also didn't look like the two were particularly close. They lived in the same neighborhood and worked together on community projects in the 1990s. Ayers hosted an event for Obama when the Democratic presidential nominee first launched his political career in Chicago. In 2001, he made a $200 donation to Obama's state senate campaign. Obama condemned the crimes committed by Ayers and the Weathermen.[4]

I asked Senator Obama why he'd even go to the house of a guy like Ayers, and he told me:

I moved to Chicago. I didn't grow up in Chicago. And after having gotten out of law school, I was involved in a whole bunch of civic activities.

The gentleman in question, Bill Ayers, is a college professor, teaches education at the University of Illinois, and that's how I met him, was working on a school reform project that was funded by an ambassador and former close friend of Ronald Reagan's, and I was sitting on this board along with a whole bunch of conservative businessmen and civic leaders and he was one of the people who was on this board. And he lives in the same neighborhood.

Ultimately, I ended up learning about the fact that he had engaged in this reprehensible act forty years ago, but I was eight years old at the time and I assumed that he had been rehabilitated.

So, you know, the central point is this: This is not somebody who advises my campaign, it's not somebody who is part of my, you know, inner circle in any way. This is somebody who I've worked on some projects with related to school reform. And I've strongly condemned his actions.[5]

That night and into the next morning, my conversation with Senator Obama was picked up in reports and discussions across the country. Of course, most of the analyses were similar in their presentation of the content of our conversation—and most honed in on Obama's statements about Ayers and the strategy of using the candidate's middle name as a way of stoking racial unease.

The one difference I noted was the way in which those news organizations described me. Politico's Ben Smith, the first respondent on the scene, referred to me as a "sympathetic conservative talk radio host" based in Philadelphia.[6] *Investor's Business Daily* echoed that description.[7] Jake Tapper of ABC News left it at "conservative Philadelphia radio talk show host."[8] As did the *New York Times'* Kit Seelye[9] and *Newsday's* John Riley.[10] Others such as the Associated Press's Liz

Sidoti,[11] *Chicago Tribune*'s Mark Silva,[12] Newsbusters' P. J. Gladnick,[13] and *National Review*'s Jim Geraghty[14] just called me a Philly-area radio show host.

The headline in my hometown *Philadelphia Inquirer* read like this: "Smerconish Grills Obama: Ayers, Guns, Mumia, Phils."[15] Sean Hannity, who I like and consider a friend, gave me a shout out and plugged the Big Talker radio station.[16] On *The Radio Factor*, Bill O'Reilly called me a "pal" and noted my "good rapport" with Senator Obama.[17] Rush Limbaugh, reading from Tapper's blog entry, was somewhat mocking when he read the "sympathetic" reference, and a few moments later gave the Larry King treatment to my last name ("Smer-cone-ish").[18]

But I got the biggest kick out of the posting on the *Daily Kos* headlined, "Obama speaks out on Ayers, on conservative talk radio!" The author included this aside: "**UPDATE:** I should note (having learned this from commenters below) that while Smerconish IS a conservative, his show is not of the wing nut variety like Limbaugh and Hannity. Also, he seems generally supportive of Obama. But given that he is a conservative, I am leaving my title as is."[19] (Thank goodness. I wouldn't want to ruin his headline with the outlandishness of independent thought.)

The whole episode was further proof: In our warped news cycle, it's no longer news to simply report what a politician or public figure says and does. Now, every little detail of the circumstances must be classified ideologically and filed accordingly. Why? I think it's because the media world we've all grown accustomed to has become so dependent on shoving everyone into his or her prescribed ideological box that we can't function without creating that context for ourselves. Would it really have been more or less newsworthy if Senator Obama had told a more like-minded figure, like Keith Olbermann, that he "assumed" Bill Ayers had been rehabilitated?

But these are the lengths we go to to satisfy our need for strictly defined political commentary. It's no wonder I've never actually met anyone so consistently partisan as the talking heads I encounter every day on the radio and cable television. They inhabit a world in which there's no such thing as thinking outside the box—and even your name tag isn't safe.

Chapter 24

Term Limits

Term limits: **We need citizen politicians, not professionals. Two Senate terms and six in the House will ensure we get grounded folks who are capable of earning a living when not serving us.**

Not to be flippant, but here's a little straight talk for you: The man running the free world should know how to "do a Google."

The fact that Senator McCain told a couple of *New York Times* reporters covering his presidential bid that he'd have this whole Internet thing down "fairly soon"[1]—as he serves on the Senate Subcommittee on Science, Technology and Innovation—should have shocked more Americans than it did. And not just because their would-be commander in chief couldn't conquer an e-mail address book.

Weeks after Senator McCain offered that statement, a *Boston Globe* story from March of 2000 resurfaced. That piece said that McCain's war injuries prevent him from typing on a keyboard.[2] I have no doubt that's true (and I have no doubt that Senator McCain is an American hero), but I think I know the real reason for Senator McCain's Internet illiteracy, and it's neither his war injuries nor his age. After all, the Pew Internet and American Life Project reported in July of 2008 that half of Americans ages fifty to sixty-four and almost 20 percent of seniors (sixty-five and older) have broadband Internet access at home.[3] Clearly, many of Senator McCain's peers can and do surf the Web.

Rather, what became clear from Senator McCain's admission is that he's a man whose technological curiosity was hampered or distracted after more than a quarter century in Washington. That's twenty-six years spent with an overattentive staff, a round-the-clock schedule, and a periodic need to raise money for the fight to keep his job. And as a result, he never had time to join the rest of the world online.

Here's the point: Had he been precluded by term limits from remaining in the U.S. Senate, I believe Senator McCain wouldn't be so clueless about that confounded Internet.

In fact, a term-limit movement swept the nation in the early 1990s, but ultimately failed to achieve comprehensive results. Activists succeeded in placing questions about congressional term limits on state ballots throughout the country, and in the end voters in twenty-three states approved such provisions.[4]

But in May of 1995, the U.S. Supreme Court struck them down. In *U.S. Term Limits, Inc. v. Thornton*, a five-to-four ruling supported by Justices Stevens, Kennedy, Souter, Ginsburg, and Breyer held that an Arkansas term-limit measure passed in 1992 was unconstitutional.[5] Individual states, the majority justices concluded, could not set qualifications for members in Congress in addition to the ones explicitly outlined in the Constitution. "Permitting individual states to formulate diverse qualifications for their representatives would result in a patchwork of state qualifications, undermining the uniformity and the national character that the framers envisioned and sought to ensure," Justice Stevens wrote.[6] After the ruling, some incumbents and their opponents volunteered to limit their terms. But thereafter, the effort died out.

Too bad. *Time* magazine reported in 1995 that two-thirds of American voters supported the idea.[7]

Of course, the *U.S. Term Limits* ruling applies only to federal officeholders. When the Nevada Supreme Court upheld the state's voter-approved term limits in July of 2008, the Battle Born State became the fifteenth to adopt term limits for its local and statewide officeholders.[8] In total, twenty-one states implemented state or local-level term limits between 1990 and 2000, though six have since dropped them due to a court overruling or repeal by the state legislature.[9]

Personally, I think the federal government would be well served by a citizen legislature. The framers of the Constitution couldn't have envisioned a nation with half a million officeholders sprawled throughout federal, state, and local governments.[10] And indeed, these days too many politicians pursue those positions as an opportunity to make a life out of politics, instead of making politics a chapter of their life.

I believe in term limits for two reasons: First, I don't want anyone incapable of earning a living on the outside making important decisions for me. Sadly, I fear we have many individuals at the state and federal level who are almost wards of the state—they're in government because they cannot hack it elsewhere. They're not our best and brightest, just our most entrenched.

Second, I believe that the country has significant problems that cannot be solved by individuals concerned primarily with getting reelected. Entitlements are a perfect example. Polling data shows that Americans don't like Congress, but they like their representative in Congress and reelect him or her with return rates in the 90 percent range. In other words, we want somebody to do something about our problems, but we excuse our own representatives when they don't take charge.

It's a disconcerting rut we've voted ourselves into, especially considering the rate at which America changes these days. And I don't mean "change" in the way Barack Obama trademarked it over the last few years. The changes I'm thinking of are tangible. Think of the progression from rotary phones to cordless ones, from car phones to BlackBerries. From snail mail to Gmail.

Indeed, it's *always* a brave new world out there, and our elected officials should be hip to how it works. So what's the solution? The people running the government should change too.

At this point, it's clear that keeping up with change necessitates turnover, especially because the forces behind congressional incumbency are too strong to allow long-serving politicians to stray far from the beaten path. Approximately 85 percent of PAC money is used to support incumbents,[11] who are already equipped with the congressional equivalent of petty cash to produce direct-mail brochures and other communications with constituents, even as their reelection campaigns heat up. Their districts are creatively redrawn every ten years by like-minded state legislators looking to protect their party's congressional incumbents.

In short, they have advantages of money and influence that manipulate their beliefs, upending the simple rationale that incumbency creates a sense of familiarity among voters. How else to explain the fact that Congress can at once tout low turnover rates and dismal approval ratings? Not to mention the fact that America's relatively low voter-turnout rate effectively serves to deaden the influence voters can drum up on election day.

Limiting terms will begin to temper the influence PACs and lobbyists have on the electoral and legislative processes. Those shadowy "Washington insiders" earn their stripes and their clients based on their extensive contacts and relationships with the entrenched forces laying dormant in the nation's Capital. The leadership shift that term limits would force upon professional insiders would leave them scrambling to reestablish control of a suddenly foreign game.

Meanwhile, limits would focus legislators' priorities on pursuing that which their peers and constituents deem most important. They will engage more Americans in an electoral process with more open seats and fewer financial barriers to mounting a viable campaign. And they will leave us with less-entrenched political institutions and more responsive citizen representatives.

I'm thinking twelve years sounds right—two terms in the Senate and six in the House, though something tells me Senator McCain wouldn't endorse my proposal. And indeed, had term limits been implemented almost twenty years ago, they'd have left him significantly shorter in the experience column in 2008. But at least he'd know how to raid Facebook for votes against a BlackBerry-wielding opponent.

Chapter 25

Pennsylvania Society

I've always had a healthy appetite for a good practical joke—one where nobody is physically injured or emotionally scarred. And I have been present for some beauties.

As I said earlier, Pat Croce, businessman extraordinaire, author, broadcaster, and former president of the Philadelphia 76ers, happens to be my next-door neighbor and a good friend. He is the master of the practical joke. I remember one hot summer night a couple of years ago when my wife and I attended a party at his house at the Jersey Shore. The food was great and the booze flowed freely. And then there was Pat's mischievous grin.

Years ago, Pat acquired what's called a "hot seat" from the prop maker for Penn and Teller, the world-famous magicians. It was a bar stool that was wired to emit one helluva shock, and it was triggered by remote control. Pat's old friends knew the routine and were important accomplices. Here was the drill: Somebody would have a camera and all the guys would gather around under the pretense of taking a group shot. Then they would grab an unsuspecting partygoer and tell him to get in the picture. One of the guys in the know would then relinquish his position on the hot seat in favor of the "mark." When that person was seated, Pat would pull the trigger and when the shock came, the camera would flash. It was hysterical. I once saw Charlie Pizzi, the CEO of Tasty Baking, jump about ten feet in the air when Cap'n Pat got him in the hot seat.

I once got Pat pretty good. My three small sons are in a gas mode. Breaking wind cracks them up, and their laughter cracks me up. But I came up with a scheme to get them to stop passing gas with such gusto. I told them that if they break wind and don't tell anybody for a day, they get a treat, like an after-dinner snack. Inevitably, when I come home from work, one of them will pull me aside and whisper in my ear, "Dad, I farted and didn't tell anybody." That usually gets a pudding snack. (If you have young kids, you may want to try this.)

Anyway, in this gaseous environment, we acquired a remote-controlled fart machine. Quite ingenious. Compact and with different sounds. One night, Pat and I took our wives to the movies and, unbeknownst to him, I planted the fart machine under the front passenger seat of the car. The tough part was not pushing the button on the ride to the movie. Showing incredible restraint, I waited until the ride home. Then I hit the button. No one said a word. Another mile down the road, I pushed it again. This time Pat asked, "What was that?" Nobody answered. Another mile, another push of the button. "That was not me," screamed Pat. "I would be proud if it were."

But my favorite practical joke of all time happened in 1991. The venue was a club where I am a member, the Union League of Philadelphia, founded at the time of the Civil War to support the Union. For most of its history, it was a men's club for the City's WASPs. Times have changed. Guys with names like Smerconish are now members.

The Union League takes up an entire city block, and the building is unique and magnificent. Beautiful moldings. Leather furniture. High ceilings. Grand staircases. Dark wood everywhere. And tons of tradition. You get the picture. One of the benefits of membership is that you get reciprocal privileges to utilize facilities of similar clubs around the globe. They include some great places, like the prestigious Union League of New York.

I have been a member of the League since law school, and have forged some great friendships there. And while the public's perception of members might be one of stiffness, the truth, in our case, is far from it.

Every December, I attend festivities in New York City related to another institution, the Pennsylvania Society. This group exists today for no other purpose than to meet annually at events surrounding and including a formal dinner in Manhattan. The Pennsylvania Society dates from a time when Philadelphia was the center of the universe. It was started back in 1899 when a group of industrialists got together at the invitation of James Barr Ferree, a Pennsylvania-born architect and historian. They called themselves the Pennsylvania Society of New York. Andrew Carnegie and Andrew Mellon were among the participants. These were Pennsylvania steel, coal, and oil tycoons who were primarily Republicans from Pennsylvania who would gather in New York City to do business and have some fun.

The tradition continues. More than 150 years later, Pennsylvanians—some two thousand strong—are still traveling to New York City for a wintry weekend of social functions and political king-making. The highlight for most is a Saturday-night black-tie dinner at the Waldorf-Astoria. During that dinner, a Gold Medal is bestowed by the Society on the likes of American presidents. In the old days, Republican candidates would get slated in smoke-filled rooms during this weekend.

Today it is largely bipartisan, but still an opportunity for candidates and officeholders on both sides of the aisle to be showcased. I have been going to New York City for that weekend for twenty years, although I have only attended the formal dinner once. Once was enough. It is quite a cattle call. But the more private events surrounding the dinner are great fun.

In the early 1990s, before I was married, some friends from the Union League of Philadelphia and I would go to the Pennsylvania Society weekend in December and use our reciprocal relationship to stay at the Union League of New York. Bill McLaughlin, a stockbroker extraordinaire, was one of the guys. Rob Gundlach, a childhood friend and an extremely successful lawyer, was another. Bruce Fiscus, my one-time roommate and now a regional manager for a publicly traded office products company, was another. Like the League in Philadelphia, New York's version on Park Avenue is a spectacular facility.

One particular Pennsylvania Society weekend we had an unusually raucous time. We'd closed the Oak Room at the Plaza on a Saturday night before we headed back to the Union League, where the drinking and shenanigans continued. Suffice it to say, things were a bit out of hand. There were some calls from the front desk made to our rooms, and we watched the sun come up on Sunday morning (did I mention we are all married now?). Later that day we headed back to Philly. Everybody had a good time and nobody got hurt.

When we were all back at our respective jobs, my wheels were turning. One of the guys along for the trip was Dave Singer (now working as a real estate investor). Back then, we called him "CCD," a moniker for Center City Dave. The New York rooms at the League had been in Dave's name—something he would soon regret.

Another of the posse was Robert M. Flood III, or "Floody." Back then, Floody's dad was the president of the Union League in Philly. That meant Floody had access to the club's stationery. Soon after the trip to New York, here is what David Singer found in his mailbox on the fancy letterhead of the Union League:

December 26, 1991

Dear Mr. Singer:

The Union League of Philadelphia is extremely proud of its reciprocal relationships with fifty-seven other similarly situated men's clubs worldwide. It is for this reason that we place great value on maintaining these relationships.

In this context, I am sorry to have learned from the Union League of New York of their displeasure with your recent visit to their facility. The President of the Union League of New York has recently corresponded with the President of the Union League of Philadelphia, outlining allegations of conduct unbecoming of a League member.

The Committee on Member Conduct has reviewed this correspondence and would like to provide you with a forum in which to discuss this matter. You should realize that we are contemplating sanctions against you and other League members that may have been with you on this occasion and are, therefore, considered to have been accessories in your misconduct.

The Committee on Member Conduct will hold its next meeting on Thursday, January 9, 1992, at 5:30 p.m. in the Binney Room. Please plan to join us at this meeting. In the event you are unable to do so, please call my office.

Sincerely,
Stanley Orr, Manager

Not bad, eh? And so Union League–ish. I'd completely made up the Committee on Member Conduct, but it would not surprise me to learn we actually had one. Dave was numb. We had correctly predicted whom he would call to authenticate the reprimand, so he took this hook, line, and sinker.

But to really pull off this stunt, we knew we needed somebody from the League community in our corner. Somebody with credibility. Somebody with stature. Somebody with a sense of humor, a real pro. Somebody like Philadelphia City Councilman W. Thacher Longstreth, the prototype Union League member.

Thacher Longstreth (or "Thach," as his friends called him) was an original. I never saw him out of argyle socks, and no matter what the temperature in winter he refused to wear an overcoat. Most importantly for our purposes, he was a great practical joker.

So I called him in his City Hall office to invite him to participate in the gag. He took my call and listened to my recap of the events. And then he laughed. And laughed. And laughed. I could tell I had made his day. Thacher told me he loved the scheme, and would do anything to support it. Just think about that for a moment. Here was the original Philadelphia WASP. The prototypical Union League member. A proud Princeton alumnus. A WWII naval veteran who early in his career was *Life* magazine's top salesman, and ended up the president of Philadelphia's Chamber of Commerce. A two-time Republican mayoral candidate who served for more than a decade as a member of city council. And he couldn't wait to help some young guys carry out a schoolboy prank. You have to love that about him. And I did.

At the appointed hour of CCD's appearance before the Committee on Member Conduct, Thacher stood in a foreboding manner on the front steps of the august Union League pacing like an expectant father as CCD approached from down the block. He greeted CCD and simply told him, "Whatever you do, be contrite." He then spun on his heel and escorted CCD into the League house and toward the meeting room, giving no hint of what was really to come. I followed closely behind. CCD was nervous about the fate that awaited him behind the big oak door. Thacher then acted like he was administering a secret knock on the door—what a great effect—and opened it wide. But instead of a dozen fuddy-duddies, it was the crew who had attended the Pennsylvania Society and a few add-ons, all with cigars and drinks, applauding and eager to greet our nervous pal. And nobody laughed harder than Thach.

My recounting this great practical joke is a bit of a long-winded intro to yet another Pennsylvania Society story. This one concerns U.S.

211

Senator Arlen Specter. Sixteen years after we pulled the prank on CCD, I was still attending the annual events in New York City, now joined by my wife, Lavinia.

The Gold Medal honoree that night was Arlen Specter, who over almost three decades had earned the distinction of being Pennsylvania's longest-serving U.S. senator. Given our friendship and my prior work on his behalf, I had listened to him deliver countless speeches. But I had never seen him talk quite as he did when he addressed a thousand people on December 8, 2007.

He began his remarks as he so often does—by taking off his wristwatch, placing it on the lectern, and telling the crowd he wished to give them "a false sense of security that I am paying attention to the time." He then injected some levity into the room.

Specter had recently won praise for his comedic skills after appearing in a stand-up routine at a Washington, D.C., comedy club. He shared some of his more mild material with the gowned and black-tied crowd. "I called Bob Dole last July 22nd on his eighty-fourth birthday and said 'Happy Birthday, Bob, how do you feel?' He said: 'I feel like a nineteen-year-old teenager—trouble is I can't find one.' Then he added: 'I just came down to breakfast and told Elizabeth that I'd just shaved and felt ten years younger.' Elizabeth scowled and said, 'Bob, why didn't you shave last night?' Bob said to me, 'Arlen, Elizabeth has been very mad at me lately because I've been complaining about the cost of Viagra. You know, Arlen, Viagra costs $10 a pill.' I replied, 'Bob, how would I know about that?' He then added: 'Elizabeth insists that I can afford $40 a year.'"

Some pretty funny stuff. The political crowd loved it. Having watched his comedy-club performance on YouTube, I was only disappointed he didn't reprise a particular one-liner on Dan Quayle. ("He thought *harass* was two words.")

But then he reached inside his tuxedo pocket and withdrew a few index cards. I knew immediately he had something important to say—and that he wanted to get it just right—because Specter rarely, if ever, speaks from notes. I was glad I had the presence of mind, despite having dined with my friend Jack Daniels, to jot down a few of my own notes. When the speech ended, I realized the notes on my program were insufficient. I asked the senator for his note cards, and he obliged. I have them now as I reconstruct what occurred.

This was Specter as Pennsylvania elder statesman, anxious to deliver a message about the need for civility and compromise, not shrillness and contempt. He spoke like an ideological moderate fed up with the left–right extremism too often seen on the split screens of America today. And he said he thought the future should have more of the camaraderie so evident in New York City that night.

Here's part of what the senator said: "Senator Barry Goldwater in his 1964 Republican Convention speech made two very provocative statements when he said, 'Extremism in the defense of liberty is no vice. Moderation in the pursuit of justice is no virtue.' Tonight I am going to discuss the national political war in the congressional partisan battlefield. My theme is that 'Moderation in the pursuit of virtue is no vice.' Moderation in the pursuit of virtue is no vice. And I will suggest that the history of Pennsylvania and American politics shows that moderation and cooperation are more successful than extremism and confrontation."

Specter then praised what he called "the most successful public figures in my lifetime" and said they were those "whose approach to government has been to listen to everyone who wanted to speak, to meet with everyone who wanted to meet, and to find common ground to accentuate the positive and narrow differences wherever possible." He named governors Bill Scranton, Dick Thornburgh, Bob Casey, and Tom Ridge; Senators Hugh Scott, Dick Schweiker, Harris Wofford, and John Heinz; and mayors like Philadelphia's Joe Clark, Richardson Dilworth, and Ed Rendell, Pittsburgh's Pete Flaherty and Dick Caligiuri, Erie's Lou Tullio, and Harrisburg's Steve Reed. He also tipped his hat to his former colleague Senator Rick Santorum, who he said "never got adequate credit for the work he did for the poor, for the people of Africa, and for promoting volunteerism."

He then said that in the Senate today, as many as ninety senators' votes can be predicted before the roll is called. "The world's so-called greatest deliberative body now looks like two knee-jerk partisan caucuses glaring at each other across the famous Senate political aisle."

Specter then told a compelling story about his own past work with current Pennsylvania governor Ed Rendell. Riding down an elevator in the southwest corner of Philadelphia's City Hall in 1967, Rendell, then a young assistant district attorney, told Specter, his boss, he was headed to private practice with the intention of running for elective office. Specter offered to provide an introduction to GOP boss Billy Meehan. "Thanks, but no thanks," Rendell, a Democrat, told Specter. Despite seven years working together in the DA's office, Specter did not know Rendell's political affiliation. Rendell, of course, would go on to be district attorney, mayor of Philadelphia, governor of Pennsylvania, and chairman of the Democratic National Committee.

Shifting his attention to the field of foreign policy, Specter said that "moderates have pursued diplomacy and dialogue as opposed to saber-rattling and bellicose threats." His introduction to the crowd at the Pennsylvania Society had been accompanied by a video presentation that rolled through the stages of his career—from hard-charging district attorney to Warren Commission staffer to unsuccessful gubernatorial candidate. Included in the high-tech scrapbook were images of Specter on the world stage—with Fidel Castro and Yasir Arafat—which prompted a round of guffaws from the audience. It now occurred to me that his office had no doubt supplied those images to underscore his point that we live in times requiring more, not less, dialogue.

That became evident when he praised President Bush for writing a letter to Kim Jong Il that began "Dear Mr. Chairman," calling that greeting of respect a good move as we strive for better relations with North Korea. He cited President Ronald Reagan's successful arms-reduction treaties with the U.S.S.R. even after Reagan had tagged that country the Evil Empire. And he credited diplomacy for the deflation of Libyan leader Muammar Gadhafi's terrorist tendencies.

Specter was well on his way to arguing the importance of courtesy and civility as critical at all levels—international negotiations as well as national, state, and local government. And then he brought the message home to this ballroom full of Pennsylvania movers and shakers.

This weekend is exactly the kind of time when we should all reflect on how much we have in common and how much harder we should try to get along.

In this room, right now, there likely are dozens of young men and women with the brains and energy to lead our state and nation through the breadth of this century. But will we have the discipline and restraint to get along with each other to do the people's business?

If you can lift a glass together with your colleague from across the aisle on a Saturday night here in New York, you can lift your pen with that same colleague across the hall on Monday morning in Philadelphia, Pittsburgh, Harrisburg, or any place in our state.

Moderation in the pursuit of virtue is the approach which must be extended to our county courthouses, to Harrisburg, to Washington and beyond to international conferences.

This is the approach that will insure that when your future Gold Medalists stand in my place on a future second Saturday in December you can declare, as do I, that we still live in the greatest country in the history of the world.[1]

Senator Specter then thanked the crowd and was greeted with a standing ovation. His words are perhaps even more appropriate today than when he offered them at the end of 2007. Nonpartisanship continues to be in decline, fueled, I suspect, by my own professions. Cable TV and the airwaves of talk radio continue to present all matters of public discourse as a left-to-right battle. The congeniality and moderation that Specter evoked that night are interpreted in this cross fire as weakness and lack of commitment. In my own life, pumping gas, buying coffee, driving our kids around town, I rarely meet people like the ideologues who are such prominent personalities in my profession. I do not come in contact with people who see the world entirely through liberal or conservative glasses. But it's easy to forget this reality check when the only individuals showcased in national media represent those polar opposites.

We'd do well to keep in mind Senator Specter's observations offered at the Pennsylvania Society.

Chapter 26

Entitlements

Entitlements: Social Security, Medicare, and other programs make up more than half our federal spending. The number of people on Social Security and Medicare will double in fifteen years, and life expectancy continues to rise. We can't afford to continue the status quo. Yo, AARP: The retirement age has to be raised to seventy.

In 2006, Senator Rick Santorum faced an uphill battle in the race against Pennsylvania state treasurer and former auditor general Robert P. Casey Jr. The senator had a number of unfavorable circumstances working against him, including a political climate that was generally hostile to Republicans, as well as his own controversial—and ultimately, too conservative—policy positions. The exchanges between the two candidates in the press and the debates often became heated, and on Labor Day, the traditional start of the fall election cycle, Tim Russert kicked off *Meet the Press*'s election season with one such episode.

Something caught my ear during that September 3, 2006, exchange. Russert ran a Casey campaign commercial and began a conversation about the need to balance the budget. He and Casey then had some give and take before Russert consulted one of his legendary charts:

> *Mr. Russert: But let me show you reality. Here was the budget, as you mentioned in 2001, a surplus of some $261 billion. And now a deficit—now it's a deficit of $260. That's the next chart. And our debt has gone from $5.7 trillion to $8.5 trillion. Senator Santorum, you voted to increase that debt every single time.[1]*

Santorum joined the fray, and got into a sharp exchange with Casey. Then Russert directed both of their attention back to his chart.

> *Mr. Russert: Let's go back to the chart where Social Security and entitlements are such a huge part of our budget. They asked Willie Sutton why he robbed banks, he said that's where the money is. Look at this pie chart. Social Security and Medicare and other entitlements make up 52 percent of our federal spending [emphasis mine]. It dwarfs defense and non-defense and interest on the public debt. There are 40 million people on Social Security and Medicare. There's going to be 80 million in the next 15 years. Life expectancy is—used to be 65, it's now approaching 80. We all know it.[2]*

Russert confronted Senator Santorum about the senator's prior assertion that the retirement age needed to be raised to seventy, and the debate continued. Meanwhile, I was thunderstruck by Russert's data. It was probably not earth-shattering for those who were already conversant in this issue of entitlements, but it was something on which I had never focused. Social Security and Medicare and other entitlements comprise 52 percent of our budget?

I needed confirmation and soon found more than I bargained for. In a July 20, 2005 op-ed, U.S. Senator Judd Gregg, then-Chairman of the Senate Budget Committee, wrote that "mandatory entitlement spending" made up 55 percent of federal spending.[3] Meanwhile, in a letter dated March 8, 2007 and addressed to Congressman Jeb Hensarling, Peter Orszag, then-Director of the Congressional Budget Office, projected that Medicare, Medicaid, and Social Security alone would account for 45 percent of the federal government's $2.7 trillion-worth of spending in fiscal 2007.[4] Each analysis predicted a sharp increase in such spending over the coming decades.

Orszag continued: "Many observers have noted that the aging of the population increases spending in all three major entitlement programs. Today, for every person age 65 or older, there are five people 20 to 64 years old. That figure is projected to fall to below three by 2030. Even after the retirement of the baby-boom generation, the population will continue to age, demographers project, as life expectancy continues to increase and fertility rates remain low by historical standards."[5]

Indeed, in 2008 life expectancy in the United States rose above seventy-eight years, a full year higher than in 2001.[6] And as life expectancy and federal spending on entitlements grow by the hour, so too does the federal deficit.

A *USA Today* analysis published in 2004 surmised that balancing Social Security would require pushing the age at which a retiree gains full benefits past seventy-three years old. (Right now, retirees begin receiving full benefits between sixty-five years and four months and sixty-seven years old, depending on when they were born.)[7]

Whatever the case may be, it's clear that something needs to be done to put the system in balance and secure it for the future. Federal Reserve Chairman Ben Bernanke echoed this sentiment when he testified before the Senate Budget Committee in January 2007: "To summarize, because of demographic changes and rising medical costs, federal expenditures for entitlement programs are projected to rise sharply over the next few decades. Dealing with the resulting fiscal strains will pose difficult choices for the Congress, the administration, and the American people. However, if early and meaningful action is not taken, the U.S. economy could be seriously weakened, with future generations bearing much of the cost."[8]

How early and meaningful must that action be? When Senate Budget Committee Chairman Keith Conrad asked Bernanke how urgently any "long-term imbalances" needed to be addressed, the Fed chairman replied, "The right time to start is about ten years ago."[9]

Perhaps that's easier for an appointed official like Bernanke to so publicly proclaim. Those running for political office could never expect widespread support and affirmation after so openly decrying the fact that some of the most celebrated federal assistance programs in American history are wiping out the budget. Indeed, aggravating our country's careening entitlements vehicle is the political stigma attached to it.

Democrats, proud of their party's role in introducing and fostering the most enduring of these entitlement programs, Social Security, welcome few efforts to reform it or temper its reach. Their stubbornness was made evident during President Bush's State of the Union address in 2006, when congressional Democrats cheered derisively when the president lamented that Congress had failed to act on his proposal to reform Social Security that year. The U.S. House went so far as to suspend a procedural rule in order to avoid addressing the question of spending on entitlements over the summer of 2008.

The positions staked out by the presidential contenders during the fall of 2008 also reflect that rocky political road towards entitlements reform. On a fact sheet entitled "Helping America's Seniors" posted on his campaign Web site, Barack Obama called maintaining the solvency of Social Security "a real but manageable problem" that would cost less than an extension of the Bush tax cuts.[10] He routinely offered to increase Social Security levies on wealthier taxpayers, but failed to note what that tax rate might be and what types of income would incur it.[11] In any event, Senator Obama positioned himself as starkly against efforts to raise the retirement age or "privatize" Social Security, the oft-maligned (and ultimately scrapped) solution proposed by President Bush in 2005.[12]

A supporter of those efforts to privatize, Senator McCain nonetheless drew the ire of fiscal conservatives during the campaign by implying—despite his vows not to raise taxes—that he'd have the courage to "do the hard things" to shore up Social Security.[13] He also vowed to modernize the workings of America's Big Three entitlements, and repeated his trademark promises to rail against congressional pork-barrel spending en route to accruing the revenue necessary to balance the country's entitlement spending. Never mind that pork-barrel spending represents 1 percent of what the federal government spends each year.[14]

The debate over entitlements is seemingly untouchable, filled with vague and idyllic promises made by politicians too cowardly to address the issue head-on. And what bothers me most is that the burden of cleaning up the mess will rest primarily on the shoulders of our kids, who will work their whole lives to pay into a system from which they will receive little or no benefit. Additionally, their generation will be accountable for the deepening deficit caused in part by the massive entitlement spending. What a tremendous burden for these kids, many of whom are not yet even old enough to vote. On this issue, we need common-sense solutions that aren't limited by political correctness or reelection fears. There is a crisis out there, and we need leaders with the courage to properly address it.

Chapter 27

Speaking Conventionally

Before 2008, I had attended several national political conventions, all of them Republican. In fact, in 1986, my senior year of college at Lehigh University, I was elected an alternate delegate to that year's RNC in Dallas, Texas. When Ed Palladino, then the acting program director at my radio station, came to me early in the 2008 presidential cycle and asked about my interest in covering the conventions, I told him I wanted to attend both or neither. I decided to cover both. And when MSNBC asked me to appear on *Race for the White House* each night at both, it confirmed that I had made the correct decision. Although it took me away from my family for two straight weeks, the content I was able to deliver to my radio audience was superb.

I left Philadelphia with two pieces of equipment: a high-quality recorder and a mobile unit called a Comrex. The recorder had a disk memory that allowed me to rendezvous with a producer every night and hand off something they could then e-mail back to my home studio. TC would come in early the next morning and have a wealth of material to choose from to play for the first two hours of my show. Then, in hour three, I'd broadcast live—from my hotel room—using the Comrex unit, which, as I understand it, enhances a telephone line and brings it up to broadcast capability. That's the extent of my knowledge. My first stop was Denver. MSNBC put me up at a hotel in the Cherry Creek section of town along with their other so-called talent. Rachel Maddow was the first person to greet me when I walked into the hotel. Her show was about to launch on MSNBC and we would be working together on *Race*. Eugene Robinson from the *Washington Post* was there too, and so was Michele Bernard, with whom I have often enjoyed appearing on *Hardball*. Pat Buchanan and his wife, Shelly, were in the room next to mine.

I am a big Buchanan fan. You may disagree with his politics (as I sometimes do), but spend time with the man and you will respect his intellect and enjoy his dry sense of humor. Bottom line: He's funny as hell. I arrived in Denver on Sunday night. The newspapers on Monday morning had stories about the arrest of several white supremacists who may or may not have come to town with evil intentions relative to Senator Obama.[1] (They eventually faced drug and firearms charges.)[2] When I saw Buchanan in the lobby soon after my arrival, he told me the three guys had been staying at our hotel, and that one of them was taken into custody after jumping out of a window on the sixth floor and breaking his ankle. Buchanan, noting that they were right-wing kooks, told me he "hoped they didn't think the hotel was a safe house because I am staying here."

My work at MSNBC afforded me opportunity to do impromptu interviews with many politicians and pundits I might otherwise have had difficulty reaching from Philadelphia.

Great example: Senator Barbara Boxer (D-CA). We disagree on a lot of issues, but we have something in common—an appreciation for *Curb Your Enthusiasm*. Boxer did a cameo in an episode from Season 6 called "The Anonymous Donor." I remember watching it and telling my wife that my opinion of Senator Boxer had gone up based on her willingness to face potential criticism for going on that show. So I introduced myself to her in the makeup trailer behind the MSNBC set, which was constructed at Denver's Union Station, and chatted about *Curb*. Then I rolled tape—no politics, just the TV show about which we have no disagreement. She was delightful in regaling me with how she came to appear on the show and how little had been scripted in the episode. (In it, Larry David and Ted Danson give money to the NRDC—only Ted does so anonymously while Larry accepts public credit.)

Speaking of Californians, later in the week I also interviewed former California governor Gray Davis. He was an amiable guy, but what most stands out is that when we parted he handed me his business card. It read: "Governor Gray Davis (ret.)." Retired? The man was recalled in 2003, making way for the election of the "Governator." Classic.

I did some of my best radio work in that MSNBC makeup trailer. One afternoon before I appeared on *Race*, Pennsylvania Governor Ed Rendell was a guest on MSNBC. The TV monitor in the trailer showed the live feed and somebody yelled out, "What did he just say?" I looked, and about five feet away stood the inquisitor, actor Richard

Dreyfuss. Thinking fast, and remembering one of my favorite movies, I replied, "He said you're going to need a bigger boat." For just a moment, I was awfully proud of myself for quickly making reference to a great scene in which Dreyfuss appeared in *Jaws*. There was just one problem, as he let me know: "That wasn't [my] line, it was Roy's," he corrected me, referring to the late great Roy Scheider.

And the week was filled with close encounters with celebrities. After I literally bumped into him as I first entered the Pepsi Center on Monday, Bill Maher asked me why I was even at the DNC. This was the first time I had seen him since my disastrous appearance on *Real Time*. Knowing of his predilections, I told him I was there for the herbal stimulation. He responded, "Tell me about it. I was nervous walking through security."

The final night of the convention, my role on *Race* was reduced to only a single segment because some protestors in the live audience kept disrupting the show by yelling out, "9/11 was an inside job." The producers reacted by lessening the show elements in front of the live crowd, which cut into my appearances. Later I had plans to meet a friend from home, Ken Smukler, a Democratic strategist and all-around good guy. We had agreed to head to Invesco Field together to watch Senator Obama's acceptance speech along with 84,000 others. One of the perks of working for MSNBC that week was that they had a number of golf carts that were used to shuttle the TV talent to the Pepsi Center, which was about a mile from the set. Ken and I were in a golf cart behind another one transporting NBC News chief White House correspondent and *Race* host David Gregory, together with his producer, Jamieson Lesko. This night there was added security, so the golf cart was supposed to take us to a bus stop, where a shuttle would ship us to the giant stadium where the Broncos play. We got to the bus stop and waited, but no shuttle came. After about a half hour, Ken and I saw a passing taxi and decided to flag it down to see how close the driver could get us to the stadium. Bad decision. We ended up waiting for about two hours to get through a security labyrinth endlessly snaking through the stadium's parking lots.

Once inside, my press badges got me into one part of the stadium, while Ken had access to another. He suggested I come with him. He told me he was being hosted by the Teamsters. At first I balked. The Teamsters? Then I remembered I was at a Democratic convention.

The Teamsters it would be. They had a super box on the equivalent of the fifty-yard line. In the box with us were several cast members from *Mad Men,* a TV show I had not seen at the time, but now appreciate for its cult following. To our immediate left was Howard Dean's box. To our immediate right was Nancy Pelosi's, where Annette Bening and her kids were seated in the front row. When the speech ended, we left the box and passed Oprah in the hallway.

That night, we attended a *Vanity Fair* party (courtesy of the Teamsters) in a warehouse district of Denver. The guy who gave us the tickets also instructed us on the etiquette of getting in. "If they try to stop you, you tell 'em you're with the fuckin' Teamsters. Don't let 'em stop ya. You're one of us tonight. Remember, you're with the fuckin' Teamsters." The message was clear: The f-bomb was essential for this routine to work. I looked forward to the impersonation (it would have come easy after drinking a few of the Teamster beers in the suite) but there were no issues. The *Vanity Fair* party was a total celeb fest full of Democrats and Hollywood types, including Chevy Chase and John Kerry.

The following day I flew back to Philadelphia on a flight that also carried Joe Biden's mom, his son Beau, and mayor Michael Nutter. I was home for the weekend, and the following Monday, Labor Day, was back on a flight, this time bound for Minneapolis–St. Paul and the Republican National Convention. As I was getting settled aboard my U.S. Airways flight, having removed my glasses and inserted my iPod buds, I looked up and saw Neil Young hustling down the aisle with a woman in tow. He settled in four rows ahead of me looking a bit scruffy and wearing that distinct hat like I had seen him wear in concert several times. I was so psyched he was on my flight that I put "After the Gold Rush" on my iPod and settled in, anxious to make him my first interview upon arrival. Neil Young didn't seem like a natural fit for the RNC, but I figured he was doing a protest concert of some kind. Maybe a FarmAid sort of thing. Anyway, I caught up with him upon arrival at baggage claim. After tapping him on his shoulder and asking for the chance to pose a question or two, "Neil Young" turned around. He was some Minnesota wannabe who bore little to no resemblance to Neil Young up close. What the hell was I thinking? This was a Republican convention. The only celebrities we have are Tom Selleck and Bo Derek.

I worked the GOP convention as I had the Democratic confab in Denver, only this time I was aided by Andy Bloom, who was recently named the operations manager for each of the CBS radio stations in Philadelphia. Andy is an interesting guy. He is largely credited with being responsible for helping to expand Howard Stern's market outreach when Stern exploded as a syndicated talent, and yet, he had worked for a Republican congressman from Ohio. I don't know about you, I just wouldn't figure that the guy who put Stern on the air in Philadelphia would be a buttoned-down type, but his politics often make mine look liberal. Andy happened to be from Minnesota, and his wife was then pregnant with twins, so he was happy to introduce me to "Minnesota nice" when the convention rolled into his state.

Sarah Palin was the big news at the RNC. She had been announced the day after the DNC ended. In fact, that Friday after Barack Obama's acceptance speech at Invesco, I was reading glowing newspaper reviews as I ate breakfast at a counter in Denver International Airport. They confirmed my opinion that the night before, I had witnessed history. A hush suddenly came over the room when a television monitor reported that John McCain had selected Sarah Palin as his running mate. Democratic activists began to hum around me. Their buzz soon turned to a group snicker. I went back to my newspaper. In *USA Today*, Ken Duberstein, onetime chief of staff to President Reagan, was quoted as saying that McCain needed to nominate a VP who Americans could immediately believe was ready to take over as president. "This is not the time for on-the-job training," he said.[3] Too bad McCain didn't read that before he made the selection, I muttered to myself. Instead of enlisting Joe Lieberman's knowledge of the Middle East, Tom Ridge's expertise on terrorism, or Mitt Romney's understanding of the economy, McCain had gone with the Alaskan equivalent of the mayor of the small town where I had grown up, Doylestown, Pennsylvania.

By the time I arrived in Minneapolis–St. Paul, revelations about the vetting process made the pick seem even worse. How could a seventy-two-year-old presidential candidate select a running mate with whom he had had only one extended face-to-face conversation? But GOP delegates whom I interviewed in the concourse were by then well schooled in the sound bites they'd been fed by the GOP and conservative talk radio hosts. They were already Palin disciples. I remained dubious.

That's when I ran into a friend from home, David L. Cohen, executive vice president of Comcast, who had been chief of staff to Ed Rendell when he was mayor of Philadelphia. David is one of the most politically astute individuals anywhere. We'd seen each other in Denver and chatted about the differences in the party conventions. When our talk turned to Palin, whose speech was about to begin, Cohen told me that he had just entertained the Alaska governor at the new Comcast Center in Philadelphia, when Palin was in Philadelphia in July to attend a reception during the National Governors Association's annual meeting.

So I asked him for a firsthand assessment of the woman few had met and the speech the nation would soon see from the RNC. "They're about to learn something different," Cohen told me. "This is a smart, engaging, very politically astute, very direct, very compelling young woman elected official who's got a great future—I think, not only in politics, but in this race. Having met her, having met John McCain on a number of occasions, I understand why he chose her. He sees a lot of him in her. She's a blunt speaker. She's very direct. She's got guts. She's tough as nails."

For the first time in two weeks, I wasn't being fed talking points. Cohen, a Democrat who has rubbed shoulders with every political player on a state and national level, was telling me there was a very special quality in the candidate about to take the stage. Until then I had not contemplated that a gun-toting hockey mom from the Last Frontier could justify the GOP's sudden and intense enthusiasm. That night, we all saw what Cohen glimpsed when he showed the new Republican superstar a gleaming slice of Philadelphia. Sarah Palin walked into the most heated, pressure-packed situation imaginable and delivered a stem-winder that rocked what could have been an uninspired convention.

Obviously that one speech did not answer the legitimate questions that had been raised about her candidacy. The notion that the former mayor of Wasilla might not be ready to be president was a valid one that Palin would spend the next two months seeking to answer. But something else Cohen told me that night resonated. He reminded me that he and Ed Rendell had questioned the bona fides of another small-state governor who had exploded out of nowhere and onto the national political scene: Bill Clinton, who was then governor of a state with a budget that was smaller than Philadelphia's. When it comes down to it, Cohen told me, nobody's really ready to be president—or even mayor of Philadelphia—before they're elected. "And the question that should be being asked is not: Is Sarah Palin qualified to be president of the United States on day one? I mean, I hate to say this, I think the answer to that question is probably obviously she isn't," Cohen told me.

"But that's not the right question. The question is: Does she have the capacity based upon her experience and her background to grow into a position where she could be an effective president if she's called upon to be president of the United States? And I think at a minimum that's a much closer question than the question other people are asking."

Her speech that night was electrifying, clearly the high point of the week. And I went home thinking about what David had told me and believing she had the capacity to be president, but my view would quickly change.

Why? Because when it came time for Palin to move to the next level in the vice presidential proving grounds, the McCain campaign kept the Alaska governor wrapped in a protective papoose instead of making her available for the normal give and take of a national campaign. Despite the fact that my radio program reaches a crucial part of a swing state, and I had already interviewed Sens. Barack Obama and John McCain, I quickly gave up hope of getting the vice presidential candidate herself. One day, I received an e-mail from a freelance scheduler who often offers me celebrities for my radio program. He had a question: "Interested in Sarah Palin's dad, Chuck Heath? His passion for the outdoors is merged with a passion for hunting that he passed on to all his children. A trailer in his driveway has a bumper sticker reading 'PETA—People for Eating Tasty Animals.'" In a column I joked that while Heath sounded interesting, I passed because I was holding out for an A-list Palin guest. Maybe her taxidermist. Or at least her optician.

The sheltering of Palin fostered suspicion that she was ill equipped to serve in the role for which McCain had selected her. On election day, exit polls revealed that a full 60 percent of voters said they believed her to be unqualified to be president.[4] And I was reminded of something I'd come to understand after years of attending those long-winded, scripted nominating events: Conventional wisdom—and the RNC and DNC are full of it—can turn out to be flat wrong.

Chapter 28

Death Taxes

Death taxes: **We work hard trying to lead a comfortable life and leave a nest egg for our children. It's un-American that when we check out, Uncle Sam will stand there with his hand out to tax our earnings for the second time. The estate tax must go.**

My family lives in a nice house—much nicer than the three-bedroom, one-bath home in which I was raised (we didn't have a shower until I was in eighth grade). Not that my family is unique. Many Americans grew up absorbing the notion that their hard work would pave the way for more fruitful and comfortable lives for their children. Sure, the stories are all different, but the goals are generally the same: Work hard, earn a living, and give your children a chance to make an even better life for themselves.

Not so fast, says the IRS. Before we reach the pearly gates, Uncle Sam stands waiting to collect his final toll in the form of an estate tax, or death tax, before letting us journey on. I just can't understand why. I feel like I'm already paying my dues—and millions of other Americans are doing likewise. When I get my paycheck, my income is taxed. The shoes I'm wearing have been taxed. The computer I'm using to type out this book was taxed. I paid a tax to get married, a tax to register a vehicle, and a tax to own property. But nevertheless, at the end of a (God-willing) long life, you're telling me that a final tax could be placed on the fruits of a lifetime of hard work?

Seem redundant, insane, and downright un-American? Welcome to the U.S. Tax Code.

According to the IRS: "The Estate Tax is a tax on your right to transfer property at your death. It consists of an accounting of everything you own or have certain interests in at the date of death. The fair market value of these items is used, not necessarily what you paid for them or what their values were when you acquired them. The total of all of these items is your 'Gross Estate.' The includible property may consist of cash and securities, real estate, insurance, trusts, annuities, business interests and other assets."[1]

The estate tax was originally established in the early twentieth century to provide a fund for national emergencies, but the government enjoyed its new piggy bank so much that it became a permanent fixture in the system. When World War II started, the rates were raised to finance the war efforts. At one point, the death tax accounted for 9.7 percent of federal revenues.[2] The Omnibus Reconciliation Act of 1987 and 1993 capped the death tax at 55 percent, and only in 2001, with the Economic Growth and Tax Relief Reconciliation Act, were measures taken to try to phase it out. This phase-out, however, was not permanent and is set to expire in 2011.[3] The Estate Tax and Extension of Tax Relief Act of 2006 attempted to extend the 2001 reconciliation act, but failed to garner enough votes in the Senate.[4]

Here's what else we know: The overwhelming majority of Americans *will not* encounter estate tax liability. In 2001, just 2.1 percent of deceased adults (just shy of 50,000 people) actually had to pony up to estate tax collectors.[5] By the conclusion of George W. Bush's presidency, the *New York Times* reports, less than 1 percent of American households paid it.[6] Nor will an overwhelming number of small businesses surpass the exemptions built into the estate tax. The Congressional Budget Office calculated that in 2000, when exemptions were granted for estates up to $675,000, 1,659 farmers had to pay the estate tax.[7] The Urban Brookings Tax Policy Center reported that in 2004, when exemptions had more than doubled to $1.5 million, just 440 estate taxpayers owned farms or small businesses.[8]

Which makes the results of the Tax Foundation's 2007 Annual Survey of U.S. Attitudes on Taxes and Wealth, conducted by Harris Interactive, particularly interesting. The survey found that two-thirds of Americans still supported completely repealing the federal estate tax, despite the fact that the overwhelming majority of those respondents would never amass enough assets to warrant filing an estate tax return form. Perhaps more revealing is this: Respondents to the 2007 study believed the estate tax to be the "least fair" federal tax—even more unfair than gas taxes.[9] Not surprisingly, Americans older than fifty-five and married Americans exhibited the strongest dislike for the levy.[10]

Why? Cynics and estate tax proponents will argue that the disdain is the result of an expensive and extensive lobbying and public relations effort that began in the early 1990s. And no doubt, that has something to do with it. (It was, after all, Republican pollster and wordsmith Frank Luntz who first convinced Republicans in Congress to replace "inheritance" or "estate" tax with the term "death tax" in their political lexicon.)[11]

But I think there's more to it than that. I think older and married Americans have the most at stake when it comes to the afterlife—that is, the lives their spouses, children, and grandchildren will lead in future decades. And their disdain for the estate tax arises not because they're easy marks for a calculated PR effort, but because they see it as counter to the notion they've been working their whole lives to achieve.

Think of it this way: Upward mobility has always been a hallmark of American society, and rags-to-riches Horatio Alger stories have always elicited a special sense of pride among us. Doesn't it make sense that middle- and working-class Americans striving to reach those upper economic echelons—knowing they'll already encounter a disproportionate amount of income taxation when they get there—would oppose the additional taxation of their families' properties and assets once they die?

It's the long-held American emphasis on individualism that is most behind the country's overwhelming support for repealing the estate tax. And maybe it's naïveté or unchecked idealism on my part, but I'm all for anything that encourages a revival of that rugged American industriousness our parents and grandparents displayed for generations. In truth, most people want to believe they have the capacity to do well enough to enter a higher tax bracket, and no doubt they realize they'll be paying higher income taxes if they do. So why further punish decades of earnings, investment, and allocation that could otherwise be dedicated towards a more comfortable life for somebody's children?

The estate tax must go. It's insulting to hardworking Americans to tax them—and perhaps more accurately, their families—after a lifetime of hard work. Particularly when it is hard enough to build and lead a successful, comfortable life while covering the cost of taxation from the day we enter the workforce until the day we head to that tax-exempt community in the sky.

Chapter 29

Time to Vote

Twenty-two miles separate Newtown, an old-fashioned township nestled in bucolic Bucks County, Pennsylvania, from Progress Plaza, a bustling shopping hub planted in the urban grit, decay, and gentrification of North Philadelphia near Temple University. To travel from one to the other is basically a straight shot on I-95 in southeast Pennsylvania, and if you make the drive at the right time of day, you can probably complete it in less than forty-five minutes.

You could say it took me four years.

On the eve of George W. Bush's reelection in 2004, I was the master of ceremonies for his final rally in Pennsylvania, an event held in a Newtown cornfield with a crowd estimated at twenty thousand. I supported W's reelection and agreed to emcee that rally because three years removed from 9/11, I believed he was better suited than John Kerry to wage the war on terror, and that issue was my most important campaign consideration.

I remember the event very well. Our eldest son, Michael Jr., was then eight years old, and the only thing I wanted in return for speaking was to introduce him to the president of the United States. When the event was winding down, the president greeted many members of the Philadelphia Eagles in attendance, but an aggressive advance man for the White House suddenly kept me and Michael at bay.

I was stunned. Michael was terribly disappointed. He'd been standing in the cornfield for five hours clutching a W sign. The president was about twenty-five yards away from where I suddenly found myself behind a snow fence. At his side was Senator Rick Santorum, who saw me and quickly sized up the situation. I saw him talk to the president and point at Michael and me. Then the president pointed at the two of us. Problem solved. Our son met the president and had some classic photographs snapped—with a big smile on his face and a Toby Keith "American Soldier" hat on his head.

One funny postscript: The next month, Michael Jr. wrote a letter to Santa for Christmas. He wrote, "You're like the President of the United States to me." Well, my wife and I had been invited to a White House Christmas party. It was the second time we had attended one in the W years, so we knew the drill. You arrive and walk through a long receiving line at the basement level, meet the president and first lady, and then retire to the first floor of the White House for hors d'oeuvres. In my suit pocket I had a picture from the Bucks County rally and our son's letter to Santa. Guests wait in the line, then a military guard announces their names before they shake hands with the president and first lady and pose for the picture. Even though everyone has already cleared security, the atmosphere is still very guarded. Well, as we approached the president, I reached into my pocket for the Santa letter and almost got tackled. The Secret Service did not take kindly to what must have looked like a sudden movement inside my suit. But I explained the circumstances to the president and he happily signed the photograph for our son.

Four years later, it was the failure to win the war on terror that topped my list of presidential considerations in the race to succeed George W. Bush. This time around, I wasn't on the stage. On a brisk Saturday morning, I was one of several thousand people who came to hear Barack Obama speak at the outset of what would be his final day of preelection appearances in Philadelphia. For me, it was a sanity check. By now, my mind was made up. I just wanted the confirmation that would come from taking another look at the first Democrat for whom I would ever vote for president.

After all, I had been giving serious consideration to my selection for quite some time. When I came home from attending both national conventions and went back on the air just after Labor Day, the traditional start of the final leg of the campaign, I offered my audience a lengthy presentation as to how I would run my program for the final eight weeks. Wanting to be precise, I had written out my words, which is a rarity for me, and posted them on my Web site. I called this offering my "September Statement."[1]

I said that I was among the minority in this cycle, as one of the 10 or 15 percent of undecided voters. I said this was a position in which I had never found myself at this stage in any previous presidential election. I reminded my audience that ever since I turned eighteen in 1980, I had registered and remained a Republican. I had never missed an election, nor had I ever pulled a straight party lever. I said I had voted for plenty of Democrats, but never one running for president.

I then explained that while I am a guy who television networks choose to label a "conservative" talk-show host, I have never used that or any other label to describe myself. I said I didn't mind it, but that I didn't think it an accurate description. I reminded longtime listeners of my Suburban Manifesto and how much agreement there appeared to be on fifteen important issues that shaped my world view. And then I summed up my personal platform:

> *What exactly do you call someone who: owns firearms; defends law enforcement to the point of spending two years writing a book about a cop killer only to give the proceeds to charity; wants to use profiling as a means of identifying terrorists; supports torture for the worst of our enemies; thinks we should leave Iraq but go into Pakistan to hunt bin Laden; is troubled that the GOP platform is not only pro-life but doesn't even have exceptions for rape, incest, or the life of the mother; doesn't want the government in his bedroom or that of two guys hooking up; wants increased land preservation; thinks we should legalize pot and prostitution; and hasn't quite figured out global warming? That person is me.*

I offered an assessment of the two presidential candidates, each of whom I believed to be honorable. And I gave some perspective on their backgrounds. Of McCain, I said, "I feel that I know him. I think he is personable. He is intelligent. He does put country ahead of self. And he is the true embodiment of an American hero. . . . As we would say in Philly, John McCain is good people."

On Obama, I offered: "Call me a hopeless romantic, but I believe he can do a world of good by bringing people of diverse backgrounds together. There is a quality about him that I find genuine, and I think he is unquestionably of fine intellect."

I detailed areas of disagreement I had with both candidates. And then I commented on how I would use my respective platforms—the radio, MSNBC, and my two newspaper columns. "For starters, I don't think it is my job to tell anyone how they should vote. I would hope that people would make up their own minds based on their own priorities and assessment of the facts. I view my role as being just one part of a listener's intelligence-gathering process, and I will continue to seek to supply that information in a way that is entertaining."

I reminded the audience of my divergent guest list and promised that policy would continue. I said that I would

continue to treat my guests and callers with dignity and respect. I have never been one to hang up on callers or seek ratings based on condescension, and I will not start now. I have never taken positions as a means of currying favor with my audience and I am not about to start. I will rely on no one's talking points but my own. The opinions that you get from me, the right and the wrong, are mine alone. In the end, I will do what I have always tried to do: entertain you with information. And it won't all be serious. There will be laughs along the way, no doubt many at my expense.

I want you to know that you, whoever you are, you are welcome. I want you to listen. Sometimes I want you to participate. I want you to take ownership in this program.

If you are one of those who is only comfortable in the company of people you believe to be ideologically pure, folks with whom you agree on all issues, I am not your man.

Instead, I am Michael Smerconish, and I approved this message.

In short, I did all that I could to separate myself from the talking point–focused, lemming-like, ruthless style of talk radio to which the nation has grown accustomed. I was wrestling with a tough decision and wanted my audience to know that my choice this time might be to vote for the Democrat, but I wanted them to know that my program would be inclusive and that I would not beat them over the head with my own thought process.

I think I was true to my word. Several weeks later I made up my mind. My next decision was whether to tell my audience. After all, there's a reason for those curtains on the ballot box. Why should I be required to allow thousands of people to peek over my shoulder?

Especially when, given my decision, there was going to be hell to pay and potentially some career disadvantages associated with my revelation.

In the end, I decided I should detail my thinking. I didn't want to run from the controversy. So I decided that I would publish my views in one of my columns. I selected the *Philadelphia Inquirer* instead of the *Daily News* because of the enormous reach of the Sunday newspaper. To avoid leaving the *Daily News* out of the equation, I thought I would tip my hand in the *Daily News* by writing a postmortem of the McCain campaign—more than two weeks before election day.

In the *Daily News* I conveyed my sense of distress at the continuation of the undue catering to the right wing of the Republican Party. Far from the rogue candidacy that triumphed in New Hampshire and Michigan and the legendary bull sessions aboard the Straight Talk Express throughout the 2000 GOP primary, Senator McCain ran scared of the conservative wing of his own political party eight years later. No doubt he emerged from 2000 and his candidacy's near collapse in late 2007 with a grave understanding of the venom of the far right, and his general election candidacy reflected that. Set up as a November 5 (meaning, the day after the election) memo from McCain campaign manager Steve Schmidt to an unsuccessful Senator McCain, the column began:

> *You fought the good fight. You lost because of a failed campaign strategy, not because of what you as an individual offered the nation.*
>
> *Last night's polling suggests this election wasn't about the GOP base. It was about the middle of the spectrum, not its fringes. Karl Rove's advice to drive our base by indirectly fueling the urban legends about Barack Obama's background with our own questions about his associations and fitness to lead appears to have backfired. We should never have run that ad with the tagline "Too Risky for America."* [2]

My point was not simply to predict an Obama victory two weeks before the ballots were actually cast. The column was my chance to lament the candidacy Senator McCain ran—a candidacy robbed of its authenticity by the continued intolerant dominance of the far right. In the end, turning an honorable man's campaign ugly had also served to turn independents and moderates away at the door.

The final words of Schmidt's "memo" were ones I wished I could speak to Senator McCain directly: "Your place in American history was secure long before this race. I regret that there will be debate over what the result would've been had you run as a maverick with moderate tendencies."[3]

Now it was time to publish my intention to vote for Obama. I had gotten to work on this column right after watching Senator Obama's appearance at Progress Plaza, in anticipation of filing soon thereafter for the following Sunday's newspaper. I employ a research assistant for my columns. His name is John McDonald and he is a graduate of Saint Joseph's University. He is a level-headed, conscientious assistant whom I am fortunate to have with me. There are many weeks where I must entrust John to carry the laboring oar of the research for my opinions, but this wasn't one of them. Like any columnist, I often struggle in putting my ideas onto paper, but not that week. It was one of the easier columns I have ever written. I knew exactly what I wanted to say, my only trouble was getting my points across in the allotted 750 words. Here is what I wrote:

I've decided.

My conclusion comes after reading the candidates' memoirs and campaign platforms, attending both party conventions, interviewing both men multiple times, and watching all primary and general-election debates.

John McCain is an honorable man who has served his country well. But he will not get my vote. For the first time since registering as a Republican 28 years ago, I'm voting for a Democrat for president. I may have been an appointee in the George H.W. Bush administration, and master of ceremonies for George W. Bush in 2004, but last Saturday I stood amid the crowd at an Obama event in North Philadelphia.

Five considerations have moved me:

Terrorism. *The candidates disagree as to where to prosecute the war against Islamic fundamentalists. Barack Obama is* *correct in saying the front line in that battle is not Iraq, it's the Afghan–Pakistani border. Osama bin Laden crossed that border from Tora Bora in December 2001, and we stopped pursuit. The Bush administration outsourced the hunt for bin Laden and instead invaded Iraq.*

No one in Iraq caused the death of 3,000 Americans on 9/11. Our invasion was based on a false predicate, so we have no business being there, regardless of whether the surge is working. Our focus must be the tribal-ruled FATA region in Pakistan. Only recently has our military engaged al-Qaeda there in operations that mirror those Obama was ridiculed for recommending in August 2007.

Last spring, Obama told me: "It's not that I was opposed to war [in Iraq]. It's that I felt we had a war that we had not finished." Even Sen. Joe Lieberman conceded to me last Friday that "the headquarters of our opposition, our enemies today" is the FATA.

Economy. *We face economic problems that are incomprehensible to most Americans, certainly they are to me. This is a time to covet intellect, and that begins at the top. Jack Bogle, the legendary founder of the Vanguard Group, told me recently that McCain's assertion that the fundamentals of the economy were "strong" was the "stupidest statement of 2008." In light of the unprecedented volatility in the market, who can dispute Bogle's characterization and the lack of understanding that McCain's assessment portends?*

VP. *I opined here that Sarah Palin demonstrated the capacity to be president in her speech to the Republican convention. Sadly, there has been no further exhibition of her abilities, and she remains an unknown quantity. We are left questioning the judgment of a candidate who bypassed his reported preferred choices, Lieberman and former Gov. Tom Ridge, and instead yielded to the whims of the periphery of his party. With two wars and a crumbling economy, Palin is too big of a risk to be a heartbeat away from a presidency held by a 72-year-old man who has battled melanoma. Advantage Joe Biden.*

Opportunity. *In a speech delivered on Father's Day, Obama lamented that too many fathers are missing from the lives of too many children and mothers. Look no further than Philadelphia for proof that the nation has a fatherhood problem at the root of its firearms crisis. And no demographic is affected by this confluence of factors like the black community. Among the many elements needed to address this crisis are role models, individuals whom urban youth can aspire to emulate. Little more than a year ago, Charles Barkley told me: "I want young black kids to see Barack on television every day. . . . We need to see more blacks who are intelligent, articulate, and who carry themselves with great dignity." Obama can be that man.*

Hope. *Wednesday morning will come and an Obama presidency holds the greatest chance for unifying us here at home and restoring our prestige around the globe. The campaigns have foretold the kind of presidency we can expect from each candidate. Last Friday in Lakeville, Minn., McCain himself had to explain to a supporter who was "scared" of an Obama presidency that those fears were unfounded. Another told McCain that Obama was untrustworthy because he is an "Arab." Those exchanges were a predictable byproduct of ads against Obama featuring tag lines such as "Too Risky for America" and "Dangerous," and a failure to rein in individuals at McCain events who highlighted Obama's middle name, all against a background of Internet lore.*

Last Saturday at Progress Plaza, I heard Obama say: "The American people aren't looking for somebody to divide this country; the American people are looking for someone to lead this country."[4]

On the Friday before publication, I thought I needed to give my radio audience advance warning of what the Sunday newspaper would contain. It was always my intention to discuss my views with my radio audience, but I now faced the dilemma of how to straddle my radio and newspaper duties. I decided that I would tell the Friday radio audience that the Sunday newspaper would include my decision on the presidential race and that I hoped it would be read in anticipation of Monday's program and discussion. Well, the floodgates of criticism opened the second my radio program ended. More than five hundred people weighed in immediately, unwilling to consider my argument before criticizing its conclusion. Many of their comments were not suited for a family radio program (or print).

"You made up your mind a long time ago, you rat," one wrote to me. "Either you have no core beliefs, or you are just like all the other elitist Main Line snobs. My guess is both," wrote another. "Smerconish, you're one awful, greedy, shameless ratings hog," said one more. "You traded your soul for socialism," said another detractor.

My heads-up to my radio audience gave me a degree of national attention for the second consecutive week (the week before, my third interview with Senator Obama had aired). And for the second consecutive week, ABC News' Jake Tapper referred to me as a "conservative."[5] A *Huffington Post* item that day referred to me as a "dependable conservative organ."[6] Organ? More like an appendage these days.

During that first day of blowback, my agent, George Hiltzik, called me. My contract with CBS to do morning drive in Philadelphia was up in just over two months, and he was involved in negotiations with the company. For quite some time I had told him I had no interest in continuing to do a show that only reached Philadelphia. And given the ratings and revenue the show generated for CBS in Philadelphia, I wanted him to use our leverage to expand my platform. There had been many discussions along that line, but none had born fruit. Until now. Unaware of the storm in which I was now centered in Philadelphia, George was calling me to tell me that CBS had a station in Washington, D.C., that had been subject to a sale that had fallen through. Now, the company was contemplating keeping it in its portfolio, changing the format from gospel to talk. He said the station's general manager, Sam Rogers, was interested in simulcasting my morning show to the nation's capital. I wasn't sure whether to laugh or cry. He also wanted me to know that a radio syndicator that had always been on the periphery of my career, Dial Global, was now back in the fold. They were wondering if I would undertake a second radio show on a daily basis that they would roll out in national syndication. None of them—CBS, the station in Washington, nor the syndicator—was aware of my soon-to-be published endorsement and I felt obliged to tell George what I was doing so that no one would be blindsided. In other words, where some very conservative listeners would see payoff, I was more realistically worried that my endorsement would ruin my prospect for a new deal. "Michael, they are interested in you because you are a talent, not because of any particular opinion you have," George reassured me. He said my choice of Obama would have no consequence to these potential partners, and he would later be proven correct.

By the time the column actually reached the newsstand, my e-mail critics numbered more than one thousand. Naïvely, I thought there would be a slight change in the tide when the column actually ran, especially once former secretary of state Colin Powell endorsed Senator Obama based on reasons uncannily similar to my own, virtually point-by-point. No luck. An additional one thousand angry e-mails came in the twenty-four hours that followed publication. And, the tone of the objectors actually escalated. Missing from most, however, was any reference to the argument I had advanced: Barack Obama properly recognizes that the central front in the war on terror is the Afghan–Pakistani border, not Iraq; he has more intellectual capacity to deal with the economy than the guy who said its fundamentals were "strong"; Sarah Palin is not ready to be president; Obama represents a role model for black youth, too many of whom are growing up and killing one another; and he presents the best opportunity to unite us after the election and restore our prestige around the globe.

All that fell mostly on deaf ears. Instead, people wondered how I could ever consider voting for a "Marxist" or "socialist" candidate like Senator Barack *Hussein* Obama. Those few willing to engage in substance said Obama's associations made him unfit to lead the country. A large bloc held me in contempt for acting as an enabler for a liberal trinity of Obama, Nancy Pelosi, and Harry Reid. Others questioned my two decades of loyalty to Maureen Faulkner, the widow of slain Philadelphia policeman Daniel Faulkner, by tying Obama to Weather Underground founder William Ayers and Ayers to Mumia Abu-Jamal, convicted in 1982 of killing police officer Danny Faulkner.

I also got a look at the best and worst my day job has to offer. One conservative talk-show host invited me on his program. At the outset,

Mike Gallagher told me he hoped things would not get "personal" between us, which I thought odd given that I wanted to talk issues. He continued to talk about me long after I was gone, and lumped me with Colin Powell, saying we'd "betrayed their party and their beliefs and their ideology and this country."[7] His demonization was classic textbook talking-points radio, all the things that have caused our medium to exclude so many. I don't know how the guy plays around the country, but now I realized why in Philadelphia he literally has no ratings. Zip.

Bill O'Reilly represented the best in the spirit of debate. I was nervous when Victor Garcia, who works for Bill, called me on Monday and said Bill wanted to interview me on *The Radio Factor* on Tuesday. I wondered if I would ever be invited back as his guest host. My fears proved unfounded. O'Reilly wanted to talk issues and challenge my beliefs, and did. He also said this:

"I think you are an American and you're entitled to vote for who you want to. I don't think people should be e-mailing you and telling you you're a traitor or anything else. But I have some questions about the endorsement." And so he asked them. That same day, I was offered and accepted my next O'Reilly radio fill-in date.

There was a different outcome after I was invited to discuss my decision on *Hardball*. Chris Matthews properly noted my "consistency" in drawing attention to our government's failure to avenge the deaths of three thousand Americans on 9/11. But the day of my appearance, I got an e-mail from David Gregory, then NBC White House correspondent and host of *Race for the White House,* who said: "Heard your news today. . . . Would have loved for you to have shared that on my program." The following day I was cancelled from a scheduled appearance on *Race* and was never invited back. In other words, I had now been appearing on that show two to three times per week for more than six months, including having worked the show from both conventions, and now after going on another MSNBC show, I was finished. Done until after the election.

I took solace in the fact that two days after my column was published, it was still the most popular item at Philly.com. Hopefully, I thought, that meant other people were reading what I had written, not just papering cages with my work.

After all, not all the correspondence I received was hatriolic. There were a few like-minded Republicans who thought John McCain ceded too much ground to the periphery of our party to get elected.

These are the folks I'm hoping are ready to begin a battle for the future of the Republican Party. I want to advance a suburban manifesto as a means of expanding the tent of the GOP. This is why I told my readers in a follow-up column that I wouldn't be bullied by the nasty, doctrinaire types who've had a stranglehold on the GOP for far too long. My work was just beginning.

Chapter 30

Guns

Guns: A symptom, not a cause. Single-parent households pose more of a threat to safety than firearms. Let's address that issue.

What would you say to inner-city high school graduates if you were their commencement speaker?

A few years ago, I had that privilege at the Multi-Cultural Academy Charter School in Philadelphia. I told the students that while I had once dreamed of material goods as a measure of success, it's my family that has given me real joy.

> *When I graduated from high school, everyone seemed to have advice for me: where to go to college, what type of career to pursue, where to live, and even what to wear. To the extent I had goals for the future, they included the usual material things: Fancy car. Big house. Money. Those, I thought, would bring me happiness and serve as the yardsticks of my success. I wanted it all. Well, a quarter-century later, my eyes aren't as sharp. My middle is a little thick, and I've lost all my hair. But by the goals I set for myself when I was graduating, I guess you could say I have been successful. Here's the funny thing: That's not how I view myself. If I were to see someone today with whom I graduated from high school over twenty years ago, and if they were to ask me about my life, I wouldn't tell them what I drive, or where I live, not even what I do for a living. I would tell them about four terrific children, a wonderful wife, and maybe even three dogs, because they are how I define my success.*

Family is not something that I was thinking about when I graduated from high school, but it should have been. I was lucky. I got where I wanted to go without thinking too much about it, but I also had some advantages that others had not been given. And that's the funny part. There is good reason to believe that if you make your family your priority, you'll find that your other needs and goals will be more easily met.[1]

Unfortunately, these are difficult times for American families, particularly in the inner city. Consider:

- The number of children living with only one parent has more than doubled since 1970.[2]

- A quarter of our children now live with a single parent, usually mom, although the number of children living in single-father families is growing fast.[3]

Perhaps you're thinking, what exactly does that have to do with a professional future? Well, keep reading:

- Children in single-parent families are more likely to be worse off financially.[4]

- Children in single-parent families are more likely to struggle with their schooling.[5]

- Children in single-parent families are more likely to develop emotional and behavioral problems.[6]

- Children raised in single-parent families display more casual attitudes toward marriage and divorce.[7]

- Children living in single-parent families are more likely to experience abuse.[8]

- The parents raising those children without a spouse tend to have problems of their own, chiefly financial.[9]

That's why I told those graduates:

Here is what it all means. If you want a happy and productive life for both you and your children, the surest way to attain those goals is to create a strong family unit, and stick with it.

No one will blame you if you are hoping that your future includes some of the finer things life has to offer. This is America. The house, the car, and the money can be yours so long as you are willing to work hard, but they can never be tops on your list of priorities.

Settling down in a stable relationship, having children in a marriage, and being a good parent has to be your number one priority. Achieve that, and the rest will fall into place."

Part of my motivation in delivering this kind of address had to do with what's been occurring in Philadelphia. Gun violence, largely in the minority community, is out of control. Consequently, so is the murder rate. In 2006, Philadelphia had the worst murder rate among the nation's ten largest cities, with 27.8 murders per 100,000 residents.[10]

So what does my commencement address have to do with gun violence? Well, a great deal, in my view. I am of the opinion that Philadelphia, like much of the nation, has a family problem more than a firearm problem. Here is how I get there:

A U.S. Census survey released in late 2006 shows that married couples with children now occupy fewer than one in every four households—the lowest ever recorded, and a figure that has declined by half since 1960. Households with married couples and their children are now the exception, not the norm. Marriage rates have declined, and social scientists say it's becoming an institution for the affluent and well educated more than for other income groups.[11]

Meanwhile, more babies are being born out of wedlock. And the rates of such births follow a disturbing pattern. About one-third of first births among white women occur before marriage, compared with three-quarters among black women, according to a recent review of research on cohabitation coauthored by University of Michigan professor Pamela Smock and Wendy D. Manning of Bowling Green State University.[12]

The result? A dismaying proportion of children—especially poor, urban children—are growing up outside of a married two-parent household, which means they're increasingly likely to encounter abuse, emotional and financial difficulties, and problems at school.

They're also the kids most susceptible to the violence that plagues too many of our cities, according to experts such as Robert J. Sampson, chairman of the department of sociology and the Henry Ford II Professor of the Social Sciences at Harvard University.

Sampson has published extensively on the link between youth violence and the marital status of their parents. In a study of Chicago neighborhoods he coauthored that was published in the February 2005 *American Journal of Public Health*, it was found that the odds of perpetrating violence were 85 percent higher for black youths than those for white youths. Importantly, the marital status of a youth's parents was a key determinant of those odds. The presence of married parents was linked to a lower probability of violence among young people, and it also significantly lessened the disparity in levels of violence between black youths and white youths.[13]

A separate 2006 study coauthored by Sampson affirms the benefits of marriage for the children, as well as for married men themselves. For this one, Sampson and coworkers closely followed a sample of five hundred at-risk men from adolescence to age thirty-two, reporting a "significant reduction"—35 percent—"in the probability of crime" among those men when they were married.[14]

To sum it up: There's a correlation between the presence of a coherent family unit, marriage, and a reduction of violence. Unfortunately, we're seeing fewer and fewer married couples with children, particularly in the city, and it's disproportionately hurting the black community.

According to the Violence Policy Center, blacks, who are only 13 percent of the nation's population, make up nearly half of all homicides. And Pennsylvania—no doubt because of Philadelphia's family problem—had the highest black homicide rate per 100,000 residents (29.52) in the country in 2004.[15]

When I spoke to Professor Sampson, he told me, "If I were in charge of policy, I would point to the link between many different social phenomena. We tend to divide this up and talk about police for crime. But the fact of the matter is, a lot of things go together: infant mortality, low birth weight, school dropout, and teenage pregnancy.

These all cluster in the same neighborhoods. We tend to only talk about one or two things in terms of policy. Politicians talk about the criminal-justice system, police, locking people up. Sociologists tend to talk about poverty. I mean, these are all relevant, but there's a more complex picture, I think, involved."[16]

The debate reminds me of the age-old question in public-housing circles: Is it better to build more high-rises or try community dispersion? Here's the short answer: It makes no difference because bricks and mortar have little to do with the underlying problems.

It's the same with guns. And unfortunately, the problem is exacerbated because too many people are unwilling to have an open, honest discussion of America's broken families and troubled kids because of the racial element involved. In 2004, when Bill Cosby criticized the behavior and values of low-income African Americans ("These people are not parenting. They are buying things for their kids—$500 sneakers for what? And won't spend $200 for 'Hooked on Phonics.' . . . They're standing on the corner and they can't speak English."), he was derided for his "classist, elitist viewpoints that are rooted in generational warfare,"[17] or his comments were pinned as a "dog-bites-man story" headlined "Billionaire Bashes Poor Blacks,"[18] to cite a few early examples.

Fortunately, not everybody is so willing to dismiss the underlying problem. Former Philadelphia 76ers great and NBA Hall of Famer Charles Barkley has been a guest on my radio program numerous times, and he makes no bones about his disappointment with African American youths. When I hosted him in September of 2007, he told me: "We as black people, we have got to do better. And like I say, I wish our neighborhoods were safer, but they're not. I wish our schools were better, but they're not. But we know that now. We know our neighborhoods are not safe. We know we're not getting a quality education in some areas. So we know that now. But to go out and kill each other, not work harder to get our education, only enhances the problem."[19]

Barkley's prognostication came in a discussion in which he told me he was supporting Barack Obama for president ("I think he'd be a great role model for the bigger picture," Barkley said in that conversation, "because all our role models now are athletes and entertainers.

And we're lost."[20] And his instincts were proven right a few months later, when Senator Obama effectively addressed that big picture in a Father's Day speech he gave in Chicago in June of 2008:

"You and I know how true this is in the African-American community. We know that more than half of all black children live in single-parent households, a number that has doubled—doubled— since we were children. We know the statistics—that children who grow up without a father are five times more likely to live in poverty and commit crime; nine times more likely to drop out of schools and twenty times more likely to end up in prison. They are more likely to have behavioral problems, or run away from home, or become teenage parents themselves. And the foundations of our community are weaker because of it. . . . We need families to raise our children. We need fathers to realize that responsibility does not end at conception. We need them to realize that what makes you a man is not the ability to have a child—it's the courage to raise one."[21]

You want to end the violence? Figure out a way to fix the family dynamics in the homes in which the students wake up each day. The dissolution of the American family, particularly in the inner city, is what really plagues too many of our schools and cities. The people who lament the skyrocketing gun violence are pointing fingers at the wrong people. The horrors perpetuated by firearms are merely a symptom of declining families.

The stakes are too high to remain silent. We need to talk, and I believe we can do so at a level that spurs public discourse without demagoguery. The presence of two stable parents, and particularly a strong father figure, dramatically decreases the possibilities for violence. Want to stand up against gun violence? Start at the dinner table.

Chapter 31

Looking Forward

Just after the 2008 election, a group of conservatives gathered to plot strategy. About twenty people were invited, including key grassroots organizers, top fundraisers, and the heads of influential conservative groups. Their aim was to ensure that the party's efforts to rebrand itself did not divert too far from traditional right-wing values. The group was said to include Brent Bozell III, president of the Media Research Center; Tony Perkins, president of the Family Research Council; Grover Norquist, president of Americans for Tax Reform; Al Regnery, publisher of the *American Spectator;* activist Richard Viguerie; and pollster Kellyanne Conway.[1]

According to published reports about the confab, the consensus was that conservatism as a political philosophy had not been defeated in 2008. Rather, the Republican Party had been punished for turning its back on that philosophy. "This was a campaign between the moderate wing of the Republican Party and the Democrats," explained Bozell.[2] "The purpose of these meetings is quite simple: The conservative movement is going to retake America," he said.[3] Viguerie echoed those sentiments: "Conservatism did not lose—big government Republicanism lost."[4] Perkins covered the obligatory Ronald Reagan name drop, urging the Republican Party to remedy its defeat by letting conservatives back into the driver's seat. "It's a return to fundamental conservative principles that Ronald Reagan showed work and that people can be attracted to."[5]

The same sort of message was being offered on talk radio. Rush Limbaugh was quick to explain to his audience that conservatism was not up for a vote in 2008. "We haven't been on the ballot since 1994.

"The conservative movement does not need to be rebuilt," he continued. "We had some people abandon the conservative movement, and they need to be abandoned." Not surprisingly, Limbaugh said

2008 wasn't a repudiation of purebred conservatism; it was actually "an opportunity for cleansing . . . like we haven't seen in a long time."[6]

Soon thereafter, the Republican Governors Association met for its annual conference in Miami, and unsurprisingly, Sarah Palin garnered most of the attention. She was in the midst of a media blitz no doubt intended to restore the damage that had been done to her national persona during the campaign. At the same time, she sounded to me like someone already sizing up the field in 2012. As she told Greta Van Susteren: "I'm like, OK, God, if there is an open door for me somewhere, this is what I always pray, I'm like, don't let me miss the open door. . . . And if there is an open door in '12 or four years later, and if it is something that is going to be good for my family, for my state, for my nation, an opportunity for me, then I'll plow through that door."[7] Perkins, for his part, invited a GOP with Governor Palin at its helm, calling her "the future of the party."[8]

Back at home in Philadelphia, I had seen this coming and did what I could to advance my own perspective, which differed from those offered by conservative leaders. Exactly one week after the election, I appeared on *Hardball* along with Ron Christie, a former aide to vice president Dick Cheney. At the outset of the segment, Chris Matthews framed the issue as follows: "Following the Democratic victories last week, the Republican Party will be regrouping and planning its return to power. But who will emerge as the leader of the party? And which Republican philosophy will prevail?"[9]

Matthews then showed his audience a part of David Brooks's column from that morning's *New York Times*. In the column, Brooks wrote that there was a divide in the Republican Party. On one side was the cultural right, the ideological purists who want to take the party back to its pure roots: orthodoxy, small government, tough foreign policy, religious in its orientation. Brooks labeled them "Traditionalists." On the other side were the "Reformers," those who believed the party must be less cultural, less orthodox, and open to all kinds of views within the center-right coalition.[10]

Matthews then asked me which way the party should go. I said this:

"The right way to go is more big-tent focus and to lose the litmus tests. I mean, the Democrats don't have any litmus tests. And they are exclusionary for us. What I agree with is Brooks's conclusion. In that final paragraph, he said, the Republicans probably will continue to veer toward a conservative doctrine, and will take it on the chin. And then they will moderate their views. Well, I would rather get to the end sooner. Let's moderate now on those social issues."

Initially, Ron Christie agreed, saying there should be more "cultural diversity in the Republican Party. We need to be as broad in coalition as possible, but still hold true to certain principles. Otherwise, we're going to get another spanking, like we saw the other week."

But the discussion took a turn when Chris Matthews showed a map that he said "stuns" him. It depicted the only part of the United States where the Republicans did better in 2008 than they had in 2004—the "Appalachian part of the country," as Matthews called it. He described it as moving "back from sort of southwestern Pennsylvania, sort of, and then goes southwestern direction across the—through the mountains, through the Appalachians, down through the Ozarks. It ends up somewhere around Oklahoma." He wanted to know what we made of the GOP growing there as it shrank throughout the rest of the country. Christie said he thought it represented the Republicans' failure to get out their message. I disagreed. I said I thought it was a result of the Republicans having the wrong message. That night on *Hardball*, I said:

> *Look, the right wing of the Republican party always viewed this as a referendum on Barack Obama. This is why I always believe that the Palin pick was a mistaken pick, because it was a pick designed to placate the base. The vote of the base was never in doubt. It's the middle. That's where John McCain lost this election. The reason that map shows growth in Appalachia is that Appalachia responded to what they were receiving in the waning days of the campaign. Chris, what they were getting was Bill Ayers, ACORN and socialism. That may have rung a bell in that part of the world, but it cost votes in suburbia.*
>
> *It's that Rovian notion of banging the drum for the base by taking it out on same-sex relationships, or talking about abortion. That may bring folks out in that territory, but in the rest of the country it costs you. It's a net negative.*[11]

I was pleased to have had a national platform to say what I had been articulating at home in Philadelphia for a long time. I had just enjoyed a front-row seat in a battleground state and I thought there were lessons to be learned from what had just played out in my backyard. In truth, Christie's theory that the GOP had failed to get out its message was impossible to square with what happened in Pennsylvania, a state that Senator McCain visited thirty times and Sarah Palin visited fourteen times (once every fifth day!).[12] Indeed, governor Ed Rendell even joked on election night that the GOP ticket had spent so much time in the state that he was thinking of assessing them a state income tax.

This while both candidates spent more money on advertising in Pennsylvania than any other state. According to CNN's Election Tracker and news reports, the McCain campaign spent around $21 million on ads in Pennsylvania between June and November 4, 2008, while Obama spent about $28 million during the same period.[13] But for all of McCain's commitment of resources, he could do no better than a ten-point deficit statewide. In other words, the problem wasn't that Pennsylvanians weren't aware of John McCain's message. The real problem was all those personal and television appearances—and the message they carried—were somewhere between meaningless and counterproductive.

Obama's victory was punctuated by victories in the traditionally Republican suburbs that surround Philadelphia in southeast Pennsylvania. Each of those counties had been dependably Republican through the 1988 presidential cycle. The question in elections past, both local and national, was not whether a particular Republican candidate would win, but by what margin.

So what happened? I think the McCain campaign was devoid of a message to the suburban voters in Pennsylvania and across the nation who once had been dependable votes for the Republican Party. People like the almost 3,500 who responded to my fifteen-point Suburban Manifesto with nearly 80 percent agreement.

I don't want to be overly simplistic. I certainly recognize that John McCain was handicapped by his association with President Bush and an economy that was in a tailspin in the final weeks of the election. But neither of those factors alone could explain the margins in the Philadelphia suburbs or suburban communities across the nation.

In my opinion, the McCain campaign repeated the mistake of Bush's efforts in 2000 and 2004 by playing to the party base to the exclusion of more independent-thinking suburbanites. Yes, Bush was victorious in those cycles, but not in Pennsylvania. And what had been a voter registration edge for the Democrats in Pennsylvania of 485,540 in 2000 had grown to 1.2 million by 2008. In the intervening time, the GOP had lost touch with a once-supportive constituency, and the McCain campaign did nothing to regain that connection.

The Republican campaign offered conservative Sarah Palin as a vice president, Joe the Plumber as an economic adviser, and socialism as a bogeyman, instead of a discussion about stem cell research, preservation of open space, or the need to end the war in Iraq regardless of whether the surge was successful. In fact, the only difference between this cycle and those overseen by Karl Rove was the issues used to incite passion among conservatives. In the past, it was opposition to same-sex marriage. This time, there was the subtle and not-so-subtle insinuation that something about Barack Obama was to be feared. Consider the GOP chairman from Lehigh County, Pennsylvania, who delivered an introductory speech just weeks before the election in which he referenced Obama's middle name.[14] Or the daily e-mail blasts from the RNC with a subject of "voter fraud alert," consisting usually of some reference to ACORN and endless embellishment of the routine incidents of voting mishap. On election day in Philadelphia, some guy who had no business showing up with a billy club at a public housing development was suddenly spun nationwide into an effort by Black Panthers to suppress white voting—overlooking the fact that he was at a polling place where only 84 of the 1,535 registered voters are Republicans.[15] Quite an extensive suppression effort, eh?

Of course, some of these activities did not directly involve the McCain campaign. For example, in the week leading up to election day, the Republican State Committee in Pennsylvania ran its own television ad featuring Rev. Jeremiah Wright,[16] a tactic Senator McCain had long before declared off-limits.[17] But meanwhile, the McCain campaign ran a radio spot on my radio program that began with a menacing voice asking, "Who is Barack Obama?" The commercial then went on to discuss health-care policies, which on the surface, at least, had nothing to do with Barack Obama's identity. So why launch it that way? I believe it was intended to communicate a subliminal message—fueling Internet fodder about the background of a man who was able to endure media scrutiny for twenty-one straight months. More great material for the base, I'm sure, but nothing in terms of an offering for those in the middle of the road.

Put it all together, and it is easy to understand why McCain and Palin each were so willing to believe their campaign volunteer in western Pennsylvania when she said an Obama supporter carved a B onto her cheek after catching a glimpse of her McCain bumper sticker while attempting to rob her at an ATM machine. Too many, including the Republican standard bearers, overlooked the fact that the B was in reverse, a telltale sign that she had done it while looking into a mirror.[18]

In the end, Barack Obama beat John McCain in the Philadelphia suburbs, in Pennsylvania, and, I would argue, in the nation because he defeated him in the political center. Indeed, exit polls revealed that Barack Obama had won the suburban areas of the country—home to 49 percent of the electorate—50 percent to McCain's 48 percent. President Bush won those areas in 2004, and in fact, no candidate since 1980 won the presidency without winning suburbia first.[19] But will the Republican Party grasp that lesson? That's the critical question going forward.

I am not optimistic.

Less than two weeks after the election, South Carolina Senator Jim DeMint complained that Senator McCain's record strayed too far from the conservative brand to appeal to a majority or plurality of Americans. "It didn't really fit the label," Senator DeMint mused, "but he was our package."[20]

DeMint would be one of those whom David Brooks had labeled a "Traditionalist." Brooks concluded that in the short term, the party traditionalists would win out over the reformers, at the cost of the next few elections. I agree with that assessment, much as I would like to change the conclusion. And here's why: The Democratic Party has grown in suburban communities like my own while the Republican Party has declined. (In 2000, there were about 348,000 more Republicans than Democrats in the four counties surrounding Philadelphia. By November 2008, the gap was just 7,583.)[21] Those who have departed from the GOP tend to be more moderate in their thinking, while the conservatives have stayed put. Which means fewer moderates will participate in GOP primaries, and conservatives will be even more favored than they have been in the past. My concern? The Republican Party will be stuck nominating candidates who placate the base early on, but are unelectable come November.

Indeed, the presidential process has long favored the more conservative candidates. That's why we so often see GOP moderates who are successful in their own states tack to the right when they seek to enter the national stage. Consider the examples of Rudy Giuliani, Mitt Romney, and Senator McCain himself. Each felt pressured to become a far more conservative presidential candidate than the very record that made them presidential timber in the first place would anticipate. None was elected president.

So what Brooks's "Reformers" need is models of leadership, candidates whose moderate credentials have produced electoral success. That's easy to ruminate about in theory and difficult to find in practice, though Senator Lamar Alexander, Senator Susan Collins, and Congressman Peter King could be the exceptions. Each was victorious in a strong Democratic cycle and said things in the aftermath of their races that acknowledge a need for caution against a move to the right. "What doesn't work is drawing a harsh ideological line in the sand," said Senator Collins, who outpaced Senator Obama 61 percent to 58 percent in her home state of Maine. "We make a mistake if we are going to make our entire appeal rural and outside the Northeast and outside the Rust Belt," said New York's Congressman King. "We can stand around and talk about our principles, but we have to put them into actions that most people agree with," Tennessee's Senator Alexander, a self-described conservative, told a *New York Times* reporter.[22]

So the question becomes, how can things change? Moderate Republicans need a message and require some leadership. That message should be one predicated on strong defense, limited government, less taxes, and a more libertarian outlook on social issues. I am not claiming that I have sole possession of the specific issues that should comprise the platform, but I do believe that my Suburban Manifesto is a good place to start.

Strong on defense means finally ridding the world of Osama bin Laden and Ayman al-Zawahiri. It means being willing to look for terrorists who look like terrorists and, once we find them, willing again to get information on impending attacks by any means necessary. It also means implementing all the recommendations of the 9/11 Commission, which was entrusted to study what went wrong pre-9/11 and recommend how to prevent its recurrence. Iraq? Stop arguing about the surge. We need to shift resources to the war along the Afghan–Pakistani border—a war we've let slip out of our hands over the last few years. Speaking of borders, let's do something to secure our own. It's a security vulnerability waiting to be exploited.

On the home front, Republicans should return to the idea that fiscal responsibility means balancing the budget, plain and simple. And that means we need to control the growth in entitlements, given that Social Security, Medicare, and other programs make up more than half our federal spending even though the number of people on Social Security and Medicare will double in fifteen years. We simply can't afford that. That said, despite the country's economic instability, less than 1 percent of Americans actually pay an estate tax. We can afford to forgo that infringement on a lifetime of hard work.

Most importantly, I think the Republican Party needs to be more libertarian on social issues. Stay out of people's individual choices and for goodness' sake, stop being a party of litmus tests. How about we get a handle on stemming heterosexual divorce before telling same-sex couples how to lead their lives? Speaking of families, let's recognize that single-parent households pose more of a threat to safety than firearms. Why not have room in our tent for both pro-life and pro-choice views? Stop treating cells bound to a petri dish with the same rights and inherent dignities afforded to people. And let us resolve that never again will we stand for politicians trying to determine for any American what his or her end-of-life plan should be.

Speaking of politicians, I continue to believe that we need citizen politicians, not professionals. Two Senate terms and six in the House will ensure we get grounded folks who are capable of earning a living when they're not serving us. And when it comes to those elections, let's give up trying to regulate donations. Someone will always find a loophole. Let anyone spend whatever he or she wants, as long as there is full and immediate disclosure.

Finally, I wish my party wouldn't cede so many issues to the other side of the aisle simply for the sake of principle. From global warming to stem cell research to urban violence and decay, the GOP has, for too long, been too absent from too many debates. I believe that this is why Barack Obama consistently made headway throughout 2008—talking about issues like taxes and national security, which the Democrats have traditionally surrendered to Republicans. At the Republican Governors Association conference, Utah Governor Jon Huntsman Jr. made a fitting point: "We as Republicans can't shy away from speaking the word 'environment,' and we shouldn't shy away from speaking the words 'climate change.' When you've got a body of science that already is rendering certain judgments about what is happening in our world, for us to shy away, say it doesn't matter as an issue, I think is foolhardy, it's shortsighted and it's bound to do us damage in the longer term."[23] Minnesota Governor Tim Pawlenty made the point on a larger scale: "We cannot be a majority governing party when we essentially cannot compete in the northeast. We are losing our ability to compete in the Great Lakes states, we cannot compete on the West Coast," Pawlenty said. "Similarly, we cannot compete and prevail as a majority governing party when we have a significant deficit as we do with women, where we have a large deficit with Hispanics, where we have a large deficit with African-American voters, where we have a large deficit with people of modest incomes. . . . The Republican Party is going to need more than just a comb-over," he concluded.[24]

A plurality of American voters—44 percent—considers itself moderate, not orthodox conservative or progressive liberal.[25] Nobody would say that 44 percent of American voters are waffling, unprincipled people who lack principles or ideological clarity. Unfortunately, those are the labels hurled at the few remaining moderates within the GOP ranks. Over the last twenty years, the Republican Party has gradually abandoned too many centrists and independents for the sake of appealing to a shrinking political base. Too often it has forsaken civility for brashness. And to what end? A political drubbing in 2006 and again in 2008.

I don't think the GOP is on the brink of extinction. But I know the roads back to congressional majorities and the White House will be long ones. And lining them will be the same voters who have been deciding national elections for years now: moderate, suburban ticket-splitters. It's time for the party to adopt a manifesto that speaks directly to them.

Afterword

Among the fifteen points in my Suburban Manifesto, the issue I am most invested in and passionate about is the failure to avenge the deaths of 3,000 Americans on 9/11 by finding and killing Osama bin Laden and Ayman al-Zawahiri. Over the span of just the last three years, my fixation on this breakdown in defense and foreign policy has been the subject of countless radio segments, several of my television appearance commentaries, and eight different newspaper columns I have written in the *Philadelphia Daily News* and *Inquirer.* Indeed, I believed that it warranted a lengthy chapter in this book, a precursor of which was a 5,643-word essay published on Salon.com. I interviewed Barack Obama three times while he was running for president, and in each discussion Pakistan was the focus. I once grilled John McCain for eleven minutes on the same matter, to the point where an aide was interrupting on his end of the conversation. In the end, Obama's promise of change from Bush policy on this matter was a key element of my decision to vote for him.

So imagine the significance of an invitation offered to me in early 2009 when a friend and neighbor asked that my wife and I come to his home to have dinner with former Pakistani President Pervez Musharraf.

My wife Lavinia and I are friendly with Raza and Sabina Bokhari. Lavinia sold them their home a few years ago. Raza is an American citizen who was born in Pakistan; Sabina is an American citizen born in India (if only their two countries could follow their lead when it comes to relations). They are a young, attractive couple. Sabina is a dentist and Raza is a medical doctor-turned-entrepreneur. He is very successful. Public acknowledgments speak of his $1 million donation to the Fox School of Business at Temple University in Philadelphia. Raza is the past president of Pakistani American Public Affairs Committee, and in that capacity has been on my radio program many times to discuss U.S.–Pakistani relations.

We had been to the Bokharis' home on a prior occasion. In the summer of 2008, Raza and Sabina invited my wife and me to come and meet Dr. Nasim Ashraf, the Minister of State and chairman of the National Commission for Human Development in Pakistan. Raza told me he was a close friend and advisor to President Musharraf. The three of us had an enjoyable discussion in the course of which we spoke of the possibility of visiting Pakistan together. Both men said they believed President Musharraf might entertain a discussion of my concerns.

Well, on August 18, 2008, Musharraf resigned from the presidency.[1] A month later, on September 20, 2008, the preferred hotel of Westerners in Islamabad, the Marriott, was bombed and more than fifty people died.[2] This is where we would have stayed. Plans for our trip were then abandoned.

Nevertheless, Raza continued to promise to put me together with President Musharraf, and said that he might soon entertain him in suburban Philadelphia. It all sounded a bit fantastical, that the former Pakistani president would literally be coming to our neighborhood, but it happened. And I was provided an extraordinary opportunity to voice my concerns about Pakistan directly to the nation's former president. Not once, but twice within three days.

The dinner date was Sunday, January 25, 2009. The day before, I caught a stomach bug and literally did not move out of bed for twenty-four straight hours. But come Sunday night, nothing could have kept me away from Raza and Sabina's house. There were ninety people at their home, plus a significant amount of security. Out front was a large SUV with New York plates. Inside were several personnel spread throughout the large home. No one had to pass through any security checkpoint, but everyone was subjected to the hairy eyeball exam by security.

Cocktails were to begin at 5:30 p.m. We arrived just before 6:00. For about an hour there was no sign of Musharraf. Reportedly, his luggage was late arriving from the airport and he was hampered in his ability to dress. Meanwhile the guests mingled on the ground level of the Bokharis' home, where Raza has a large entertainment space including both a humidor and wine cellar (my kind of guy).

The assembled group was very impressive. They were both Republicans and Democrats, men and women, business leaders and elected officials. They included U.S. Senator Arlen Specter and his wife Joan, a former member of the Philadelphia City Council. Congressman Joe Sestak was there. So too was Congressman Chris Carney. The newly elected state Treasurer of Pennsylvania Rob McCord, and state Senator Daylin Leach were there. Mark Alderman, one of the state's most prominent lawyers and a Democratic fundraiser, was present, as was Patrick Meehan, the former U.S. attorney and potential Pennsylvania gubernatorial candidate, as well as Moshe Porat, the dean of the Fox School of Business at Temple University. The namesake of the school himself, Dick Fox, was there, too. I was thrilled that our neighbors, Pat and Diane Croce, came as well. Only Pat could pull off a custom-made pinstripe suit with a black mock turtleneck and a pirate tattoo on his hand.

Suddenly, in walked Pervez Musharraf. He was dressed in a blue-and-white striped shirt (no tie) and a sport coat. With Raza, he quickly walked through the room while many took photographs. Although he greeted most of the people in the room, I did not have a chance to say hello. Raza then quieted the attendees and introduced his guest. He asked if there were any questions from the group. Senator Specter, standing directly next to Musharraf, asked something generic about the future of U.S.–Pakistani relations and Musharraf offered an answer in which he said our two countries must defeat terrorism (and that Pakistan needs to defeat terror independent of the U.S.). Everyone then moved upstairs, where tables were set for dinner throughout several different rooms.

Raza had told me I would sit at the president's table in his main dining room, so I headed there. I saw that sixteen places had been set. Across from President Musharraf was going to be Senator Specter. To his left would be Congressman Carney. Also at the table was Jim Brown, U.S. Senator Bob Casey Jr.'s chief of staff. Raza later told me that Senator Casey, as well as Senator John Kerry (the chair of the Senate Foreign Relations Committee), visited with Musharraf later that week at the Ritz-Carlton in Washington, D.C.

Eventually, I found my own place card. I was seated at Musharraf's immediate right.

Alderman was to my right. Initially, it was just the two of us awaiting Musharraf in the main dining room. We didn't realize he was in the buffet line, and soon he arrived with a plate of food. So now the question was whether to get in line and give up this time with him, or just sit and speak. It was yet another Larry David moment in my life. I choose to sit and when Musharraf arrived, introduced myself by extending a hand. A waitress then interrupted and asked him for his drink order. He asked for a Merlot. I did likewise. I had no food in front of me. I just wanted to talk.

Senator Specter was also seated. As he had once done for me in the presence of Fidel Castro, Specter gave me a nice introduction, mentioning my role in the media and my radio show in particular. Musharraf told me he wasn't doing interviews on this visit. He'd made an exception for CNN's Wolf Blitzer just two days prior, a conversation which got a bit contentious, and he had no intention of doing any more. He said that perhaps in the future he would speak to me on my radio show, but not during this trip. He did, however, give me permission to ask whatever I wanted, so without my recorder and forgoing any note taking, I proceeded to question him.

I wasn't sure how long I'd have him to myself, so I got right to the point. I said that many of us wanted to know how the Pakistani government could reach an accord promising non-intervention with the leaders of the Federally Administered Tribal Areas in fall of 2006 and again in 2007, while at the same time the U.S. Department of Defense was sending $80 million a month in reimbursements for Pakistan's role in combating terror.[3] It sounded like he had committed to not looking where bin Laden was most likely hiding.

Musharraf spoke decent English in a low but audible voice. He didn't look at me, but interrupted his meal and stared straight ahead while speaking. This was a conversation between only the two of us.

Defiant is probably the best description of his tone. He said many Americans were naïve. People don't understand Pakistan, he said. There are Pakistani troops in those tribal areas (overlooking my point that they weren't doing anything) and 1,500 Pakistani soldiers had died in the war on terror. There are important matters of strategy, he said, and at one point told me: "Don't tell us what to do in our country."

I wanted to know what we had to show for the $11 billion the U.S. had paid the Pakistani government for its counterterrorism efforts. He said it was very "frustrating," that there had been many successes by the Pakistanis in the war against terror and that many leaders of al-Qaeda had been killed. He lamented that in his own country he is perceived as a U.S. "lackey," and in the U.S., he is seen as "double-dealing."

Incidentally, the buzz in the room was that he's not well-off. More than one individual surmised over cocktails that for all the money that was paid to Pakistan, you'd think Musharraf wouldn't need to do the U.S. lecture circuit, which was the reason for this visit.

I told him of my trip to Qatar, and how I had visited CENTCOM headquarters and seen the maps depicting military activity in real time, including how all U.S. troop activity stopped at Pakistan. Thinking of Marcus Luttrell and others, I told him that American soldiers had expressed to me frustration at not being able to pursue al-Qaeda when it retreats into Pakistan.

He said that wasn't true. Soldiers had crossed the border, but it's foolish for them to do so. Because of the terrain and the nature of life in the tribal areas, they could get sucked in and killed in great numbers. According to Musharraf, crossing from the Afghanistan border was not an option for American troops. He also said that terrorism was created in Afghanistan and imported to Pakistan, not vice versa.

I asked him about a *New York Times* story that had run that day about a Taliban leader who used a radio to rally (and intimidate) supporters. President Musharraf said it is impossible to stop such communications because of cheap Chinese radios.

With some reluctance, because I was sure he'd heard it thousands of times, I asked where bin Laden was. In the Swat Valley? He laughed and said no. In Waziristan? More grimly, he said, "I don't know."

I asked what he thought when Barack Obama said in August 2007 that if Musharraf didn't act on intelligence regarding high-level al-Qaeda targets, the U.S. would. Musharraf said they are doing that. He said that we mix up strategy and tactics. Tactics, he said, are how to deal with al-Qaeda. There is disagreement there, he said, but overall, strategically, we agree. I expected him to say that Obama was wrong to make that assertion. He did not, but did offer that personality changes don't change policy, only changes in policy do. He said that the aims he had pursued with President Bush represented the best policy. He also said that through last March, things in his country were "pretty good," which I found to be odd. (Remember, he left office in August.)

I asked if Pakistani condemnation of U.S. predator strikes is simply to save face. Do they really disapprove, or do they say that to "placate" the people? When I rephrased the question without that word (one he didn't understand), Musharraf took this as an opportunity to tell me how angry Pakistani people are with the Americans. He said the man on the street doesn't like the U.S., but the U.S. needs Pakistan and vice versa.

When I asked what we Americans don't understand about the situation in Pakistan, he said that the Mumbai coverage had been all about the Pakistani role, with very little said of the Indian role. He said that Americans don't appreciate the danger posed by India, which had sided with the Soviets during the Cold War, and that for more than 40 years, we'd been allies of the Pakistanis. In short, people were too quick to question Pakistan's loyalty to the U.S. He repeatedly made a case for continued U.S. economic aid to Pakistan.

By then, others had taken their places at the table. I felt I was monopolizing the conversation. I finally left the table to get some food, ultimately not having the patience to be away for too long, and returned with just a salad on my plate. The former president wanted to know whether I was dieting. Switching to a lighter topic, I asked him how he relaxed. He mentioned reading and tennis, describing himself as a good defensive player. He also sang the praises of bridge. I then asked him—since he wouldn't sit down for an interview—would he at least sign his place card for our children? So he did:

To Michael, Wilson, Lucky and Caitlin, wish all of you good health, happiness, success and contentment in life. May the wind always favour you. Pervez Musharraf. 25 Jan 09

When the night was winding down, my wife, (who had been seated in a different room with Sabina) Mrs. Musharraf, and Dr. Nasim's wife greeted the former president and made apologies for my monopolization of his time. He seemed to get a kick out of that. I am not sure my tablemates did. We then went home and I immediately sought to recreate all that had been said, given my lack of tape or notes.

I was elated about having had the encounter. I believed that Musharraf was on notice that I had been critical of the U.S.–Pakistani relationship, but probably had not read any of my columns. He was most anxious to defend his policies. From my first words, he was very forceful but never scolding. He was always measured, never ungentlemanly, but very determined. "Frustrated" might be a good word to describe his demeanor. His basic argument is that Americans like me don't understand the dynamics of his nation, cannot appreciate the situation on the ground, and that in Pakistan, entrusting his government was the only way to defeat terrorism. The United States could never do it alone. I went to bed thinking that perhaps he is right that I don't understand the situation with which he was confronted. But similarly, I thought, he cannot appreciate the consternation here in the United States, where the fact remains that seven years removed from 9/11, we have nothing to show for the hunt for bin Laden and al-Zawahiri. One thing we could both agree on is that in the bigger picture, as our limited foreign-policy attention focuses on Gaza, Iraq, and Afghanistan, real American security is being determined in Pakistan.

The following morning, a Monday, I did my best to reconstruct on the air for my radio audience what had occurred the night before. I recounted what was said between us and began preparing a written summary of the conversation for publication in the next day's *Daily News*.

When I got off the air, I received an e-mail from Raza Bokhari requesting a CD of my radio show that morning so he could play it for the president, who was scheduled that night to address the World Affairs Council in Philadelphia. I quickly obliged. By midday, Raza wrote again to tell me that the president had said he would be willing to sit for "his friend's interview" and that I should come back to the house on Tuesday morning at 10 a.m. Pay dirt. This time it would all be recorded.

On Tuesday morning after my radio show I returned to Raza and Sabina Bokhari's home. The Musharrafs were not just their dinner guests—they were their house guests, too. This was their day of departure. This time, as soon as I arrived, a security person got out of the big SUV in front and told me I would have to enter through the garage to be "wanded" with a metal detector. I did and I was. When I entered the kitchen, I was greeted by Raza, who told me that the president was not yet downstairs but was expected shortly. In the meantime I had tea with Raza and Dr. Nasim before the president appeared in a sport coat and shirt with no tie. He and Raza invited me to sit with them for breakfast. Also joining us were Sabina Bokhari, Dr. Nasim's wife, and Mrs. Musharraf, with whom I really never had a chance to converse. I did not want to talk substance at breakfast—thinking it in poor taste and wanting to avoid the risk that something would be said when I was not in a position to record. So for about twenty minutes we touched on various subjects, namely dogs. I learned that President Musharraf and I share a passion for our pets. As he ate fruit and I ate an omelet, he told me he personally spends about ninety minutes each day training his dogs. I asked him if he had ever seen *Dog Whisperer with Cesar Millan* and he told me he had not. (I think he would love that show.) Then we got up from the table and went downstairs to Raza's wine cellar and humidor for a quiet conversation. I carried with me a recorder and microphone necessitating that we be close, and so we shared the leather sofa within three feet of one another. I had notes in my sport coat pocket but never pulled them out. What followed was a forty minute, one-on-one conversation.

Here I was, someone who for years had voiced frustration over the U.S. policy with President Musharraf, now sitting with Musharraf himself for an on-the-record interview. There were no handlers. There were no rules. I wanted to be courteous both to the president and the Bokharis, but I had the opportunity to ask him whatever I saw fit, and this interview was one I could record for my radio show, columns, and posterity.

I broke the ice by again making reference to his dogs. I also asked him about this trip he was making to the United States. I was aware of the fact that upon leaving me, he was traveling to Washington to sit with former Vice President Cheney and Gen. Colin Powell, and I was curious as to whether his views were being solicited during this trip by anyone in the Obama administration. The answer was no. Then I inquired about his take on the planned closure of the detention camp at Guantanamo Bay and his view on coercive interrogation measures.

He offered nothing of significance in either regard. So I got down to business. Here is what I said:

Mr. President, here has been my criticism, that from a distance it looked like we had outsourced, that we had given the responsibility for the hunt for bin Laden and Ayman al-Zawahiri and others to your government in return for which we were paying a lot of money, eighty million dollars a month, by one account in the New York Times, *maybe as much as eleven billion dollars and that at a time when that figure was revealed, you had reached an agreement with the FATA leaders, the Federally Administered Tribal Leaders, where it seemed as if you were saying to them, "I'm not going to intrude on your territories, please don't intrude on my government." Which left me as an American wondering who then is pursuing bin Laden and al-Zawahiri? In a nutshell, that has been my criticism and I would be less than honest with you, sir, if I didn't face-to-face share that with you because I'm most interested in hearing what response you can offer.*

After listening intently, President Musharraf said, "I think, let me be very, very frank. None of what you are saying is true." He proceeded to speak for thirteen minutes without stopping. He was both respectful and defiant, while making it very clear that he believed me to be naïve. I found that his earnest rebuttal raised as many questions as it sought to answer.

The mission, he told me, is far broader than just finding or killing bin Laden and al-Zawahiri:

So we were not using the army just moving around trying to look at two people and doing nothing else. Armies are given a mission to accomplish. That mission certainly was not, "OK, you will go in and hunt for Osama and Zawahiri only." No, that was not their mission. Their mission was to eliminate any foreigners, the al-Qaeda, from that area, wherever they were.

So in the process, if Zawahiri or Osama came in, very good, like all the other al-Qaeda leaders who we got, whether from the tribal areas or from the settled areas where they had escaped. We weren't hunting for that particular man, but we had a long list of what the al-Qaeda hierarchy is, developed by the intelligence jointly.

My assumption had never been that Pakistani military was solely focused on finding the two, however, nor did I expect that such a responsibility was unassigned. We have no troops on the ground in Pakistan tracking the duo. It sounded like neither does he.

With regard to my concern about his accord with the leaders of the tribal regions, Musharraf said, "Nothing could be farther from the truth. We went in and we killed, I don't know how many, about seven hundred, eight hundred of them. We killed them. So what kind of agreement is this?"

He said there had been no such agreements between 2001 and 2006 (before the reemergence of the Taliban, which he noted), "We didn't have any kind of a deal. We were only operating in the valleys. We operated first in South Waziristan, in the valleys and we eliminated those hundreds of al-Qaeda from the valleys. We killed them, eliminated them, got their command and control structures destroyed from those places."

He added that his agreements with the tribal leaders were part of a broader political, military, social and economic strategy. He did concede, however, that the 2006 deal "fell flat" because, according to him, "it was not from a position of strength as it ought to be." He argued that the accord negotiated in 2007 was stronger because it contained four central elements: signers would eradicate al-Qaeda from their area; halt all cross-border Taliban activity; punish any violator; and specifically delineate a system to ensure that the punishments were carried out.

He made agreements with tribal leaders knowing the potential that a good number of them were unreliable or worse. "Maybe half of them are double-crossing. But I always believe . . . doesn't matter, get it signed. This is the reason: Let them double-cross, we'll pressurize them. But at least fifty percent, half of them will be on your side.

So please understand these things are complicated. I've been saying that the misunderstanding here is that when you disagree on tactics, people here start saying that we are double-dealing. No, we are not double-dealing. Double-dealing would be if—what you said—that we had agreed we are not going to do anything, if you don't disturb us we will not disturb you. In other words, we are not after al-Qaeda and Taliban," he told me.

I respected the breadth of his explanation and told him so. But however complicated the political and social dynamics are within those tribal regions, the fact remains that a July 2007 National Security Estimate concluded that Musharraf's accord had given bin Laden's forces the leeway to regroup. And his refusal to recognize the importance of capturing bin Laden and al-Zawahiri belied the April 17, 2008 Government Accountability Office report that declared al-Qaeda not only undestroyed, but revitalized. That report also revealed that no comprehensive plan to eradicate terrorism at its home base had ever been conceived.

In short, Musharraf seemed to acknowledge that there was no U.S. presence in his country assigned to look for the al-Qaeda leadership. Nor was his military so narrowly focused. This while he had reached an accord with individuals he suspected would double-cross him at a time when it was presumed by intelligence experts that those individuals were harboring terrorists responsible for 9/11.

It became clear that the disconnect between us was fundamental. He again balked at my emphasis on the hunt for bin Laden and al-Zawahiri: "You must know that the bigger menace in that area is Taliban. Al-Qaeda may be threatening to attack you in the mainland here. But there, in Pakistan and Afghanistan, it is a Taliban threat which is the stronger threat because they have the mass population there," he said.

I responded that the difference between the two countries was the lack of U.S. troops in his, which is why his comments about reliance on tribal leaders who play both sides is troubling. If no troops are combing that area—and a sizeable number of FATA leaders are double-crossing the Pakistani government—then who is hunting the bad guys?

President Musharraf then took umbrage at my reference to the $11 billion that the U.S. has spent in Pakistan. Half of that that money, he told me, was payment for the "services and facilities provided by Pakistan to you, reimbursement of that. So it's our money, not yours. You pay us for what we are doing for you, so it's reimbursement of that." But don't those services include hunting bin Laden and al-Zawahiri, I wondered? "No, not at all. Not at all. Not zero. Absolutely not," he answered. The other half of the money is split between military support and social sector improvements and education projects, Musharraf told me.

In fact, he continued, the $11 billion price tag (one that I've so often cited as the money trail behind the futile effort to bring two murders to justice) is a sign of the unfairness with which the U.S. has treated Pakistan. How could the United States, he wondered, spend $143 billion in Afghanistan (where there has been a Taliban resurgence and a failure to apprehend Mullah Mohammad Omar, Musharraf pointed out) and expect Pakistan to uproot al-Qaeda and capture its leaders for $11 billion? "We need more money, we must be given more money, we deserve more money. So please don't hold this against Pakistan."

I told him my frustration comes from seven years without resolution for those who perpetrated 9/11.

"I do understand your concern. I do understand the concerns of people here," he responded, before offering a refrain that over the last few years became a familiar chorus for the Bush administration and others. "But those concerns are because of lack of understanding of the terrain, lack of understanding of the people."

The Pakistani military had deployed 80,000 troops to cover three of seven tribal agencies, Musharraf told me. But that force is "incapable of combing the whole area" for a host of reasons: The people look the same. They all carry weapons. There are no defense lines. "They are all fighters. They all fight. They are tribes and they don't want [or] like intrusion on their area. This area, even the British never intruded in the area for three centuries. They never went in. The deal that they struck was only one road, no moving on any other road. They dared not because they were fighters," he said.

"They were very, very sensitive to any outside intrusion, including Pakistan, into their area. Hardly any roads, all mountains. Ferocious fighters, all of them. If you go into some area to comb that area, the whole village will fight you. If you take two hundred people, maybe thousands of people will surround you and kill you."

Later in our discussion he said, "Maybe you need hundreds of thousands of soldiers to do all that, and you don't have that.

All that I would like to say is yes, it's very difficult to understand what I'm saying for a person who's living here in very settled and developed conditions. We can't even imagine what this area is and what the people are. We can't imagine what a tribal society is, uneducated. They are maybe living in Middle Ages; they are living two, three hundred years behind us."

Fearing I was again overstaying my welcome, I thanked the former president profusely for his time, said so long to the Bokharis and left, praying that my tape recorder was functioning properly. It was.

So did I find his argument compelling? There is not a simple yes or no answer.

First, I respect enormously his willingness to engage on such critical matters. There was no trepidation on his part. I would like to think that was attributable in part to him recognizing that my interest is legitimate even when he might think my understanding is flawed.

He seemed earnest. He seemed determined. There was no hesitancy in his voice. He was clear-speaking and appeared clear-thinking. I can understand how the Bush administration came to the conclusion that this was our best ally in a troubled part of the world. He transcends the East–West divide. No doubt he was correct in saying there is a fundamental misunderstanding by many Americans, including me, about the intricacies of Pakistan and the fight against terror. But certain aspects of his explanation are problematic based on my extensive reading and interviews.

The concerns I sought to express to the former president are more fully set forth in the chapter titled "Pakisourced." Nothing Musharraf said convinced me that the 2007 National Security Estimate or the 2008 GAO report (bluntly titled, "Combating Terrorism: The United States Lacks Comprehensive Plan to Destroy the Terrorist Threat and Close the Safe Haven in Pakistan's Federally Administered Tribal Areas") were off base.

Moreover, the former president acknowledged that right now, there is no concerted effort solely focused on finding bin Laden and al-Zawahiri. He also admitted that he had reached an accord with FATA leaders, knowing many of them double-cross.

Which leaves a question even more basic than the ones I've been asking over the last four years. Forget "Where the hell are Osama bin Laden and Ayman al-Zawahiri?" Perhaps the most egregious reality of the post 9/11 world is that we haven't even progressed that far yet.

The question now is: Who exactly is avenging the deaths of 3,000 Americans?

Acknowledgments

Two individuals were most involved on an ongoing basis with this book. Alex Smith is a student at Catholic University who was organized, thorough, and conscientious even when supporting political views of mine that were at odds with her own. Bravo, Alex! John McDonald works in support of my newspaper columns, and was invaluable to me when it came time for Alex to resume being a college student. I have much to learn from John's steady hand and unassuming style. I am most appreciative of the two of you.

Thanks to my literary agent, Larry Kirshbaum, and the folks at The Lyons Press, including Scott Watrous, Gene Brissie, and Inger Forland. And I never forget that I am an author because of the support and friendship of Buz Teacher.

My radio show thrives because of the intellect and drive of TC Scornavacchi, my executive producer. TC is a whirling dervish who never balks at my undertaking of responsibilities that in one form or another end up on her desk. She willingly lent her talents to this project as a perpetual sounding board and sanity check, for which I am grateful. As of this writing, Greg Stocker remains employed as my radio program's technical producer and I thank him for whatever it is that he does. I am the daily beneficiary of enormous support from others with whom I work at the Big Talker 1210, including Marc Rayfield, David Yadgaroff, Mike Baldini, Andy Bloom, and Ed Palladino, all of whom are in management; each has been very supportive. So too was John Cook, who was briefly my program director and made a critical change to my time clock. Grace Blazer was a supportive program director during the time many of the events I describe here occurred and remains a good friend; I miss her. She is now the PD at a Boston station, and I am hoping our paths cross again soon. Walter Kosc is a delightful man who capably takes on orchestrating live events and promotional campaigns that I dream up. My home VCR still blinks "12:00," which is why I so value the technical expertise of Frank Canale, Dave Skalish, "Dr." Bart Feroe, and Tommy MacDonald. Rob Kaloustian and Corey Purcell convert my bloviation into cash, thanks guys. And Sid Mark, you, sir, are a prince.

Dial Global and CBS put my radio show program into national syndication as I was concluding this book. For that I thank David Landau, Spencer Brown, Amy Bolton, and Chris Oliviero.

Then there is George Hiltzik, who represents me in all matters pertaining to radio and television. We're a married couple driving one another crazy but headed for a silver anniversary.

Believe it or not, the cover photograph for this book was taken by a (then) high school intern named Olivia Dubendorf. Look out Annie Leibovitz. Alex Carella is yet another high school wunderkind who for several years has been an audio archivist and able research assistant to me. Thanks as well to Eddy Silverman, who lent a hand with some important fact checking along the way.

Then there are the former interns who I refuse to let cut the cord: Anthony Mazzarelli, M.D./Esq.; "Notre Dame" Ben Haney; and Josh Belfer. I'm guessing one of them will be elected to the U.S. Senate, another appointed as a U.S. ambassador, and the third will be a business baron, but I won't say which ends up where.

For several years now, I have had the pleasure of guest hosting for Bill O'Reilly on *The Radio Factor*. This has been a great honor, and for it, I thank the big man himself, as well as David Tabacoff, Victor Garcia, Rick Buser, Joe Muto, and Elan Kriegel.

My radio profile has been greatly enhanced by my association with MSNBC. For that relationship I thank Steve Capus, Phil Griffin, and Chris Matthews.

One more important category is of those who are regular contributors to the radio program and on whose expertise I regularly rely. Thank you: Lloyd George Parry, Esq.; "Liberal" Paul Lauricella; Sal Paolantonio; Art Caplan, M.D.; Jonathan Newman; Steve Cordasco; Kurt Schreyer; George Anastasia; Dick Jerardi; Pat McLoone; Ed Turzanski; Michael Scheuer; Dan Giancatarino; Vai Sikahema; Marci Hamilton; the guys at TheSmokingGun.com; Louis Barson from Hymies; Armand Ferrante from Ferrante's Meats; Larry Platt; Lisa DePaulo; Ike Richman; Debbie Schlussel; Ray Diddinger; Denny Somach; Ken Smukler; Carrie Budoff Brown; Larry Ceisler; Walt Hunter; Gail Madison; Roger Stone; Michael Klein; Dan Gross; and John Brazer (Go Phils).

Jim Kurek does a terrific job keeping my Web site current (check out www.mastalk.com). And another Jim, Jim Batty, makes my public speaking run smoothly.

And one final note: Blended into this book are pieces of columns that I have written that have appeared in the *Philadelphia Daily News* and *Philadelphia Inquirer.* Thank you to Brian Tierney, Michael Schefer, and Harold Jackson.

(P.S. I was only kidding when I said that "as of this writing" Greg is employed with the show. He'll be sticking around for the long haul. The guy is a terrific talent, and I am very fortunate to have him associated with my program.)

Endnotes

Preface

1   Chris Matthews, "The Washington Read," *Washington Post,* July 2, 2006, www.washingtonpost.com/wp-dyn/content/article/2006/06/30/AR2006063001345.html.

Introduction

1   Paul De La Garza, "In Search of Ground Truth," *St. Petersburg Times,* September 3, 2006, www.sptimes.com/2006/09/03/Floridian/In_search_of_ground_t.shtml.

2   President George W. Bush, "Remarks to Firemen and Rescue Workers" (Murray and West Sts., New York, September 14, 2001).

3   President George W. Bush, "Address to a Joint Session of Congress and the American People" (U.S. Capitol, Washington, D.C., September 20, 2001).

4   Michael A. Smerconish, "Post-Election Blues: Where's My Party?" *Philadelphia Daily News,* November 9, 2006.

5   Robert E. Lang and Thomas W. Sanchez, "The New Metro Politics: Interpreting Recent Presidential Elections Using a County-Based Regional Typology," in Metropolitan Institute 2006 Election Brief (Alexandria, VA: Metropolitan Institute at Virginia Tech, 2006), www.mi.vt.edu/uploads/NationalElectionReport.pdf.

6   Senator John McCain, interview by Michael Smerconish, Michael Smerconish Book Club meeting, December 2, 2006, Philadelphia.

7   Maria Newman, "Bush Backs Gay Marriage Ban as Senate Debates," *New York Times,* June 5, 2006, www.nytimes.com/2006/06/05/washington/05cnd-bush.html?scp=2&sq=Barry%20Goldwater%20pocketbooks%20bedrooms&st=cse.

Chapter 1

1   Christopher Hepp, "Rizzo, Protégé Part Company over Bush Post," *Philadelphia Inquirer,* April 19, 1988.

Chapter 2

1   Sam Roberts, "In a Generation, Minorities May Be the U.S. Majority," *New York Times,* August 13, 2008, www.nytimes.com/2008/08/14/washington/14census.html.

2   Patrick J. Buchanan, *State of Emergency: The Third World Invasion and Conquest of America* (New York: Thomas Dunne Books, 2006), 8–10.

3   Michael A. Smerconish, "The Immigration Fraidy-Cats," *Philadelphia Daily News,* April 10, 2008.

4   Julia Preston, "City's Immigration Restrictions Go on Trial," *New York Times*, March 13, 2007, www.nytimes.com/2007/03/13/us/13hazleton.html?ref=us.

5   "Mayor Wins Both GOP, Democrat Primaries," WorldNetDaily.com, May 17, 2007, www.worldnetdaily.com/news/article.asp?ARTICLE_ID=55741.

6   Josh Drobnyk, "Barletta to Candidates: Hazleton Wants You!" Allentown Morning Call's Pennsylvania Ave. blog, March 14, 2008, http://blogs.mcall.com/penn_ave/2008/03/barletta-to-can.html.

7   Lou Barletta, interview by Michael Smerconish, *Michael Smerconish Show*, WPHT 1210 AM, Philadelphia, March 20, 2008.

8   Governor Richard D. Lamm, "I Have a Plan to Destroy America" (speech, Federation for American Immigration Reform, Washington D.C., 2004).

9   Ibid.

10 Governor Richard D. Lamm, interview by Michael Smerconish, *Michael Smerconish Show*, WPHT 1210 AM, Philadelphia, April 28, 2006.

11 Governor Richard D. Lamm, "I Have a Plan to Destroy America" (speech, Federation for American Immigration Reform, Washington D.C., 2004).

Chapter 3

1   Laura Sullivan, "Philadelphia MOVE Bombing Still Haunts Survivors," *All Things Considered*, NPR, May 13, 2005, www.npr.org/templates/story/story.php?storyId=4651126.

2   "Protestors Continue to Block Delaware River Pumping Station," *New York Times*, June 4, 1987, http://query.nytimes.com/gst/fullpage.html?res=9B0DE6D6173AF937A35755C0A961948260&scp=1&sq=Point%20Pleasant%20Pumping%20Station&st=cse.

3   William K. Stevens, "Bucks County's Long Water War: Decision Time," *New York Times*, June 12, 1987, http://query.nytimes.com/gst/fullpage.html?res=9B0DEFDA163FF931A25755C0A961948260&sec=&spon=&pagewanted=2.

4   "Candidate Survey," Citizens Awareness Network, 1986.

Chapter 4

1   Kenny O'Dell, "Behind Closed Doors," performed by Charlie Rich (Sony Records, 1973).

2   Governor James E. McGreevey, "Resignation Statement" (State House, Trenton, NJ, August 12, 2004).

3   Governor James E. McGreevey, interview by Michael Smerconish, *Michael Smerconish Show*, WPHT 1210 AM, Philadelphia, September 25, 2006.

4   James E. McGreevey, *The Confession* (New York: Harper Collins, 2006), 255.

5   Governor James E. McGreevey, interview by Michael Smerconish, *Michael Smerconish Show,* WPHT 1210 AM, Philadelphia, September 25, 2006.

6   Ibid.

7   Ibid.

8   The Platform Committee, "Republican Platform, 2000," CNN's AllPolitics.com, www.cnn.com/ELECTION/2000/conventions/republican/features/platform.00/#19 (accessed November 19, 2008); Nick Anderson, "Republican Party's Platform Embraces Constitutional Ban on Same-Sex Marriage," *Los Angeles Times,* August 26, 2004, http://articles.latimes.com/2004/aug/26/nation/na-gopplatform26.

9   National Conference of State Legislators, "Same-Sex Marriage Measures on the 2004 Ballot," November 17, 2004, www.ncsl.org/programs/legismgt/statevote/marriage-mea.htm.

10 James G. Wiles, "Calling the Obama Girl," *Evening Bulletin,* April 18, 2008, www.thebulletin.us/site/news.cfm?newsid=19497112&BRD=2737&PAG=461&dept_id=653414&rfi=6.

11 Peter Baker and Jim VandeHei, "Bush Chooses Roberts for Court," *Washington Post,* July 20, 2005, www.washingtonpost.com/wp-dyn/content/article/2005/07/19/AR2005071900725.html.

12 Mike Celizic, "Same-Sex Talk in Diversity Video Divides Town," TODAYShow.com, September 17, 2007, www.msnbc.msn.com/id/20825559/.

Chapter 5

1   Michael Decourcy Hinds, "Pennsylvania Campaign Fizzles, but Not Quietly," *New York Times,* October 11, 1990, http://query.nytimes.com/gst/fullpage.html?res=9C0CE7DE173FF932A25753C1A966958260.

2   "Best of Philadelphia" recognition for Part-Time Radio Work, Philadelphia, August 1993.

3   Opening Monologue, *Michael Smerconish Show,* WWDB 96.5 FM, Philadelphia, October 3, 1993.

4   Art Carey, "Did Exercise Lengthen or Shorten Life of Dr. Jim?" *Philadelphia Inquirer,* March 19, 2001.

Chapter 6

1   "Bush Opposes 9/11 Query Panel," CBS News, May 23, 2002, www.cbsnews.com/stories/2002/05/15/attack/main509096.shtml.

2   "Bush Prepares for Appearance Before 9/11 Panel," CNN.com, April 28, 2004, www.cnn.com/2004/ALLPOLITICS/04/27/bush.911 .commission/index.html.

3   "Bush Backs Independent 9-11 Probe," CBS News, September 20, 2002, www.cbsnews.com/stories/2002/09/24/attack/main523156. shtml.

4   Associated Press, "House Democrats Take Up Remaining 9/11 Commission Recommendations," FoxNews.com, January 9, 2007, www .foxnews.com/story/0,2933,242520,00.html.

5   Judy Keen and John Diamond, "Bush to Act on Some of 9/11 Report Today," *USA Today,* August 1, 2004, www.usatoday.com/news/ washington/2004-08-01-bushterror-usat_x.htm?csp=22_tnt.

6   House Republican Leadership, "Democratic Promise #31: Implement ALL 9/11 Commission Recommendations," *House Democrats' Top 100 Broken Promises,* June 2008, http://republicanleader.house.gov/ brokenpromises/p_security.html.

7   Alvin Felzenberg, interview by Michael Smerconish, *Michael Smerconish Show,* WPHT 1210 AM, Philadelphia, July 31, 2008.

8   Michael Isikoff and Mark Hosenball, "The Civil Liberties Board Goes Dark Under Bush," *Newsweek,* July 9, 2008, www.newsweek.com/id/ 145140.

9   Brett J. Blackledge and Eileen Sullivan, "WMD Report: U.S. Remains 'Dangerously Vulnerable,'" *Associated Press,* September 9, 2008, http://abcnews.go.com/Politics/wireStory?id=5757824.

10 Editorial, "Not Safe Enough," *New York Times,* September 13, 2008, www.nytimes.com/2008/09/14/opinion/14sun2 .html?_r=1&ref=opinion&oref=slogin.

11 Mark Mazzetti, "9/11 Panel Study Finds that CIA Withheld Tapes," *New York Times,* December 22, 2007, www.nytimes.com/2007/12/ 22/washington/22intel.html?pagewanted=1&_r=1&hp&adxnnl=1& adxnnlx=1198350491-9XKfuW5/RLUihEnpPBCEzQ9/11.

Chapter 7

1   "Fatal Attraction: Behind the Facade," CBS News, July 23, 2002, www .cbsnews.com/stories/1999/10/14/48hours/main66462.shtml.

2   Richard Rhys, "The Big Talker: Radio host Michael Smerconish has better ratings than Rush Limbaugh—but his own station doesn't want you to know it. That's part of the reason Smerconish is threatening to quit. Is he all talk?" *Philadelphia,* October 2001.

3   Ibid.

4   Ibid.

5   "Talker Smerconish Says He's Leaving WPHT," *Philadelphia Inquirer,* November 22, 2001.

6   Michael Klein, "B101, News and 'Opie' Big Hits in Arbitrons,"
     Philadelphia Inquirer, April 23, 2002.
7   WPHT, press release, May 9, 2002.

Chapter 8
1   President George W. Bush, "Address to a Joint Session of Congress and
     the American People" (U.S. Capitol, Washington, D.C., September 20,
     2001).
2   Eric Schmitt and Mark Mazzetti, "Bush Said to Give Orders Allowing
     Raids in Pakistan," *New York Times*, September 11, 2008, www.nytimes
     .com/2008/09/11/washington/11policy.html?ref=todayspaper.
3   Transcript, *Hardball with Chris Matthews*, April 23, 2008, www.msnbc
     .msn.com/id/24293399/.
4   Mark Mazzetti, "C.I.A. Closes Unit Focused on Capture of bin Laden,"
     New York Times, July 4, 2006, www.nytimes.com/2006/07/04/
     washington/04intel.html.
5   Ismail Khan and Carlotta Gall, "Pakistan Lets Tribal Chiefs Keep
     Control Along Border," *New York Times*, September 6, 2006, http://
     query.nytimes.com/gst/fullpage.html?res=9D01E2DB1631F935A3575
     AC0A9609C8B63.
6   "Pakistan 'Taleban' in Peace Deal," BBC.co.uk, September 5, 2006,
     http://news.bbc.co.uk/2/low/south_asia/5315564.stm.
7   "General Plays Down Value of Capturing Bin Laden," *Washington Post*,
     February 24, 2007, www.washingtonpost.com/wp-dyn/content/
     article/2007/02/23/AR2007022301799.html.
8   President George W. Bush, "Press Conference by the President" (White
     House, Washington, D.C., May 24, 2007).
9   David E. Sanger and David Rohde, "U.S. Pays Pakistan to Fight Terror,
     but Patrols Ebb," *New York Times*, May 20, 2007, www.nytimes.com/
     2007/05/20/world/asia/20pakistan.html.
10   Mark Mazzetti and David E. Sanger, "Bush Aides See Failure in Fight
     with al-Qaeda in Pakistan," *New York Times*, July 17, 2007, www
     .nytimes.com/2007/07/17/washington/17cnd-terror.html?hp.
11   Transcript, *Meet the Press*, July 22, 2007, www.msnbc.msn.com/id/
     19850951/.
12   Senator Barack Obama, "The War We Need to Win" (speech,
     Washington, D.C., August 1, 2007).
13   Perry Bacon Jr., "Democratic Candidates Discuss Gay Rights Tonight,"
     Washington Post, August 8, 2007, www.washingtonpost.com/wp-dyn/
     content/article/2007/08/08/AR2007080802573_3.html.
14   Senator John McCain, "Remarks at News Conference" (Columbus
     Hotel, Columbus, Ohio, February 20, 2008).

15 James Pindell, "McCain Says He Wants to Shoot Osama," *Boston Globe,* October 23, 2007, www.boston.com/news/local/politics/ primarysource/2007/10/mccain_says_he.html.

16 Susan Milligan, "Democrats Court Labor Backing," *Boston Globe,* August 8, 2007, www.boston.com/news/nation/articles/2007/08/ 08/democrats_court_labor_backing/.

17 Senator Barack Obama, interview by Michael Smerconish, *Michael Smerconish Show,* WPHT 1210 AM, Philadelphia, March 21, 2008.

18 Senator Barack Obama, interview by Michael Smerconish, *Michael Smerconish Show,* WPHT 1210 AM, Philadelphia, April 18, 2008.

19 Associated Press, "Missile Strike in Pakistan May Have Killed Senior Qaeda Operative," *International Herald Tribune,* July 29, 2008, www .iht.com/articles/2008/07/29/asia/pakistan.php.

20 U.S. Government Accountability Office, "Combating Terrorism: The United States Lacks Comprehensive Plan to Destroy the Terrorist Threat and Close the Safe Haven in Pakistan's Federally Administered Tribal Areas," GAO-08-622, April 17, 2008, www.gao.gov/docsearch/ abstract.php?rptno=GAO-08-622.

21 Charles Johnson, interview by Michael Smerconish, *Michael Smerconish Show,* WPHT 1210 AM, Philadelphia, April 24, 2008.

22 Ismail Khan and Carlotta Gall, "Pakistan Asserts It Is Near a Deal with Militants," *New York Times,* April 25, 2008, www.nytimes.com/2008/ 04/25/world/asia/25pstan.html.

23 Eric Schmitt and Mark Mazzetti, "Pakistan's Planned Accord with Militants Alarms U.S.," *New York Times,* April 30, 2008, www.nytimes .com/2008/04/30/washington/30policy.html?fta=y.

24 Jane Perlez, "Pakistan and Taliban Agree to Army's Gradual Pullback," *New York Times,* May 22, 2008, http://query.nytimes.com/gst/ fullpage.html?res=9505EEDB173EF931A15756C0A96E9C8B63.

25 Habibullah Khan and Gretchen Peters, "U.S. Officials Call Pakistan Deal 'Bin Laden Victory,'" May 21, 2008, ABCNews.com, http:// abcnews.go.com/Blotter/story?id=4901559&page=1.

26 Marcus Luttrell, interview by Michael Smerconish, Michael Smerconish Book Club meeting, May 21, 2008, Collingswood, NJ.

27 Ibid.

28 Will Bunch, "Breaking News: Man with '9/11 Fixation' Endorses Obama in Primary (Sort Of)," *Philadelphia Daily News'* Attytood blog, April 16, 2008, www.philly.com/philly/blogs/attytood/Breaking_ news_Man_with_911_fixation_endorses_Obama_sort_of.html.

29 Senator John McCain, interview by Michael Smerconish, *Michael Smerconish Show,* WPHT 1210 AM, Philadelphia, June 13, 2008.

30 Ibid.

31 Ibid.

32 Know the Facts, "Fact Check on Republican Claims that Obama Opposes the Death Penalty for bin Laden," BarackObama.com, June 19, 2008, http://factcheck.barackobama.com/factcheck/2008/06/19/bin_laden_death_penalty.php.

33 Reza Sayah and Saeed Ahmed, "Musharraf's Resignation Accepted," CNN.com, August 18, 2008, www.cnn.com/2008/WORLD/asiapcf/08/18/musharraf.address/index.html.

34 Jane Perlez and Pir Zubair Shah, "Cease-Fire by Pakistan in Attacks on Militants," *New York Times,* August 31, 2008, www.nytimes.com/2008/09/01/world/asia/01pstan.html?partner=rssnyt.

35 Pir Zubair Shah, Eric Schmitt, and Jane Perlez, "American Forces Attack Militants on Pakistani Soil," *New York Times,* September 3, 2008, www.nytimes.com/2008/09/04/world/asia/04attack.html?ref=worldspecial&pagewanted=all.

36 Craig Whitlock, "In Hunt for Bin Laden, a New Approach," *Washington Post,* September 10, 2008, www.washingtonpost.com/wp-dyn/content/article/2008/09/09/AR2008090903404.html?hpid=topnews.

Chapter 9

1 Transcript, *Real Time with Bill Maher,* March 30, 2007, Episode #507.

2 Ibid.

3 Dave Itzkoff, "For Once CNN Takes News Less Seriously," *New York Times,* October 25, 2008.

4 Larry McShane, "Imus's Apology Does Nothing to Quiet a Chorus of Critics," *Washington Post,* April 9, 2007, www.washingtonpost.com/wp-dyn/content/article/2007/04/08/AR2007040801059.html.

5 Michael A. Smerconish, "Guilty as Charged: I Don't Support Imus' Firing," *Philadelphia Inquirer,* April 15, 2007.

6 "It's Not Just Imus," Media Matters for America's County Fair blog, April 12, 2007, http://mediamatters.org/items/200704120010.

7 Associated Press, "MSNBC Fires Michael Savage After Anti-Gay Comments." *USA Today,* July 7, 2003, www.usatoday.com/news/nation/2003-07-07-talk-host-fired_x.htm.

8 "It's Not Just Imus," Media Matters for America's County Fair blog, April 12, 2007, http://mediamatters.org/items/200704120010.

9 Ibid.

10 Ibid.

11 Media Matters Statement, "Imus Replacement Tryouts," Media Matters for America's County Fair blog, April 20, 2007, http://mediamatters.org/items/200704200008.

12 Transcript, *Real Time with Bill Maher,* April 13, 2007, Episode #508.

Chapter 10

1   Michael A. Smerconish, "C'mon, Mr. President, Show Us the Evidence," *Philadelphia Daily News,* January 2, 2003.

2   Ibid.

3   Michael A. Smerconish, "Iraq for Dummies," *Philadelphia Daily News,* March 19, 2003.

4   "Philadelphia Rally for America Draws 10,000+," GlennBeck.com, March 16, 2003, http://archive.glennbeck.com/news/03102003.shtml.

5   Richard W. Stevenson and Thom Shanker, "Ex-Arms Monitor Urges an Inquiry on Iraqi Threat," *New York Times,* January 29, 2004, http://query.nytimes.com/gst/fullpage.html?res=9D07EFD81338F93AA1575 2C0A9629C8B63.

6   Colin Powell, interview by Michael Smerconish, *Michael Smerconish Show,* WPHT 1210 AM, Washington, D.C., January 21, 2004.

7   Ibid.

8   Michael A. Smerconish, "The Real Reason We're in Iraq," *Philadelphia Daily News,* March 11, 2004.

9   Ibid.

10 Ibid.

11 Michael A. Smerconish, "Any Common Ground in the Eye of the Storms?" *Philadelphia Daily News,* September 8, 2005.

12 Ned Parker, "The Conflict in Iraq: Saudi Role in Insurgency," *Los Angeles Times,* July 15, 2007, http://articles.latimes.com/2007/jul/15/world/fg-saudi15.

13 Helene Cooper, "Saudis' Role in Iraq Frustrates U.S. Officials," *New York Times,* July 27, 2007, www.nytimes.com/2007/07/27/world/middleeast/27saudi.html?hp.

14 Bob Kerrey, "The Left's Iraq Muddle," *Wall Street Journal,* May 22, 2007, www.opinionjournal.com/editorial/feature.html?id=110010107.

Chapter 11

1   Rupert Cornwell, "Guantanamo Guards Tortured Prisoner with Music," *Independent,* June 13, 2005, www.independent.co.uk/news/world/americas/guantanamo-guards-tortured-prisoner-with-music-494007.html.

2   "Gibson: 'I am not an anti-Semite,'" CNN.com, August 2, 2006, www.cnn.com/2006/SHOWBIZ/Movies/08/01/gibson.dui/index.html.

3   Associated Press, "Richards Says Anger, Not Racism, Sparked Tirade," MSNBC.com, November 22, 2006, www.msnbc.msn.com/id/15816126/.

4   "Retired NBA Star Hardaway Says He Hates 'Gay People,'" ESPN.com, February 16, 2007, http://sports.espn.go.com/nba/news/story?id=2766213.

5   "Ann Coulter Attacks 9/11 Widows," CBSNews.com, June 7, 2006, www.cbsnews.com/stories/2006/06/07/entertainment/main1690954.shtml.

6   "Coulter Under Fire for Anti-Gay Slur," CNN.com, March 4, 2007, www.cnn.com/2007/POLITICS/03/04/coulter.edwards/index.html.

7   Jake Tapper, "Obama Apologizes for Saying Troops' Lives 'Wasted,'" February 13, 2007, http://abcnews.go.com/Politics/story?id=2872135&page=1.

8   Liz Sidoti, "McCain Says U.S. Lives 'Wasted' in Iraq," *San Francisco Chronicle,* March 1, 2007, www.sfgate.com/cgi-bin/article.cgi?f=/n/a/2007/03/01/politics/p074811S21.DTL&type=politics.

9   Jim VandeHei and Chris Cillizza, "Bush Calls Kerry Remarks Insulting to U.S. Troops," *Washington Post,* November 1, 2006, www.washingtonpost.com/wp-dyn/content/article/2006/10/31/AR2006103100649.html.

10 Xuan Thai and Ted Barrett, "Biden's Description of Obama Draws Scrutiny," CNN.com, February 9, 2007, www.cnn.com/2007/POLITICS/01/31/biden.obama/.

11 Alex Mooney, Ted Barrett, and Scott Anderson, "Top Democrat Blasts Limbaugh for 'Phony Soldiers' Comment," CNN.com, October 1, 2007, www.cnn.com/2007/POLITICS/10/01/reid.limbaugh/index.html.

12 Jonah Goldberg, "Behold the Ego of Chris Matthews," *National Review*'s Corner blog, October 5, 2007, http://corner.nationalreview.com/post/?q=ZTlhNDcwODA0NmQzNGQlYWNiOGE5ZTU4YzE2MDNiZTE=.

13 David Wright and Sunlen Miller, "Obama Dropped Flag Pin in War Statement," ABCNews.com, October 4, 2007, http://abcnews.go.com/Politics/story?id=3690000&page=1.

14 Gerri Peev, "'Hillary Clinton's a Monster': Obama Aide Blurts out Attack in Scotsman Interview," *Scotsman,* March 7, 2008, http://thescotsman.scotsman.com/latestnews/Inside-US-poll-battle-as.3854371.jp.

15 Transcript, *Face the Nation,* March 9, 2008, www.cbsnews.com/stories/2008/03/09/ftn/main3920027.shtml.

16 Rebecca Sinderbrand, "Ferraro: 'They're Attacking Me Because I'm White,'" CNN.com, March 11, 2008, www.cnn.com/2008/POLITICS/03/11/ferraro.comments/index.html.

17 Ibid.

18 Transcript, *Hardball with Chris Matthews,* March 13, 2008, www.msnbc.msn.com/id/23611992/.

19 John Whitesides, "Clinton Aide Likens Obama to Ken Starr," Reuters, March 6, 2008, www.reuters.com/article/vcCandidateFeed7/ idUSN06239362.

20 "McCain Apology Angers Conservative Host," CNNPolitics.com, February 27, 2008, www.cnn.com/2008/POLITICS/02/27/ cunningham.mccain/.

21 Geoff Earle, "Wild Bill Clinton Strikes Again," *New York Post,* January 27, 2008, www.nypost.com/seven/01272008/news/nationalnews/ wild_bill_clinton_strikes_again_534042.htm.

22 Nedra Pickler, "McCain Camp Angry over Obama's 'Lipstick' Comment," Associated Press, September 10, 2008, www.guardian.co .uk/uslatest/story/0,,-7787228,00.html.

Chapter 12

1   "Michael Smerconish," NewsMeat.com, www.newsmeat.com/media_ political_donations/Michael_Smerconish.php.

2   "Newsmeat Power Rankings," NewsMeat.com, www.newsmeat.com/ fec/power_rank.php?rank=749.

3   *Buckley v. Valeo,* 424 U.S. (1976), http://caselaw.lp.findlaw.com/ scripts/getcase.pl?navby=CASE&court=US&vol=424&page=1

4   Zachary Coile, "Lobbyist Parties for Lawmakers Bend Rules," *San Francisco Chronicle,* August 19, 2008, www.sfgate.com/cgi-bin/article .cgi?f=/c/a/2008/08/19/MNLA12D4DE.DTL.

5   Ibid.

6   CQ MoneyLine Glossary, "Key Campaign Finance and Lobbying Definitions," CQ.com, http://moneyline.cq.com/pml/show.do?page= flatfiles/editorialFiles/moneyLine/glossary/glossary (accessed November 20, 2008).

7   David M. Halbfinger, "Bush Promotes His Plan for Missile Defense System," *New York Times,* August 18, 2004, www.nytimes.com/2004/ 08/18/politics/campaign/18bush.html?ex=1250568000&a mp;en=78d15ed4549c2e04&ei=5090&partner=rssuserland.

8   Adam Liptak, "Supreme Court Strikes Down 'Millionaire's Amendment.'" *New York Times,* June 27, 2007, www.nytimes.com/ 2008/06/27/washington/27money.html.

Chapter 13

1   Steve Kroft, "Barack Obama Makes His Case, Steve Kroft Interviews," CBSNews.com, February 10, 2008, www.cbsnews.com/stories/2008/ 02/07/60minutes/main3804268.shtml.

2   Brian Ross and Rehab El-Buri, "Obama's Pastor: God Damn America, U.S. to Blame for 9/11," ABCNews.com, March 13, 2008, http:// abcnews.go.com/Blotter/Story?id=4443788.

3   Barack Obama, "On My Faith and My Church," *Huffington Post,* March 14, 2008, www.huffingtonpost.com/barack-obama/on-my-faith-and-my-church_b_91623.html.

4   Peter Nicholas, "Obama's Ex-Pastor Strides Back on Stage," *Los Angeles Times,* April 29, 2008, http://articles.latimes.com/2008/apr/29/nation/na-wright29.

5   Alex Mooney, "Controversial minister off Obama's campaign," CNN .com, March 15, 2008, www.cnn.com/2008/POLITICS/03/14/obama.minister/index.html.

6   Barack Obama, *Dreams from My Father* (New York: Three Rivers Press, 2004).

7   Ibid.

8   Ibid.

9   Ibid.

10 Jodi Kantor, "Disinvitation by Obama Is Criticized," *New York Times,* March 6, 2007, www.nytimes.com/2007/03/06/us/politics/06obama .html.

11 Ibid.

12 Ibid.

13 Transcript, *Hardball with Chris Matthews,* March 18, 2008, www.msnbc .msn.com/id/23707778/.

14 Senator Barack Obama, interview by Michael Smerconish, *Michael Smerconish Show,* WPHT 1210 AM, Philadelphia, March 21, 2008.

15 Ibid.

16 Peter Mucha, "Obama, Smerconish Talk Church, bin Laden," *Philadelphia Inquirer,* March 24, 2008, www.philly.com/philly/hp/news_update/20080324_Obama__Smerconish_talk_church__bin_Laden.html.

17 Peggy Noonan, "A Thinking Man's Speech," *Wall Street Journal,* March 21, 2008, http://online.wsj.com/public/article_print/SB120604775960652829.html.

18 Glenn Beck, *Glenn Beck Program,* WPHT 1210 AM, Philadelphia, March 28, 2008.

19 Michael Smerconish, interview by Glenn Beck, *Glenn Beck Program,* WPHT 1210 AM, Philadelphia, March 28, 2008.

Chapter 14

1   *Discover* magazine, December 1, 2008.

2   Sheryl G. Stolberg, "House Votes to Ban All Human Cloning," *New York Times,* February 28, 2003, http://query.nytimes.com/gst/fullpage .html?res=9A0CE7D6123CF93BA15751C0A9659C8B63.

3   Dr. Arthur Caplan, interview by Michael Smerconish, *Michael Smerconish Show,* WPHT 1210 AM, Philadelphia, July 29, 2005.

4   "400,000 Embryos and Counting," *New York Times,* May 15, 2003, http://query.nytimes.com/gst/fullpage.html?res=9C01E5DB1F3FF93 6A25756C0A9659C8B63.

5   Dr. Thomas Marino, interview by Michael Smerconish, *Michael Smerconish Show,* WPHT 1210 AM, Philadelphia, June 9, 2004.

6   Ibid.

7   Ibid.

8   International Society for Stem Cell Research, "International Legislation on Human Embryonic Stem Cell Research," www.isscr.org/public/regions/index.cfm.

9   United Press International, "Public Funding Impacts Stem Cell Research," UPI.com, June 10, 2008, www.upi.com/Science_News/2008/06/10/Public_funding_impacts_stem_cell_research/UPI-78701213111552/.

10 "Frist Knocks Edwards over Stem Cell Comment," CNN.com, October 12, 2004, www.cnn.com/2004/ALLPOLITICS/10/12/edwards.stem.cell/.

11 Stem Cell Information, "Federal Policy," The National Institutes of Health, http://stemcells.nih.gov/policy/.

12 President George W. Bush, "Address to the American People about Stem Cell Research" (Bush Ranch, Crawford, TX, August 9, 2001).

Chapter 15

1   David Halberstam, *The Powers That Be* (New York: University of Illinois Press, 2000), 21.

2   Jeremy Gerard, "William S. Paley, Who Built CBS into a Communications Empire, Dies at 89," *New York Times,* October 28, 1990, http://query.nytimes.com/gst/fullpage.html?res=9C0CE5DA1F 30F93BA15753C1A966958260&sec=&spon=&pagewanted=2.

3   Transcript, *Early Show,* April 14, 2008.

Chapter 16

1   Abby Goodnough, "Schiavo Autopsy Says Brain, Withered, Was Untreatable," *New York Times,* June 15, 2005, www.nytimes.com/2005/06/16/national/16schiavo.html?_r=1&scp=1&sq=Jury%20 award%20Michael%20Schiavo&st=nyt&oref=slogin.

2   "Timeline: Terri Schiavo Case," BBC.co.uk, March 31, 2005, http://news.bbc.co.uk/2/hi/americas/4358877.stm.

3   "Terri Schiavo's Final Years," CNN.com, www.cnn.com/interactive/us/0503/timeline.schiavo.case/frameset.exclude.html.

4   Charles Babington, "GOP Is Fracturing over Power of Judiciary," *Washington Post,* April 7, 2005, www.washingtonpost.com/wp-dyn/articles/A32485-2005Apr6.html.

5   Elisabeth Bumiller, "Supporters Praise Bush's Swift Return to Washington," *New York Times,* March 21, 2005, www.nytimes.com/2005/03/21/politics/21bush.html.

6   Mike Allen, "Counsel to GOP Senator Wrote Memo on Schiavo," *Washington Post,* April 7, 2005, www.washingtonpost.com/wp-dyn/articles/A32554-2005Apr6.html.

7   Manuel Roig-Franzia, "High Court Rejects Requests by Schiavo's Parents," *Washington Post,* March 31, 2005, www.washingtonpost.com/wp-dyn/articles/A12216-2005Mar30.html.

8   Charles Babington, "Senator Links Violence to 'Political' Decisions," *Washington Post,* April 5, 2005, www.washingtonpost.com/wp-dyn/articles/A26236-2005Apr4.html.

9   Associated Press, "Schiavo Autopsy Shows Irreversible Brain Damage," MSNBC.com, June 15, 2005, www.msnbc.msn.com/id/8225637/.

10   Carl Huse and Maria Newman, "Judge Hears Schiavo Arguments, But Does Not Rule Yet," *New York Times,* March 21, 2005, www.nytimes.com/2005/03/21/politics/21cnd-debate.html.

11   Scott Schiavo, interview by Michael Smerconish, *Michael Smerconish Show,* WPHT 1210 AM, Philadelphia, March 21, 2005.

12   Katharine Q. Seelye, "G.O.P. Holds to Firm Stance on Abortion," *New York Times,* August 30, 2008, www.nytimes.com/2008/08/31/us/politics/31abortion.html?partner=rssnyt&emc=rss.

13   "John McCain: 'I Believe in Less Government, Smaller Government, Lower Taxes and the Family Making Decisions on Health Care,'" *Glamour,* August 31, 2008, www.glamour.com/magazine/2008/08/mccain-interview.

14   Associated Press, "Mitt Romney Says He Opposes Abortion," MSNBC.com, February 7, 2007, www.msnbc.msn.com/id/17023959/.

15   Janet Hook, "On Abortion, Many Have Flip-Flopped," *Los Angeles Times,* March 11, 2007, http://articles.latimes.com/2007/mar/11/nation/na-abortion11.

16   Elisabeth Bumiller, "Palin Disclosures Raise Questions on Vetting," *New York Times,* September 1, 2008, www.nytimes.com/2008/09/02/us/politics/02vetting.html.

17   Michael Smerconish, "Just Phoneying It In," *Philadelphia Daily News,* January 25, 2007.

Chapter 17

1   "Trial of the Yellow Chair," *Michael Smerconish Show,* WPHT 1210 AM, Philadelphia, February 23, 2006.

Chapter 18

1   Les Waas, interview by Michael Smerconish, *Michael Smerconish Show,* WPHT 1210 AM, Philadelphia, April 1, 2008.

2   Ibid.

3   Mark Kinver, "TV 'Sleep' Button Stands Accused," BBC.co.uk, http://news.bbc.co.uk/1/hi/sci/tech/4620350.stm.

4   Rebecca Clarren, "Put a Stake in It," Salon.com, January 24, 2008, www.salon.com/mwt/good_life/2008/01/24/vampire_energy/.

5   U.S. Department Energy, "Appliances & Electronics," www.energy.gov/applianceselectronics.htm.

6   Richard Conniff, "Counting Carbons," *Discover,* August 6, 2005, http://discovermagazine.com/2005/aug/25-counting-carbons.

7   Intergovernmental Panel on Climate Change, "About IPCC," www.ipcc.ch/about/index.htm (accessed October 9, 2008).

8   Intergovernmental Panel on Climate Change, "Climate Change 2007: Synthesis Report Summary for Policymakers," IPCC Fourth Assessment Report, www.ipcc.ch/pdf/assessment-report/ar4/syr/ar4_syr_spm.pdf.

9   Transcript, "Exposed: The Climate of Fear," CNN, May 2, 2007, http://transcripts.cnn.com/TRANSCRIPTS/0705/02/gb.01.html.

10 Ellen Goodman, "No Change in Political Climate," *Boston Globe,* February 9, 2007, www.boston.com/news/globe/editorial_opinion/oped/articles/2007/02/09/no_change_in_political_climate/.

11 John Coleman, "Comments About Global Warming," International Climate and Environmental Change Assessment Project, November 15, 2007, http://icecap.us/index.php/go/joes-blog/comments_about_global_warming/.

12 Ibid.

Chapter 20

1   "Iran Hostage Anniversary: Saturday Is 20 Years Since Americans Held in Iran Were Released," CBSNews.com, January 21, 2001, www.cbsnews.com/stories/2001/01/18/iran/main265244.shtml.

2   Rick Hampson, "25 Years Later, Bombing in Beirut Still Resonates," *USA Today,* October 18, 2008, www.usatoday.com/news/military/2008-10-15-beirut-barracks_N.htm.

3   David Ensor, "U.S. Captures Mastermind of Achille Lauro Hijacking," CNN.com, April 16, 2003, www.cnn.com/2003/WORLD/meast/04/15/sprj.irq.abbas.arrested/.

4   Anne Swardson, "Lockerbie Suspects Delivered for Trial," *Washington Post,* April 6, 1999, www.washingtonpost.com/wp-srv/inatl/longterm/panam103/stories/handover040699.htm.

5   U.S. Department of State, "Appendix C: Libya's Continuing Responsibility for Terrorism," in *Patterns of Global Terrorism,* 1991, April 1991.

6   "'Proud Terrorist' Gets Life for Trade Center Bombing," CNN.com, January 8, 1998, www.cnn.com/US/9801/08/yousef.update/.

7   Barton Gellman and Dana Priest, "U.S. Strikes Terrorist-Linked Sites in Afghanistan, Factory in Sudan," *Washington Post,* August 21, 1998, www.washingtonpost.com/wp-srv/inatl/longterm/eafricabombing/stories/strikes082198.htm.

8   Benjamin Weiser, "In Terrorism Case, a Plea Bargain Secretly Two Years in the Making," *New York Times,* October 24, 2000, http://query.nytimes.com/gst/fullpage.html?res=9C04E4DD1431F937A15753C1A9669C8B63.

9   "Two Sentenced to Death for *Cole* Bomb," CNN.com, September 29, 2004, http://edition.cnn.com/2004/WORLD/meast/09/29/yemen.cole/index.html.

10 Associated Press, "Judge: Sudan Liable in USS *Cole* Attack," MSNBC.com, March 14, 2007, www.msnbc.msn.com/id/17598388/.

11 Cathy Booth Thomas, "Courage in the Air." *Time,* September 1, 2002, www.time.com/time/covers/1101020909/aattendants.html.

12 Maria Ressa, "Sources: Reid Is al Qaeda Operative," CNN.com, December 6, 2003, www.cnn.com/2003/WORLD/asiapcf/southeast/01/30/reid.alqaeda/.

13 "Bali Bomber Sentenced to Die," CNN.com, February 26, 2004, www.cnn.com/2003/WORLD/asiapcf/southeast/08/07/bali.verdict/index.html.

14 Tracy Wilkinson, "21 Convicted in Madrid Train Blasts," *Los Angeles Times,* November 1, 2007, http://articles.latimes.com/2007/nov/01/world/fg-verdict1.

15 Adam Fresco, Daniel McGrory, and Andrew Norfolk, "Video of London Suicide Bomber Released," *Times Online,* July 6, 2006, www.timesonline.co.uk/tol/news/uk/article683824.ece.

16 Ramola Talwar Badam, "India Demands Strong Action from Pakistan," Associated Press, December 1, 2008, http://news.yahoo.com/s/ap/as_india_shooting; Robert F. Worth, "In Wake of Attacks, India-Pakistan Tensions Grow," *New York Times,* December 1, 2008. www.nytimes.com/2008/12/02/world/asia/02mumbai.html?pagewanted=1&em.

17 National Commission on Terrorist Attacks Upon the United States, *The 9/11 Commission Report* (New York: W. W. Norton & Company, 2004), 394.

18 Ibid.

19 National Commission on Terrorist Attacks Upon the United States, *Seventh Public Hearing,* U.S. Capitol, Washington, D.C., January 26, 2004.

20 Secretary John Lehman, interview by Michael Smerconish, *Michael Smerconish Show,* WPHT 1210 AM, Philadelphia, September 15, 2004.

21 National Commission on Terrorist Attacks Upon the United States, *The 9/11 Commission Report* (New York: W. W. Norton & Company, 2004), 394.

22 Rand Office of Media Relations, "U.S. Should Rethink 'War on Terrorism' Strategy to Deal with Resurgent Al Qaida," press release, July 29, 2008, www.rand.org/news/press/2008/07/29/.

23 Secretary John Lehman, interview by Michael Smerconish, *Michael Smerconish Show,* WPHT 1210 AM, Philadelphia, April 10, 2004.

Chapter 21

1 Transcript, *Seinfeld,* episode #5-22, "The Opposite," transcribed by Astrid Humstad, SeinfeldScripts.com, www.seinfeldscripts.com/TheOpposite.htm.

2 Lt. Col. Orson Swindle, interview by Michael Smerconish, *Michael Smerconish Show,* WPHT 1210 AM, Philadelphia, October 9, 2008.

Chapter 22

1 John McCain, *Faith of My Fathers* (New York: Random House, 1999), 189.

2 Michael A. Smerconish, "Wild Bill's Lesson for P.O.W. John," *Philadelphia Daily News,* November 17, 2005, www.mastalk.com/daily_news2/11_17_2005.htm.

3 Foster Klug, "McCain: Torture Ban Protects U.S. Image," *Washington Post,* November 14, 2005, www.washingtonpost.com/wp-dyn/content/article/2005/11/14/AR2005111400247.html.

4 Rick Jervis, "Iraqi Woman Confesses on Jordanian TV," *USA Today,* November 13, 2005, www.usatoday.com/news/world/2005-11-13-jordan-arrest_x.htm.

5 "CIA Admits Waterboarding Inmates," BBC.co.uk, February 5, 2008, http://news.bbc.co.uk/2/hi/americas/7229169.stm.

6 Scott Shane, "Inside a 9/11 Mastermind's Interrogation," *New York Times,* June 22, 2008, www.nytimes.com/2008/06/22/washington/22ksm.html?pagewanted=3&ref=opinion.

7 Brian Ross and Richard Esposito, "CIA's Harsh Interrogation Techniques," ABC News, November 18, 2005, http://abcnews.go.com/WNT/Investigation/story?id=1322866.

8 "How the CIA Broke the 9/11 Attacks Mastermind," ABCNews.com's Blotter blog, September 13, 2007, http://blogs.abcnews.com/theblotter/2007/09/how-the-cia-bro.html.

9   Dan Eggen and Walter Pincus, "FBI, CIA Debate Significance of Terror
     Suspect," *Washington Post,* December 18, 2007, www.washingtonpost
     .com/wp-dyn/content/article/2007/12/17/AR2007121702151_pf
     .html.

Chapter 23

1   Transcript, Larry King Live, May 29, 2008, http://transcripts.cnn
     .com/TRANSCRIPTS/0805/29/lkl.01.html.
2   Catherine Donaldson-Evans, "*Washington Post,* Other Newspapers
     Won't Run 'Opus' Cartoon Mocking Radical Islam," Fox News, August
     28, 2007, www.foxnews.com/story/0,2933,294779,00.html.
3   Transcript, *Today,* August 29, 2007, video at www.youtube.com/
     watch?v=WrWCmohqtqM&eurl=www.truveo.com/Hussein-Ibish-and-
     Michael-Smerconish-on-Freedom-of/id/623931468.
4   Scott Shane, "Obama and '60s Bomber: A Look into Crossed Paths,"
     New York Times, October 4, 2008, www.nytimes.com/2008/10/04/
     us/politics/04ayers.html?th&emc=th.
5   Senator Barack Obama, interview by Michael Smerconish, *Michael
     Smerconish Show,* WPHT 1210 AM, Philadelphia, October 8, 2008.
6   Ben Smith, "Obama on Ayers: 'I Assumed That He Had Been
     Rehabilitated,' Politico.com, October 9, 2008, www.politico.com/
     blogs/bensmith/1008/Obama_on_Ayers_I_assumed_he_had_been_
     rehabilitated.html.
7   "Talk Turns to Jive About Ayers," *Investor's Business Daily,* October 10,
     2008, www.investors.com/editorial/editorialcontent.asp?secid=1501&st
     atus=article&id=308530627185173.
8   Jake Tapper, "Obama: I Assumed Ayers Had Been Rehabilitated,"
     ABCNews.com's Political Punch blog, October 9, 2008, http://blogs
     .abcnews.com/politicalpunch/2008/10/obama-i-assumed.html.
9   Katharine Q. Seelye, "Obama Picks the Phillies," *New York Times'*
     Caucus blog, October 9, 2008, http://thecaucus.blogs.nytimes.com/
     2008/10/09/obama-picks-the-phillies/.
10   John Riley, "Obama: Thought Ayers Was Rehabilitated," *Newsday*'s Spin
     Cycle blog, October 9, 2008, http://weblogs.newsday.com/news/
     local/longisland/politics/blog/2008/10/obama_thought_ayers_was_
     rehabi.html
11   Liz Sidoti, "McCain TV Ad Raises Obama's Links to Ex-Radical," *USA
     Today,* October 10, 2008, www.usatoday.com/news/politics/2008-10-
     09-2824987828_x.htm.
12   Mark Silva, "McCain: Obama 'Decent' but 'Lied,'" *Chicago Tribune*'s
     Swamp blog, October 10, 2008, www.swamppolitics.com/news/
     politics/blog/2008/10/mccain_obama_decent_but_lied.html.

13 P. J. Gladnick, "Will MSM Challenge Obama Assumption that Bill Ayers Was 'Rehabilitated'?" Newsbusters.org, October 10, 2008, http://newsbusters.org/blogs/p-j-gladnick/2008/10/10/will-msm-challenge-obama-assumption-bill-ayers-was-rehabilitated.

14 Jim Geraghty, "In the End, the Candidate Has to Make the Argument," *National Review*'s Campaign Spot blog, October 10, 2008, http://campaignspot.nationalreview.com/post/?q=Y2ZhN2I4M2M2NWNlOTZjNzAwMjI4MTEyN2E1YjBiOGE=

15 Peter Murcha, "Smerconish Grills Obama: Ayers, Guns, Mumia, Phils," *Philadelphia Inquirer,* October 10, 2008, www.philly.com/philly/news/30741724.html.

16 *Michael Smerconish Show,* WPHT 1210 AM, Philadelphia, October 10, 2008.

17 Ibid.

18 Ibid.

19 "Obama speaks out on Ayers, on conservative talk radio!" *Daily Kos,* October 9, 2008, www.dailykos.com/storyonly/2008/10/9/195431/223/841/625641.

Chapter 24

1 Adam Nagourney and Michael Cooper, "McCain's Conservative Model? Roosevelt (Theodore, that is)" *New York Times,* July 13, 2008, www.nytimes.com/2008/07/13/us/politics/13mccain.html?pagewanted=1#.

2 Mary Leonard, "McCain Character Loyal to a Fault," *Boston Globe,* March 4, 2000, http://graphics.boston.com/news/politics/campaign2000/news/McCain_character_loyal_to_a_fault+.shtml.

3 Pew Internet and American Life Project, "Home Broadband Adoption 2008," July 2008, www.pewinternet.org/pdfs/PIP_Broadband_2008.pdf.

4 Linda Greenhouse, "High Court Blocks Term Limits for Congress in a 5–4 Decision," *New York Times,* May 23, 1995, http://query.nytimes.com/gst/fullpage.html?res=990CEEDC1539F930A15756C0A963958260&sec=&spon=&pagewanted=1.

5 *U.S. Term Limits, Inc. v. Thornton,* 514 U.S. 779 (1995).

6 Linda Greenhouse, "High Court Blocks Term Limits for Congress in a 5–4 Decision," *New York Times,* May 23, 1995, http://query.nytimes.com/gst/fullpage.html?res=990CEEDC1539F930A15756C0A963958260&sec=&spon=&pagewanted=1.

7 "Term Limits: The Fight Dies Hard," *Time,* June 5, 1995, www.time.com/time/magazine/article/0,9171,983018,00.html.

8 Rebecca Cathcart, "Campaigns Halt as Nevada Court Upholds Term Limits," *New York Times,* July 26, 2008, www.nytimes.com/2008/07/26/us/26nevada.html?partner=rssnyt&emc=rss.

9   Brad Bumstead, "Term Limits 'Weaken' Pa. Legislators," *Pittsburgh Tribune Review*, May 30, 2007, www.pittsburghlive.com/x/pittsburghtrib/search/s_510041.html.

10 Doug Bandow, "Real Term Limits: Now More Than Ever," CATO Institute, CATO Policy Analysis No. 221, March 28, 1995, www.cato.org/pubs/pas/pa-221.html.

11 Thomas Patterson, "Why the Re-election of Incumbents Year After Year Is a Threat to Democracy," History News Network, December 9, 2002, http://hnn.us/articles/1144.html.

Chapter 25

1   Senator Arlen Specter speaking to the Pennsylvania Society, New York City, December 8, 2007.

Chapter 26

1   Transcript, *Meet the Press*, September 3, 2006, www.msnbc.msn.com/id/14568263/.

2   Ibid.

3   Sen. Judd Gregg, "It's time to stretch short-term deficit cuts into long ones," thehill.com, July 20, 2005, http://thehill.com/op-eds/its-time-to-stretch-short-term-deficit-cuts-into-long-ones-2005-07-20.html.

4   Peter Orszag, director of Congressional Budget Office, letter to Congressman Jeb Hensarling, March 8, 2007, http://cbo.gov/ftpdocs/78xx/doc7851/03-08-Long-Term%20Spending.pdf.

5   Ibid.

6   David Brown, "Life Expectancy Hits Record High in United States," *Washington Post*, June 12, 2008, www.washingtonpost.com/wp-dyn/content/article/2008/06/11/AR2008061101570.html; National Center for Health Statistics, "HHS Study Finds Life Expectancy in the U.S. Rose to 77.2 Years in 2001," press release, March 14, 2003, www.cdc.gov/nchs/pressroom/03news/lifeex.htm.

7   "Raise the Retirement Age," *USA Today*, October 4, 2004, www.usatoday.com/news/nation/2004-10-04-retire-age_x.htm.

8   Chairman Ben S. Bernanke, "Testimony Before the Committee on the Budget" (U.S. Senate, Washington, D.C., January 18, 2007).

9   Associated Press, "Bernanke Warns of 'Vicious Cycle' in Deficits," MSNBC.com, January 18, 2007, www.msnbc.msn.com/id/16688089/.

10 BarackObama.com, "Barack Obama: Helping America's Seniors," www.barackobama.com/pdf/seniorsFactSheet.pdf.

11 Associated Press, "Obama's Social Security Plan Missing Details," MSNBC.com, July 28, 2008, www.msnbc.msn.com/id/25889673/.

12 BarackObama.com, "Barack Obama: Helping America's Seniors," www.barackobama.com/pdf/seniorsFactSheet.pdf.

13 Associated Press, "McCain: Social Security Funding System a 'Disgrace,'" *USA Today,* July 10, 2008, www.usatoday.com/news/ politics/election2008/2008-07-09-mccain-social-security_N.htm.

14 Rob Hotakainen, "Pork Barrel Spending: McCain Slams It; Obama Says It Isn't the Real Problem," McClatchy Newspapers, November 4, 2008, www.mcclatchydc.com/173/story/53912.html.

Chapter 27

1 Christopher N. Osher and Carlos Illescas, "Police Probe Possible White-Supremacist Plot Against Obama," *Denver Post,* August 26, 2008, www.denverpost.com/nationalpolitics/ci_10302666.

2 David Gardner, "White Supremacists Cleared of Gun Plot to Assassinate Barack Obama," *Daily Mail* Online, August 28, 2008, www.dailymail .co.uk/news/article-1049169/White-supremacists-cleared-gun-plot-assassinate-Barack-Obama.html.

3 David Jackson, "McCain Picks VP, Plans Friday Event," *USA Today,* August 29, 2008, www.usatoday.com/news/politics/election2008/ 2008-08-28-mccain-vp_N.htm.

4 "Schneider: Palin Gets Low Marks on Experience," CNNPolitics.com's Political Ticker blog, November 4, 2008, http://politicalticker.blogs .cnn.com/2008/11/04/schneider-palin-gets-low-marks/.

Chapter 28

1 Internal Revenue Service, "Estate Tax," U.S. Department of the Treasury, www.irs.gov/businesses/small/article/0,,id=164871,00.html.

2 DeathTax.com, "The Death Tax—Where Did It Come From?" www .deathtax.com/deathtax/comefrom.htm.

3 Congressional Budget Office, "Effects of the Federal Estate Tax on Farms and Small Businesses," A CBO Paper, July 2005, www.cbo.gov/ ftpdocs/65xx/doc6512/07-06-EstateTax.pdf.

4 Jeffrey H. Bimbaum, "Senate Plan to Repeal Inheritance Tax Fails," *Washington Post,* June 9, 2006, www.washingtonpost.com/wp-dyn/ content/article/2006/06/08/AR2006060800138.html.

5 Jonathan Weisman, "Erosion of Estate Tax Is a Lesson in Politics," *Washington Post,* April 13, 2005, www.washingtonpost.com/wp-dyn/ articles/A48025-2005Apr12.html.

6 Times Topics, "Inheritance and Estate Taxes," NYtimes.com, http:// topics.nytimes.com/top/reference/timestopics/subjects/i/inheritance_ and_estate_taxes/index.html (accessed November 10, 2008).

7 Congressional Budget Office, "Effects of the Federal Estate Tax on Farms and Small Businesses," A CBO Paper, July 2005, www.cbo.gov/ ftpdocs/65xx/doc6512/07-06-EstateTax.pdf.

8   Leonard E. Burman, William G. Gale, and Jeffrey Rohaly, "Options to Reform the Estate Tax," Tax Policy Issues and Options, March 10, 2005, www.urban.org/uploadedPDF/311153_IssuesOptions_10.pdf.

9   Andrew Chamberlain, "Special Report: What Does America Think About Taxes? The 2007 Annual Survey of U.S. Attitudes on Taxes and Wealth," Tax Foundation, April 2007, www.taxfoundation.org/files/sr154.pdf.

10   Ibid.

11   Jonathan Weisman, "Erosion of Estate Tax Is a Lesson in Politics," *Washington Post,* April 13, 2005, www.washingtonpost.com/wp-dyn/articles/A48025-2005Apr12.html.

Chapter 29

1   Michael Smerconish, "September Statement of Michael Smerconish," September 1, 2008, www.mastalk.com.

2   Michael Smerconish, "McCain: The First Obituary," *Philadelphia Daily News,* October 16, 2008, www.mastalk.com/daily_news2/101608.htm.

3   Ibid.

4   Michael Smerconish, "McCain Fails the Big Five Tests," *Philadelphia Inquirer,* October 19, 2008, www.mastalk.com/inquirer/101908.htm.

5   Jake Tapper, "In Philly, Conservative Talk Radio Host Backs Obama," ABCNews.com's Political Punch blog, October 17, 2008, http://blogs.abcnews.com/politicalpunch/2008/10/in-philly-conse.html.

6   Rachel Weiner, "Newspapers that Backed Bush Shift to Obama," *Huffington Post,* October 17, 2008, www.huffingtonpost.com/2008/10/17/conservative-talk-radio-h_n_135684.html.

7   *Mike Gallagher Show,* October 20, 2008 .

Chapter 30

1   Michael Smerconish speech to Multi-Cultural Academy Charter School, Philadelphia, June 2004.

2   Ron Haskins and Isabel Sawhill, "Introducing the Issue," in "The Next Generation of Antipoverty Policies," *The Future of Children* 17, no. 2 (Fall 2007): 6, www.futureofchildren.org/information2827/information_show.htm?doc_id=521587.

3   Ron Haskins, "Testimony Before Committee on Senate Appropriations, Subcommittee on District of Columbia" (U.S. Senate, Washington, D.C., October 6, 2005).

4   Sarah McLanahan, Elisabeth Donahue, and Ron Haskins, "Introducing the Issue," in "Marriage and Child Wellbeing," *The Future of Children* 15, no. 2 (Fall 2005): 5, www.futureofchildren.org/information2827/information_show.htm?doc_id=290792.

5   Shelia Rafferty Zedlewski Ph.D., "Family Economic Resources in the Post-Reform Era," in "Children and Welfare Reform," *The Future of Children* 12, no. 1 (Winter/Spring 2002): 3, www.futureofchildren.org/information2827/information_show.htm?doc_id=102658.

6   Paul R. Amato, "The Impact of Family Formation Change on the Cognitive, Social, and Emotional Well-Being of the Next Generation," in "Marriage and Child Wellbeing," *The Future of Children* 15, no. 2, (Fall 2005): 5, www.futureofchildren.org/information2827/information_show.htm?doc_id=290708.

7   Michael A. Smerconish, "The Real Prescription for Success," *Philadelphia Daily News,* June 17, 2004.

8   Ibid.

9   Ibid.

10 Jon Hurdle, "Perfect Storm Behind Murder in Philadelphia," Reuters, June 7, 2007, www.reuters.com/article/domesticNews/idUSN0135160820070607.

11 Blaine Harden, "Numbers Drop for the Married with Children," *Washington Post,* March 4, 2007, www.washingtonpost.com/wp-dyn/content/article/2007/03/03/AR2007030300841.html.

12 Pamela J. Smock and Wendy D. Manning, "Living Together Unmarried in the United States: Demographic Perspectives and Implications for Family Policy," PSC Research Report, Report No. 04-555, March 2004, www.psc.isr.umich.edu/pubs/pdf/rr04-555.pdf.

13 Robert J. Sampson, Ph.D., Jeffrey D. Morenoff, Ph.D., and Stephen Raudenbush, Ed.D., "Social Anatomy of Racial and Ethnic Disparities in Violence," *American Journal of Public Health* 95, no. 2 (February 2005), www.ajph.org/cgi/content/full/95/2/224.

14 Robert J. Sampson, John H. Laub, and Christopher Wimer, "Does Marriage Reduce Crime? A Counterfactual Approach to Within-Individual Causal Effects," *Criminology* 44, no. 3 (2006): 465–508, www.wjh.harvard.edu/soc/faculty/sampson/articles/2006_Criminology_LaubWimer.pdf.

15 Violence Policy Center, "Black Homicide Victimization in the United States: An Analysis of 2004 Homicide Data," January 2007, www.vpc.org/studies/blackhomicide.pdf.

16 Dr. Robert Sampson, interview by Michael Smerconish, *Michael Smerconish Show,* WPHT 1210 AM, Philadelphia, March 5, 2007.

17 Felicia R. Lee, "Cosby Defends His Remarks About Poor Blacks' Values," *New York Times,* May 22, 2004, http://query.nytimes.com/gst/fullpage.html?res=9B05E5D71E3FF931A15756C0A9629C8B63&sec=&spon=&pagewanted=1.

18 Barbara Ehrenreich, "The New Cosby Kids," *New York Times,* July 8, 2004, http://query.nytimes.com/gst/fullpage.html?res=9402E3DB15 3BF93BA35754C0A9629C8B63&sec=&spon=&pagewanted=1.

19 Charles Barkley, interview by Michael Smerconish, *Michael Smerconish Show,* WPHT 1210 AM, Philadelphia, September 19, 2007.

20 Ibid.

21 Barack Obama, "Fatherhood" (speech, Apostolic Church of God, Chicago, IL, June 15, 2008).

Chapter 31

1 Terence P. Jeffrey, "Conservative Leaders Meet, Plan to Battle Obama's Agenda—With or Without Republicans," CNSNews.com, November 6, 2008, www.cnsnews.com/public/content/article.aspx?RsrcID=38961.

2 Ibid.

3 Susan Davis, "Republicans Seek to Regroup After Loss," *Wall Street Journal,* November 7, 2008, http://online.wsj.com/article/ SB122602106707807253.html?mod=googlenews_wsj.

4 Terence P. Jeffrey, "Conservative Leaders Meet, Plan to Battle Obama's Agenda—With or Without Republicans," CNSNews.com, November 6, 2008, www.cnsnews.com/public/content/article.aspx?RsrcID=38961.

5 Scott Anderson, "Moderates to Blame for GOP Losses, Conservative Leader Says," CNN.com, November 7, 2008, www.cnn.com/2008/ POLITICS/11/07/conservatives.election/.

6 Joe Kovacs, "Limbaugh: Time to Cleanse Republican Party," WorldNetDaily.com, November 5, 2008, www.worldnetdaily.com/ index.php?fa=PAGE.view&pageId=80181.

7 "Sarah Palin Defends Herself Against Criticism in FOX News Interview," FoxNews.com, November 10, 2008, http://elections .foxnews.com/2008/11/10/sarah-palin-defends-criticism-post- election-interview/.

8 "Palin Urges Republican Governors to Stick to GOP's Bedrock Values," FoxNews.com, November 13, 2008, http://elections.foxnews.com/ 2008/11/13/palin-addresses-gop-governors-association/.

9 Transcript, *Hardball with Chris Matthews,* November 11, 2008, www .msnbc.msn.com/id/27683178/.

10 David Brooks, "Darkness at Dusk," *New York Times,* November 11, 2008, www.nytimes.com/2008/11/11/opinion/11brooks.html.

11 Transcript, *Hardball with Chris Matthews,* November 11, 2008, www .msnbc.msn.com/id/27683178/.

12 Karen Heller, "Oh, So Sweet a Love for Pa.," *Philadelphia Inquirer,* November 4, 2008, www.philly.com/inquirer/columnists/karen_ heller/20081104_Karen_Heller__Oh__so_sweet_a_love_for_Pa_.html.

13 Gail Shister, "Pa. Ranks First in Campaign TV Revenue," *Philadelphia Inquirer,* October 5, 2008, www.philly.com/inquirer/columnists/ gail_shister/20081005_Pa__ranks_first_in_campaign_TV_revenue.html; "Election Tracker: Ad Spending," CNN.com, www.cnn.com/ ELECTION/2008/map/ad.spending/ (accessed November 17, 2008).

14 Josh Drobnyk, "Platt Remark Draws Rebuke from McCain Camp," *Allentown Morning Call*'s Pennsylvania Ave. blog, October 8, 2008, http://blogs.mcall.com/penn_ave/2008/10/mccain-to-lehig.html.

15 John Sullivan, "Black Panthers, FoxNews Create Stir at Polling Place," *Philadelphia Inquirer,* November 5, 2008, www.philly.com/inquirer/ local/20081105_Black_Panthers__FoxNews_create_stir_at_polling_ place.html.

16 Michael Cooper and Michael Falcone, "In Pennsylvania, Wright and Clinton Remarks Are Revived," *New York Times'* Caucus blog, November 2, 2008, http://thecaucus.blogs.nytimes.com/2008/11/ 02/in-pennsylvania-gop-highlights-wright-and-clinton-remarks/.

17 Mosheh Oinounou, "McCain Declares Rev. Wright Issue Off Limits," FoxNews.com's Embed Producers blog, April 23, 2008, http:// embeds.blogs.foxnews.com/2008/04/23/for-mccain-rev-wright-is-off- limits/.

18 Jim King Greenwood, "McCain Supporter Robbed, Assaulted," *Pittsburgh Tribune-Review,* October 23, 2008, www.pittsburghlive.com/ x/pittsburghtrib/news/breaking/s_594853.html.

19 "National Exit Polls Table," *New York Times,* November 5, 2008, http://elections.nytimes.com/2008/results/president/national-exit- polls.html (accessed November 18, 2008).

20 Peter Hamby, "GOP Senator: McCain Betrayed Republican Principles," CNNPolitics.com's Political Ticker blog, November 14, 2008, http:// politicalticker.blogs.cnn.com/2008/11/14/gop-senator-mccain- betrayed-republican-principles/.

21 Pennsylvania Department of State, "Voter Registration Statistics," www .dos.state.pa.us/elections/cwp/view.asp?a=1310&q=447072 (accessed November 6, 2008).

22 Carl Hulse, "3 Successful Republicans Caution Against a Move to the Right," *New York Times,* November 3, 2008, www.nytimes.com/2008/ 11/14/us/politics/14cong.html?partner=rss&emc=rss.

23 Jonathan Martin, "Republicans Ask: Just How Bad Is It?" Politico.com, November 17, 2008, www.politico.com/news/stories/1108/15676 .html.

24 Ibid.

25 "National Exit Polls Table," *New York Times,* November 5, 2008, http://elections.nytimes.com/2008/results/president/national-exit- polls.html (accessed November 18, 2008).

Afterword

1   Reza Sayah and Saeed Ahmed, "Musharraf's Resignation Accepted," CNN, August 18, 2008, www.cnn.com/2008/WORLD/asiapcf/ 08/18/musharraf.address/index.html.

2   Laura King, "Islamabad Marriott Reopens Three Months After Truck Bombing," *Los Angeles Times,* December 29, 2008, www.latimes.com/ news/nationworld/world/la-fg-pakistan-hotel29-2008dec29,0,3897834 .story.

3   Robin Wright, "U.S. Payments to Pakistan Face New Scrutiny," *Washington Post,* February 21, 2008, www.washingtonpost.com/ wp-dyn/content/story/2008/02/20/ST2008022002819.html.